MYANMAR DILEMMAS AND OPTIONS

The **Institute of Southeast Asian Studies** was established as an autonomous organization in May 1968. It is a regional research centre for scholars and other specialists concerned with modern Southeast Asia, particularly the multi-faceted problems of stability and security, economic development, and political and social change.

The Institute is governed by a twenty-two member Board of Trustees comprising nominees from the Singapore Government, the National University of Singapore, the various Chambers of Commerce, and professional and civic organizations. A ten-man Executive Committee oversees day-to-day operations; it is chaired by the Director, the Institute's chief academic and administrative officer.

The **ASEAN Economic Research Unit** is an integral part of the Institute, coming under the overall supervision of the Director who is also the Chairman of its Management Committee. The Unit was formed in 1979 in response to the need to deepen understanding of economic change and political developments in ASEAN. The day-to-day operations of the Unit are the responsibility of the Co-ordinator. A Regional Advisory Committee, consisting of a senior economist from each of the ASEAN countries, guides the work of the Unit.

MYANMAR DILEMMAS AND OPTIONS

The Challenge of Economic Transition in the 1990s

Edited by
MYA THAN & JOSEPH L.H. TAN

ASEAN Economic Research Unit
INSTITUTE OF SOUTHEAST ASIAN STUDIES

Published by
Institute of Southeast Asian Studies
Heng Mui Keng Terrace
Pasir Panjang
Singapore 0511

Cataloguing in Publication Data

Myanmar dilemmas and options: the challenge of economic transition in the 1990s / editors, Mya Than and Joseph L.H. Tan
1. Burma—Economic policy.
2. Burma—Economic conditions—1948–
I. Mya Than.
II. Tan, Joseph L.H.
III. Institute of Southeast Asian Studies (Singapore)
HC422 M99 1990 sls90-4959

ISBN 981-3035-55-2 (soft cover)
ISBN 981-3035-58-7 (hard cover)

Typeset by Letraprint
Printed in Singapore by Kin Keong Printing Co. Pte. Ltd.

CONTENTS

PREFACE

Many rapid and dynamic changes in the political, social, and economic sectors in the Union of Myanmar have occurred since the present government, the State Law and Order Restoration Committee (SLORC), took over power from the defunct Burmese Socialist Programme Party (BSPP) in September 1988. The most important change has been the government's decision to switch the economy from a "socialist" one to free market capitalism by abolishing the "Burmese Way to Socialism". Furthermore, the words "Socialist Republic" in the official title of the nation have been removed so that Burma has become "The Union of Myanmar" or "Myanmar Naing-Ngan", and the Union of Burma Foreign Investment Law which was promulgated has become a symbol of an "open-door policy". Moreover, border trade with China has been formalized, and fishing and logging rights have been sold to friendly nations in Asia. Many joint venture companies are also being set up in the agricultural, trade and oil sectors.

At the same time, the government has announced that a general election would be held in May 1990 and all contesting political parties would be allowed to start their election campaign three months prior to the election date. This means that the political parties have to formulate and present their policies for public discussion and debate in early 1990. Presumably, all the policies, despite their differences in political and ideological persuasions, would mainly focus on various issues concerning the development of Myanmar.

Although the final shape and outcome of such innovations and initiatives are uncertain, Myanmar is indeed at a critical crossroad in its history and development, and it was accordingly thought appropriate and timely that the Institute of Southeast Asian Studies should get together a group of scholars interested in Myanmar to produce a volume on Myanmar's options in terms of restructuring its economy. It was understood too that such options would have to be set in the context of global as well as regional trends.

The papers in this volume attempt to identify the major issues concerning the role of the state and economic management, the new directions in resource, agricultural and industrial development and the challenges arising from the opening up of the economy to the stimuli of external trade and capital movements.

Contributors to this volume include not only Myanmar economists inside and outside the country but also foreign specialists who analyse the different aspects of economic development in Myanmar from both macro- and micro-level perspectives. However, as in most developing countries, economic data on Myanmar are very limited. Even the scanty official data suffer from weaknesses in terms of accuracy and reliability. Despite these limitations, overall trends may be reasonably accurate and on that basis the contributors have attempted to find a helpful prescription for the development of Myanmar in the 1990s.

Finally, while we encourage all points of view, needless to say, the individual contributors are solely responsible for the facts and opinions expressed in their respective papers, and their interpretations do not necessarily reflect the views and policies of the Institute or its supporters.

CONTRIBUTORS

Dr U Tun Wai is an International and Economic Consultant. Formerly Deputy Director at the IMF Institute, he has also been consultant to the IMF, UNCTAD, UNDP, and various governments. In 1987–88, he was the Distinguished Fellow in International Banking and Finance at the Institute of Southeast Asian Studies. His research interests focus on financial policies and problems of developing countries, as well as problems of economic development.

U Myat Thein is Associate Professor of Economics and currently head of the Department of Economics, Institute of Economics, Yangon. He has undertaken many research projects covering a wide range of subjects related to the Myanmar economy.

Nobuyoshi Nishizawa, Associate Professor in the Faculty of Integrated Arts and Science at Hiroshima University, is currently a Visiting Fellow at the Institute of Southeast Asian Studies, Singapore. He was formerly with the Institute of Developing Economies in Tokyo and was attached to the Embassy of Japan in Rangoon from 1977 to 1979.

U Tin Soe is a lecturer at the Department of Economics, Institute of Economics, Yangon. He is currently a Ph. D. full-time candidate at the Department of Agricultural Economics, University of Sydney, Australia.

Dr Brian S. Fisher is currently the Director of the Australian Bureau of Agricultural and Resource Economics (ABARE), Canberra, Australia. He was formerly Professor of Agricultural Economics and dean of the Faculty of Agriculture, University of Sydney.

Dr Wilfried Lütkenhorst is working with the Regional and Country Studies Branch of the United Nations Industrial Development Organization (UNIDO) in Vienna, Austria. In his research and publications, he has mainly focused on economic development issues in the Asia-Pacific region, with special emphasis on trade and investment related subjects.

Dr Richard W.A. Vokes is a lecturer in Economics and Southeast Asian Studies at the Centre of Southeast Asian Studies, University of Kent at Canterbury, United Kingdom. He has published several articles on the Myanmar and Indochinese economies.

Dr John Badgley is presently Curator, Echols Collection, Olin Library, Cornell University, Ithaca, New York. He has published several books and articles on Myanmar political economy, institutions, and leadership.

U Soe Saing has served in the Government of the Union of Burma in the Ministry of Planning and Finance. He was seconded to the United Nations Economic and Social Commission for Asia and the Pacific (ESCAP). He is currently a Visiting Fellow at the Institute of Southeast Asian Studies, Singapore.

Dr Mya Than is a Research Fellow at the Institute of Southeast Asian Studies. He was formerly with the Department of Research and Management Studies, Institute of Economics, Yangon. He has written extensively on the social and economic aspects of agricultural and rural development.

Dr Joseph L.H. Tan is a Senior Fellow at the Institute of Southeast Asian Studies and Co-ordinator of the ASEAN Economic Research Unit.

1

INTRODUCTION
Optimism for Myanmar's Economic Transition in the 1990s?

MYA THAN and JOSEPH L.H. TAN

Any realistic or reasonable prognosis on Myanmar's (Burma's) economic future should begin with an understanding of not only the country's present economic situation, but also its past economic history (see Appendix I).[1] The modern history of Burma started in 1948 when it gained independence from Britain, after more than a century under the colonial yoke. Since most of the leaders of the independence movement were staunch nationalists and socialists (to some degree), the government then supposedly modelled a democratic, socialist-oriented welfare state. Many development economists, United Nations and academic planners as well as Burma watchers were optimistic of the potential for rapid economic development in Burma because of its abundant natural resources, a relatively high literacy rate, absence of population pressure and a rigid caste system, favourable land–man ratio, and a relatively high social status given to women in the society.[2] Socialist economic planning began with the introduction of a Two-Year Plan soon after independence, which was followed by an Eight-Year Plan known as the "Pyidawtha (peaceful, pleasant welfare state) Plan", drawn up by American advisers.

However, the Pyidawtha Plan failed because of its emphasis on industrialization at the expense of the agricultural sector, inefficiency in the public sector, decline in rice prices in the international market and a rise in consumer prices, and corruption. This was compounded by the civil war and ethnic insurgency problems which resulted in economic stagnation and inflation during the second half of the 1950s. Furthermore, there was a split in the ruling party, the Anti-Fascist People's Freedom League (AFPFL), caused by a power struggle among the groups that formed it. All these factors led to the "constitutional transfer of power" to the military in 1958 with the promise of free and fair elections. During the period of eighteen months under this caretaker government, the economy seemed stable. Then the power was transferred to the democratically elected government in 1960. However, this government survived for less than two years as the Revolutionary Council formed by the army took over power "to prevent the secession of some ethnic areas". The Revolutionary Council ruled the country from 1962 to 1973.

Soon after the take-over, the Revolutionary Council introduced the Burmese Way to Socialism. This was the blueprint for action to restructure the economic and political institutions in line with "socialism". The military founded the only ruling party, the Burma Socialist Programme Party (BSPP or the Lanzin Party) along with mass peasant and worker groups to mobilize the populace in implementing the goals of the government. Self-reliance, independence and strict neutrality were emphasized in its foreign policy. In the mid-1960s, the government carried out the nationalization and Burmanization of trade, industry and commerce. In short, an inward-looking policy had been formulated and implemented.

Although some of the objectives in the political agenda and social programmes were achieved to a certain extent during this period, Burma's economy remained stagnant: average annual growth rates of real gross domestic product (GDP) and per capita GDP were 2.5 per cent and 0.5 per cent respectively. Paddy production increased from 7.5 million tons in 1962/63 to 8.5 million tons in 1973/74. However, per capita paddy production declined from 0.33 ton to 0.29 ton during the same period. Exports of rice in 1962 amounted to 1.5 million tons but it dropped to 0.2 million tons in 1973/74. This resulted in rice riots and escalating consumer prices in 1967. The consequence was mounting political opposition while the economy adjusted by producing a huge black market. Government investment was insufficient to replace foreign and (declining) private investment. This forced the government to reform some of its policies, practices and even institutional structures. Thus, in 1972 the ruling party adopted a Twenty-Year Plan, which is known as the Long-Term and Short-Term Economic Policies of the Socialist Programme Party (see Appendix II).[3]

In 1974, a new (East-European style) constitution was introduced, and the Revolutionary Council handed over power to the Pyithu Hluttaw, the national assembly. Although the First Four-Year Plan (FYP) was introduced in October 1971, it was dropped in 1974 because of new policies which modified the "Burmese Way to Socialism". Thus, the Long-Term Plan really began with the Second FYP in 1974. The Plan is remarkable in the sense that it gave the agricultural sector priority over the industrial sector and recognized the role of the private sector in economic development. It also called for the establishment of an economic system on a commercial basis and indicated the requirement for external assistance. A bonus system was introduced in the state economic enterprises (SEEs) and incentives were given to farmers in the form of inputs to stimulate individual efforts to improve efficiency and productivity. During the Second FYP period (1974/75 to 1977/78), the growth rate was impressive at 4.8 per cent, which exceeded the target of 4.5 per cent, mainly because of the good weather and institutional reforms. This momentum of growth accelerated in the second half of the Second FYP and continued to the Third FYP (1978/79 to 1981/82) with a growth rate of 6.7 per cent. This was largely due to achievements in the agricultural sector which recorded an annual growth rate of 8.6 per cent, attributed mainly to the "Whole Township Special Paddy Production Programme" introduced during the Third FYP along with policy changes in the marketing system (for details, see Chapter 4 of this volume by Mya Than and Nishizawa). Although the momentum of growth in the agricultural sector weakened significantly after 1982/83 as a result of the slowing down of the "Green Revolution" effect, the performance of the Fourth FYP (1982/83–1985/86) was still better than Burma's neighbouring countries, with an average annual growth rate of 5.5 per cent. The impressive rates of growth in the agricultural sector (6.6 per cent), forestry sector (12.7 per cent), electricity sector (14.6 per cent), and communication sector (13.2 per cent) were the main factors contributing to the exceptional overall growth achievement. In short, the substantial recovery of Myanmar's economy during this period was made possible mainly because of the introduction of political as well as economic reforms since 1974. However, it is important to note that the economy started to deteriorate after 1983 when export earnings began to decline as a result of the decrease in rice procurement and the falling world price of rice.

A Brief Assessment of Recent Economic Trends[4]

The collapse of the Burmese economy was witnessed in the mid-1980s. Table 1 shows the recent trends of the economy since April 1985.

The growth rates, foreign trade figures, balance of payments, debt service ratios and inflation rates shown in the table confirm the above statement that the Myanmar economy began to decline from the mid-1980s. Although the GDP growth rate of 5.5 per cent during the first half of the 1980s was impressive, that of the second half (that is, from 1985/86 to 1989/90) was very disappointing, with negative growth rates. Export performance was also depressing: earnings fell from US$0.31 billion in 1985/86 to US$0.15 billion in 1989/90. This reduction in export earnings resulted in a decline in foreign currency reserves — down to less than US$30 million at one point in 1988. This forced the government to borrow more money from external sources and thus, Myanmar's foreign debt rose from US$1 billion in 1979 to more than US$4 billion in 1988/89. To alleviate this problem, the government applied to the United Nations for "Least Developed Country" status in 1986 and was accordingly granted it in December 1987. By this move, the government tried to secure more concessional foreign aid and to reschedule the country's

TABLE 1
Myanmar: Major Economic Indicators
(At 1985/86 constant prices)

	1985/86	*1986/87*	*1987/88*	*1988/89*
GDP % change	(100) 1.0	−1.1	−4.2	(100) 0.2
Agriculture —	(48) 2.6	0.4	−6.4	(50) 2.2
Industry —	(13) 2.2	−7.9	−6.1	(11) −1.5
Services/Trade —	(39) 4.9	3.6	3.1	(39) −4.2
Per Capita GDP (kyat)	1509	1464	1374	1351
% change		−3.1	−6.6	−1.7
Gross Domestic Investment (% of GDP)	15.4	14.6	12.9	11.6
Gross Domestic Saving (% of GDP)	11.4	12.4	12.3	11.7
Exports (US$ billion)	0.31	0.32	0.26	0.15
Imports (US$ billion)	0.59	0.55	0.62	0.22
Trade Balance (US$ billion)	−0.28	−0.23	−0.36	−0.07
Current Account (US$ billion)	−0.01	−0.16	0.18	−0.01
Balance (% of GDP)	−1.63	−0.20	0.02	−0.07
Inflation Rate (1986=100)	90.4	103.7	126.5	155.0
Foreign Exchange Reserves (US$ million)	59.7	60.1	47.6	57.1
Debt Service Ratio (% of Exports)	36.2	41.4	42.1	59.4
External Debt* (US$ billion)	2.9	3.7	4.3	n.a.

NOTE: Numbers in parentheses are shares of the sectors in GDP, in per cent.

SOURCES: Ministry of Planning and Finance, Burma, *Review of the Financial, Economic and Social Conditions for 1989/90* (Rangoon, 1989); Central Statistical Organization (CSO), *Selected Monthly Economic Indicators* (March and April 1989); and Economic Intelligence Unit, *Thailand and Burma*, Country Report No 3 (1989).

external debt repayments. At the same time, the inflation rate rose month after month. The price of rice (*ngasein*), which is the staple food of the people, increased from 72.80 kyat per basket (75 pounds) in 1987 to 320 kyat in mid-1989.[5]

Looking at the Myanmar economy from a regional context[6] (see Table 2), its per capita income of US$190 places it as one of

TABLE 2

Comparative Economic and Social Indicators for Myanmar and Selected Asian Developing Countries

I. ECONOMIC

	Population		*GNP per capita (US$)*				*Average Annual Inflation (%)*	*Distribution of GDP*		*Exports plus Imports as % of GNP*	*Terms of Trade 1987*	*Growth of Exports (%)*	
	Number (million)	*Density*			*Average Growth*			*Agriculture (%)*	*Manufacturing (%)*				
	(mid-1987)	*(per km²)*	*1987*	*1960*	*1960–70*	*1965–87*	*1980–87*	*1987*	*1987*	*1987*	*(1980=100)*	*1965–80*	*1980–87*
1. Myanmar	39.3	58	190	59	0.4	2.5	8.2	49	9	11	65	−2.1	−4.7
ASEAN													
2. Indonesia	171.4	111.1	450	94	1.8	4.5	8.5	26	14	41	69	9.6	2.7
3. Malaysia	16.5	50	1810	270	3.7	4.1	1.1	21	—	102	72	4.4	9.7
4. Philippines	58.4	188	590	251	2.1	1.7	16.7	24	25	37	98	4.7	−0.4
5. Thailand	53.6	104	850	94	5.3	3.9	2.8	16	24	54	81	8.5	10.2
SOUTH ASIA													
6. Bangladesh	106.1	736	160	59	1.2	0.3	11.1	47	7	22	91	—	6.2
7. Sri Lanka	16.4	248	400	151	2.2	3.0	11.8	27	16	53	96	0.5	6.5
8. Low Income Countries* (excluding India and China)	956.9	40	280	n.a.	2.0	1.5	13.3	33	12	74	84	5.9	−0.1

TABLE 2 (*cont'd*)

Comparative Economic and Social Indicators for Myanmar and Selected Asian Developing Countries

II. SOCIAL

	Education		*Nutrition*	*Health*		
	Adult Literacy (%)	*Primary School Enrolments as % of Age Group*	*Daily per Capita Calorie Supplies*	*Life Expectancy at Birth (years)*	*Infant Mortality Rate (aged under one)*	*Population per Physician*
	1980	*1986*	*1986*	*1987*	*1985*	*1984*
	(1)	*(2)*	*(3)*	*(4)*	*(5)*	*(6)*
1. Myanmar	66	102**	2609	60	66	3740
ASEAN						
2. Indonesia	62	118	2579	60	96	9460
3. Malaysia	65	101	2730	70	28	1930
4. Philippines	75	106	2372	63	48	6700
5. Thailand	86	99	2331	64	43	6290
SOUTH ASIA						
6. Bangladesh	26	60	1927	51	123	6730
7. Sri Lanka	85	103	2401	70	36	5520
8. Low Income Countries* (excluding India and China)	40	76	2227	54	112	13550

*Low Income Economies in which GNP per capita is less than US$450 in 1987.

**For 1984.

SOURCE: World Bank, *World Development Report 1989*; and Ministry of Planning and Finance, *Review of the Financial, Economic and Social Conditions for 1989/90.*

the poorest countries in the region. In the last twenty-five years, the Myanmar economy has grown very slowly, in per capita terms, averaging about 2.5 per cent annually, the second lowest after Bangladesh. Its economic structure reflects its resource endowments and low level of development. It is one of the most heavily agriculture-based economies in the world and "as a corollary it is also one of the world's least industrialized countries".[7]

In terms of the degree of openness (the share of total merchandise trade in GDP), Myanmar's is the smallest with 11 per cent, which reflects its position as the most inward-looking country in the region. However, its social indicators fare more favourably in comparison with other Asian developing countries, reflecting the abundant agricultural and resource potential, relatively low population density and the government's concern more with the distributional rather than the growth objective.

Options and Dilemmas

The very depressing state of the economy, as discussed above, suggests the comparison of Myanmar to a sick *homo economicus* anxiously seeking remedy from various specialists who have conducted diverse tests and scannings on the patient. All the tests made by the eight "specialists" seem to have led to the same conclusion: that the patient is still seriously ill and suffering from various diseases. Unlike the proverbial six blind Brahmins and the elephant, these "specialists", in one way or another, have been involved and are familiar with the economic affairs of Myanmar for a long time. Thus, each of them is able to provide a particular viewpoint with a comprehensive rather than a complete perspective of the country's economic malady. (However, it sometimes happens that a surgeon may think of a remedy in terms of using the scalpel on some cancerous tissues, while a psychiatrist may recommend treating the mind to cure the diseased body, and a physician may prescribe injections and oral medication to the same patient. It is hoped that this does not happen in our collective attempt to find a helpful prescription for our Myanmar *homo economicus*.)

One of the "specialists", U Tun Wai, a veteran IMF high official and an international and economic consultant, after comparing Burma's economic performance with that of Thailand, singles out management (or mismanagement) of the economy as the fundamental reason for the failure of the economy, in general; and points to investment and savings policy, fiscal policy, the management of SEEs, monetary and pricing policy, and balance of payments and exchange policy in particular. He has also conducted a systematic "stocktaking" of the weaknesses and strengths of the Myanmar economy as a basis for prescribing a pragmatic framework for medium-term economic programming in the next three to four years.

Myat Thein, a resident economist in Yangon, goes into more detailed historical analyses of the monetary and fiscal problems which have played an important role in retarding the economy. His study reveals that the present financial sector of the Myanmar economy is less developed in many respects than the one which existed before the 1963 nationalization; that the fiscal deficits have been largely responsible for the twin problems of external and internal imbalances; and that the over-extension of the public sector, particularly to the state economic enterprises, has, in turn, been chiefly responsible for the fiscal deficits. Based on these findings, he proposes a "supply-leading" type of financial development as the single most important aspect of monetary policy for development in the 1990s.

However, Mya Than, a Myanmar development economist, along with Nobuyoshi Nishizawa, a Japanese specialist on Burma, demonstrate that incorrect agricultural marketing policy, especially the pricing policy, was one of the key problems that dragged the economy into collapse. They found that Myanmar farmers are very responsive to marketing policy and prices, and the government's interventions in the agricultural sector seemed to hinder the development of this sector. This is because most of the government's policies are based on equity rather than on efficiency considerations. They therefore suggest that the policies could yield better performance results if the efficiency criterion is given greater emphasis although the equity concern should not be neglected.

Another resident Myanmar economist from Yangon, Tin Soe, together with his Australian counterpart, Brian S. Fisher, studied the development in rice price policies and their impact on production, procurement, and export, and the domestic use of rice in Burma during the period 1948–87. Their research unambiguously showed that rice price policies prior to 1961/62 had only minor effects, while those adopted after 1962/63 had serious consequences. In a way, their paper complements that of Mya Than and Nishizawa.

Soe Saing, formerly a high official in the Ministry of Finance and Revenue in Burma and a retired senior ESCAP official, suggests that the primacy of politics over the economy, weakened administration, consequences of the nationalization of the trade and industry, and banking and education sectors, unviable and inefficient state enterprises, over-valued currency, inflation and the black market, as well as restrictive trade and unrealistic pricing policies were the reasons for the failure of the economy. After highlighting some of the economic maladjustments found existing in the economy, he posits that, in order to overcome the impediments to economic recovery, it is essential to substantially increase external technical aid first before obtaining large capital aid. In such attempts, he suggests, the United Nations system would be the most suitable avenue.

On the other hand, Lütkenhorst, a UNIDO specialist in industrial development, attributed such macro-economic factors as the foreign exchange situation and the debt service crisis, as well as the inability of the state to mobilize sufficient domestic capital for investment, among other things, to be the underlying causes for the economic malaise. According to him, the increasingly precarious foreign exchange situation has led to serious bottlenecks and constraints in the country's economy, especially with regard to essential import requirements for the efficient and smooth operation of production activities in the manufacturing sector. He points out some important issues which need to be resolved urgently, such as the exchange rate problem, the promotion of domestic investment, the identification of priority areas for future development in the industrial sector, and measures to promote integration of the whole industrial structure.

In addition, Mya Than, in his contribution on "The Union of Burma Investment Law", attempts to analyse this particular legal instrument for foreign investment promotion in the light of the increasingly difficult and competitive environment *vis-à-vis* other developing countries in the effort to mobilize foreign capital for economic development. His major findings include the facts that the law is limited by its preoccupation merely with short-term development, and that it is inadequate as a tool to mobilize foreign capital when compared with those of Myanmar's competitors. He also points out that unless the fundamental political, bureaucratic machinery and infrastructural situation improves there is little chance that Myanmar can attract much needed foreign or quality capital and technology.

A long-standing scholar on the political economy of Burma, John Badgley, gives his comprehensive perception of the problems and prospect of "remodelling Myanmar". He suggests that the absence of free markets, efficient production, revolutionary information and transportation technologies, and participant societies are the negative forces that have defeated Burma's development plans in the past. His call for "remodelling" includes measures for a radical restructuring of the political economy so that effective and systematic tax collection can be made, for increasing the productivity of farmers through correct price incentives based on real market conditions, and for releasing pent-up entrepreneurial energies in the commercial and industrial sectors. Assuming, like others with measured optimism, that rapid economic growth is possible, he says that: "there is no structural reason, nor any behavioral quality among the people, nor any lack of investment capital, nor lack of management expertise among Burmese who could be recruited from around the world to serve the administration with a goal. . . . In short, the future is bright if the correct measures are taken now".

To complete the diagnosis, Myanmar should be seen (and indeed viewed by many in the past and presently that it has the *potential* to be) as part of the fast growing Asia-Pacific region. This is put forward by Richard Vokes, a long-time Burma watcher from the University of Kent. He first gives an account of the factors causing the deterioration and collapse of the economy, such as the adoption of an inward-looking economic strategy aimed at eliminating foreign control of the economy; reducing the country's dependence on foreign markets; and the official policy of strengthening the state's role over all spheres of economic life at the expense of the operation of free-market processes and private enterprise — the perverse economic restructuring and mis-development — which are, in fact, the features of the Burmese Way to Socialism introduced in 1962. Viewing the prospects of export-oriented growth in Burma in the 1990s in the light of the dynamism of the Asia-Pacific region, Vokes emphasizes the following major points:

1. Myanmar should give first priority to rebuilding and diversifying its export sector and simultanously restructure its small and inefficient industrial sector;
2. In the short to medium term, Myanmar's wealth of natural resources and primary commodities derived would provide the best hope for enhancing its export earnings and for attracting foreign investors. This is especially important at this time when raw material shortages are experienced in several resource-based industries (timber and fisheries) in the ASEAN countries. Moreover, as the ASEAN countries begin to lose their comparative advantage in labour-intensive industries in the face of rising wages and other costs of production, Myanmar might attract such labour-intensive as well as resource-based industries to its shores.

In sum, most, if not all, of the "specialists" seem to share a consensus that the chronic, though not incurable or terminal, malady of the Myanmar economy was rooted in the malfunctioning inward-looking development strategy and compounding mismanagement of the economy practised since the military takeover in 1962. To turn the tide, as U Tun Wai puts it (which others like Soe Saing, Vokes, Mya Than, and Lütkenhorst endorse) "Myanmar's rate of economic progress will be negligible unless it can succeed in getting assistance from abroad. . . . Inflow of foreign capital is linked to many factors, including domestic financial stability, handling of the debt overhang, and how efficient the government is in processing applications for foreign investment, besides the basic incentives provided to attract such investment. When all is said and done, there is hope for Myanmar". Unless the above-mentioned issues are resolved, the hope for the recovery of the Myanmar economy in the near future remains illusive.

It seems inevitable, however, that by opening its economy and society to world trade and finance Myanmar would invite not only the global transfer of goods, services and financial resources but also the positive and negative (desirable or undesirable) developmental influences of the transfer of production technologies, organizational or institutional arrangements, consumption patterns, educational, health and social systems as well as more general values of life-styles of developed countries, whether capitalist or socialist.

To a considerable extent, the quest for speedy and sustained economic growth and development will depend on the acquisition of appropriate modern technology, and even more importantly, on increasing the efficiency in the use of all resources for production. In this light, Myanmar urgently needs to increase its external economic contacts and interactions mainly to acquire new technology which will contribute to greater efficiency and expansion of production capacity. Opening the economy to foreign trade will also help to enhance efficiency through specialization and achieving economies of scale by concentrating resources in low-cost production for export, and importing cheaper goods and services from abroad.

Myanmar could benefit in diverse ways from an increase in external economic interactions. Most notably, with increasing liberalization of the economy, new technology, new products, new standards and new ideas would undoubtedly flow into the country. Furthermore, foreign trade could stimulate improvements in domestic efficiency and productivity through healthy competition for domestic producers. Admittedly, there may be some serious costs in increasing external economic relations. Foreign competition can be adverse should it stifle infant industries which Myanmar could economically develop after a period of learning, or industries which are of strategic national importance, such as those providing essential goods and services like power, water, and military supplies. Other disadvantages include repercussions on the domestic economy arising from such undesirable phenomena as product price volatility, general inflation, and fluctuations in world demand for industrial products; increased regional inequalities; and the possible adverse effects on trade and undesirable inflows and outflows of capital. However, the possibility of benefiting from increased external economic interactions also brings with it the necessity to bear some of its potential costs and risks. A way out of such a dilemma is the establishment of an effective and efficient management system and skilful and appropriate use of policy instruments capable of dealing effectively with the foreign sector, thereby reducing costs while obtaining as much benefit as possible. In this light, and at this point, it is appropriate to invite readers to ponder the observations and prognoses of the contributors in this volume as they attempt, from their respective perspectives and professional expertise, to address the key question: What are the options and dilemmas facing Myanmar and its economy in the 1990s?

APPENDIX I
Myanmar's Reform and Revolutionary Cycles: A Brief Chronology

		Politics	*Economics*
Revolution	1948	Revolt against British colonialism and Japanese occupation, headed by General Aung San Independence Formation of civilian Government headed by Prime Minister U Nu	Buddhist Socialism (economic nationalism)

APPENDIX I (*cont'd*)

Myanmar's Reform and Revolutionary Cycles:
A Brief Chronology

		Politics	Economics
Reform	1958	Constitutional transfer of power to the military headed by Gen. Ne Win General elections	Continuation of economic policies practised previously Introduction of the first foreign investment law
Reform	1960	Formation of Civilian Government headed by Prime Minister U Nu	Continuation of economic policies practised before
Revolution	1962	Military coup Revolutionary Government Establishment of Burma Socialist Program Party	Burmese Way to Socialism Nationalization and Burmanization (command economy)
Reform	1974	Socialist Republic Expansion of Burma Socialist Program Party	Internal rice price raised Loans from World Bank, Asian Development Bank, and foreign countries Introduction of incentives
Reform or Revolution?	1988	(U) Ne Win's abdication Political upheavals Military coup State Law and Order Restoration Committee (SLORC) government	Liberalization in trade and some industries Opening of economy to foreign firms Abolition of socialist economic system
Reform or Revolution?	1990	General elections	Continuation of open economy after the elections?

SOURCE: Modified version of the table in James F. Guyot's, "Burma in 1988: *Perestroika* with a Military Face", *Southeast Asian Affairs 1988* (Singapore: ISEAS, 1989), p. 107.

APPENDIX II

Twenty-Year Plan (1973/74–1993/94) and Performance

(In per cent)

	Beginning (1973/74)	*Actual Performance (1986/87)*	*Target (1993/94)*
Shares in Total Economy			
Public	36	37	48
Co-operative	3	7	26
Private	61	56	26
Agriculture[1]	38	37	30
Manufacturing	10	10	22
Services/Trade	49	47	44
Shares in Agriculture			
Public	—[2]	2	10
Co-operative	—[2]	6	50
Private	99	92	40
Agricultural growth	4.8 annually	0.4	n.a.
Industrial growth	9.4 annually	7.9	n.a.
GDP	5.9 annually	−1.1	n.a.

[1] Including fisheries and forestry

[2] Less than 1%

n.a. Not applicable

NOTE: The plan was never published in its entirety.

SOURCE: Ministry of Planning and Finance, Burma, *Report to the Pyithu Hluttaw*, various issues; and *The Review of the Financial, Economic and Social Conditions for 1989/90* (Yangon, 1989); and Burma Socialist Program Party (BSPP), *Political Report of the Central Committee to the Fifth Party Conference* (in Burmese) (Rangoon, 1985).

NOTES

1. For further information, see James F. Guyot, "Burma in 1988: Perestroika with a military face", in *Southeast Asian Affairs 1989* (Singapore: Institute of Southeast Asian Studies, 1989), pp. 107–33; and Josef Silverstein, ed., *Independent Burma at Forty Years: An Assessment* (Ithaca: Cornell Southeast Asia Program, 1989).
2. See particularly D. Steinberg, "The Development Outlook for Burma", in *Burma's Road to Development* (Colorado: Westview Press, 1981).
3. It seems that planning essentially consisted of sectoral goals presented in percentage terms and modified and updated annually, and discrete lists of

projects, without an overall rationale for their choice. For a concise discussion on the topic of economic planning in Myanmar, see D. Steinberg, *Burma's Road toward Development* (Colorado: Westview Press, 1981), especially Chapter 3; and Tin Maung Maung Than, "Burma in 1987: Twenty-five years after the revolution", in *Southeast Asian Affairs 1987* (Singapore: Institute of Southeast Asian Studies, 1988), pp. 76–83.

4. A number of useful publications which provide more details and analyses of recent economic developments in Myanmar are: ADB, *Asian Development Outlook 1989* (Manila, 1989); Asian Productivity Organization (APO), *Challenge of Asian Developing Countries: Issues and Analyses*, edited by S. Ichimura (APO, 1988); Economic Intelligence Unit, *Country Report: Burma, 1989* (London, 1989); and J. F. Guyot, op. cit., pp. 107–33.
5. For details, see Table 4 in Chapter 5 of this volume by Tin Soe and Fisher.
6. See William E. Jones, S. Naya, and G. M. Meier, eds., *Asian Development: Economic Success and Policy Lessons* (University of Wisconsin Press for International Center for Economic Growth, 1987), especially Chapter 1; and Asian Productivity Organization, *Challenges of Asian Developing Countries*, especially Chapter 1.
7. Hal Hill and Sisira Jayasuriya, "An Inward-Looking Economy in Transition", Occasional Paper No. 80 (Singapore: Institute of Southeast Asian Studies, 1986), p. 4.

2

THE MYANMAR ECONOMY AT THE CROSSROADS
Options and Constraints

U TUN WAI

Introduction

Before World War II, the Myanmar economy was slightly ahead of the Thai economy. The value of exports from Myanmar in 1937 was US$195 million (US$1,300 million at 1989 prices) while Thailand's exports amounted to only US$76 million (US$500 million at 1989 prices). National income figures are not available for Thailand, but that for Myanmar in 1937 was US$516 million (US$3,440 million at 1989 prices), giving a per capita income of US$33 (US$220 at 1989 prices).

Myanmar was fought over twice during World War II and the economy was badly damaged while Thailand was left relatively unscathed. Despite the adoption of an active post-war rehabilitation and economic recovery programme, the Myanmar economy began to fall behind the Thai economy. In 1950, Thailand's exports of US$304 million were 2.2 times those of Myanmar, and its national income of US$1,012 million (US$4,086 million at 1989 prices) was 28 per cent larger than that of the latter. By 1962, Myanmar's national income was only one-half that of Thailand and by 1987 it had fallen to less than one-fifth. Only a very small part of the explanation lies in the more rapid increase in Thailand's population, which grew from 19.6 million in 1937 to 53.0 million in 1987, while Myanmar's population increased from 18.8 million to 39.1 million during the same period. Neither was it due to differences in natural resources, because both countries are equally rich in factor endowments. For example, Myanmar has large mineral deposits, possesses three-fourths of the world's teak reserves, and the country is not over-populated. The main reason lies in the relative efficiency in national economic management in the two countries and the different perceptions and economic policies followed by the two authorities.

Socialism, Capitalism, and Pragmatism, 1962–88

The economic development of Myanmar in pre-war years under the British took place mainly through the stimulus and participation of foreign investment under a *laissez-faire* policy. The author has estimated that about one-quarter of the capital stock in pre-war years was of foreign origin. In addition to foreign investment there was a large foreign population consisting mainly of about a million Indians and a quarter million Chinese who obtained their livelihood by working in all fields of economic activity — as landlords, agricultural labourers, small businessmen, professionals such as money-lenders, doctors, lawyers, and accountants, and even as civil servants. The British, though smaller in number, were investors in large businesses and occupied key positions in the government. In 1938, remittances of profits, interest, and dividends of foreign investors amounted to about 6 per cent of gross domestic product (GDP). The per capita income of the Myanmar people was much lower than that of the foreigners. Most foreigners returned to Myanmar after the war and stayed on after independence in 1948. These facts influenced the thinking of successive governments which desired to lift the standard of living of the local people through development programmes. They were also not averse to pushing the foreigners out of the country through various limitations on qualifications for citizenship and on the issuance of work permits.

Another fact which influenced the thinking of the authorities in the early post-war years was the war damage, estimated at

US$2,000 million and the consequent need to reconstruct the economy through public investment. The system of government state-trading monopolies for the export of agricultural products (State Agricultural Marketing Board) and timber (State Timber Board) was inherited from the British by the national government upon independence.

The Land Nationalization Act was passed in 1948 as part of the government's programme of agrarian reform. The other key components of this programme were the Disposal of Tenancies Act, 1948, which provided the tenant with security of tenure, and the Tenancy Standard Rent Act, 1950, which restricted rents on agricultural land to twice the land revenue payable on rice lands and similar limitations on land used for other crops. However, the land was not collectivized and, until the eighties, decision-making on the type of crop and the acreage to be sown for each of them was left to the farmer.

During 1948–62, the government encouraged the Myanmar people to take a more active role in trade and industry, while also welcoming foreign investment, especially in large-scale projects. Joint ventures were also established with both domestic and foreign businesses. The Myanmar businesses, though establishing a niche for themselves, were unable to compete very well with the large foreign firms.

The above facts have been mentioned to indicate that, besides political considerations, the establishment of the Burmese Way to Socialism had its antecedents in the economic history of pre-war and early post-war years. Nationalization of both foreign and domestic businesses was considered essential to bring about the Burmanization of the economy. By the early seventies, all major economic enterprises except agriculture, small-scale trading and minor services had been nationalized. Over the years, the socialist government established state economic enterprises (SEEs) and by the end of 1988 there were about fifty of them in all sectors of the economy, including agriculture, forestry, fishery, livestock, industry, mining, energy, construction, transport and communication, exports and imports, hotel and tourism, and banking and insurance.

Apart from the specifics of the Myanmar case, socialists are wont to compare the possible benefits of a socialist system to the observed defects of a capitalist system — for example, prevalence of business cycles, excessive business profits stemming in part from monopolies, market failure, exploitation of labour, and unequal distribution of incomes. But socialism also has many obstacles which must be overcome, especially in a developing country, before it can become a viable option. Since markets are not used to allocate resources in a socialist economy, the central planner has to decide on production targets based on estimates of the needs of the consumer for every type of good to be sold at fixed prices. If goods are in short supply, prices can be adjusted upwards, production increased, or rationing introduced. If there is an accumulation of unsold goods, prices can be lowered or output reduced. In order to make an intelligent and meaningful decision, the planner must have precise knowledge of consumer behaviour, of the relationships among domestic sectors, and of the inter-connections between the national economy and other countries.

The economic performance of Myanmar has been influenced by the manner in which socialism was introduced and operated, by the macro-economic policies adopted by the authorities, and by events in the world economy. Had the authorities been more careful on how socialism was managed, and if more appropriate economic policies had been used, perhaps Myanmar would have had an opposite experience.

Method of Implementing the Burmese Way to Socialism

Soon after the Burmese Way to Socialism was introduced, the central planners and the economic advisors began to collect masses of information and attempted to compile input–output tables to set quantitative targets. Since the administrative machinery was not geared to carry out this task, the data supplied were fairly inaccurate for assessment and planning. Later, even after this effort of compiling sophisticated statistics was abandoned, it was still necessary to report on the state of the economy and the effects of government activity on production. Over-optimistic reporting on the economic situation and the down-playing of difficulties, especially in the oil sector, continued for a long period because officials feared they would lose their jobs. It was only in the late seventies, when the seriousness of the deteriorating economic situation became clear, that the flow of information became less unreliable and the authorities gradually realized the need to change some of their policies — for example, they began to accept Overseas Development Assistance (ODA).

In the socialist regime, practically all Cabinet posts and heads of the state economic enterprises were filled by military personnel as only they had the confidence of General Ne Win (later U Ne Win). This was understandable from the political viewpoint because in the fifties, when he was in power, U Nu had also appointed people he could trust. But the difference was that U Nu's appointees had some administrative experience running the country, whereas the military had practically no experience. Furthermore, under a socialist economic system, there was a growing need for economic expertise, which the socialist government did not have.

Some of the military personnel learned on the job but, as soon as they were trained, they were either moved to new posts or relieved from their duties, in part for political reasons and in part because of the Burmese socialist view that things must be shared as equally as possible. In other words, important civilian posts were used to reward deserving military personnel on a rotational basis. Furthermore, the military felt that they did not need to accept the advice of technocrats and quite often took decisions based on socialist principles rather than on pragmatism. There are interesting anecdotes of the way imported goods were distributed equally to all regions without considering variations in income levels, taste, climate, and the size of local production. The country-wide sale of goods at a uniform retail price, irrespective of differing transport costs, is another example of socialistic principles taking precedence over pragmatic considerations.

The decision-making process was also very cumbersome and too centralized. In order to have checks and balances, most decisions were taken in committees which did not have powers to decide on important issues. These committees in turn had to submit proposals to the Cabinet for matters considered small in other countries, such as the issuance of passports to government service personnel and the sending of students for training abroad. This means, of course, that key officials were kept busy with small matters and they were unable to devote time and attention to more important issues.

In the first decade of the socialist regime, the authorities wished to be self-reliant and not only did they not accept any foreign investment, but they were also reluctant to accept foreign aid. Socialism and foreign investment do not generally mix, but foreign assistance could have been accepted on a large scale from the beginning. The effect of this socialist policy of "going it alone" greatly limited the size of domestic investment and the rate of economic growth, details about which are taken up next.

Macro-Economic Policies

The scope of macro-economic policies covers a broad spectrum of governmental attitudes and decisions on many questions, including the allocation of resources between current and future consumption or how much to invest, establishing priority sectors for development, deciding upon methods for the mobilization of domestic financial resources, motivating people to work hard, ensuring the absence of inflationary pressure, and preventing balance of payments difficulties despite changing world economic conditions.

Governments take good and bad economic decisions, but the balance must be very positive in order that a country prospers. The Myanmar governments in power from 1948 to 1962 took bad economic decisions such as embarking on an over-ambitious Eight-Year Plan (Pyidawtha Plan) in 1952, which had to be abandoned after three years and substituted with two less unrealistic Four-Year Plans. However, the second one for the period 1961/62–1964/65 could not be implemented because the military took over in 1962.[1] Probably, the balance of economic decisions during that period was slightly positive and, furthermore, each government tried to learn from the mistakes of its predecessor.

The major macro-economic policies of the socialist regime will be examined under the headings of Investment and Savings

Policy, Fiscal Policy, Management of State Economic Enterprises, Monetary and Pricing Policy, and Balance of Payments and Exchange Rate Policy. Each of these policies interacted upon one another and with economic events in a vicious circle of lower rates of economic growth and increasing rates of inflation.

Investment and Savings Policy. The Myanmar economy is centrally planned and regulated, but less so since the trade liberalization measures of 1988 and 1989, and the encouragement given to private enterprise. Investments are carried out within the framework of a twenty-year plan, Four-Year Plans, and an annual economic budget.

Table 1 provides information on the level of investment, savings, and growth achieved by the Myanmar economy during the past twenty-seven years. The performance has been well below those of its neighbours in the Association of Southeast Asian Nations (ASEAN). Growth rates were low because investment was greatly constrained by low national savings and the fact that, in the first fifteen years, the socialist government was reluctant to accept foreign assistance. As mentioned by Kazushi Hashimoto, growth rates rose in the late seventies and early eighties only

TABLE 1
Investment, Savings, and Growth in Myanmar, 1962–88
(In per cent of GDP)

Years	*Growth*	*Investment*	*National Savings*	*Resource Gap*
1962–65	4.9	13.5	15.4	−1.9
1966–69	2.2	10.9	8.7	2.2
1970–73	1.3	11.2	10.5	0.7
1974–77	4.7	10.9	10.0	0.9
1978–81	6.5	20.9	16.5	4.4
1982–85	4.7	17.7	12.5	5.2
1986–88	−1.7	12.5	9.7	2.8

SOURCES: Ministry of Planning and Finance, *Report to the Pyithu Hluttaw on the Financial, Economic and Social Conditions for 1988/89*, and *Review of the Financial, Economic and Social Conditions for 1989/90*; International Monetary Fund, *International Financial Statistics* (monthly), and *Yearbook, 1988*.

after Myanmar began to accept ODA. Other factors cited were the management reform of the state economic enterprises and the implementation of the "Whole Township Special Paddy Production Programme".[2] It also began to borrow from commercial banks but this policy was not in the country's long-run interests because interest rates were high and the projects were not as successful as expected. Even during 1982–85, when the growth rate was still good, the country was experiencing financial difficulties, with reserves declining by US$196 million between 1982 and 1985. Imports were cut drastically and this adversely affected both government revenues, public sector savings and investment, and growth during 1986–88.

In the fifties, public and private investments were approximately the same size. Under the socialist regime, as more and more sectors of the economy were taken over by the government and the SEEs, the share of private sector investment declined. During 1982–85, of the total gross investment rate, equivalent to 17.7 per cent of gross domestic product (GDP), the public share was 13.9 per cent and the private, only 3.8 per cent. In 1986–88 about three-quarters of total gross investment was by the public sector, with state enterprises accounting for about 60 per cent of public sector investments.

Another reason for the low rates of growth was that agriculture was given lower priority than industry. State investments in that sector declined from 13 per cent of the total in 1962/63 to 12 per cent in 1985/86, and still further to 9.2 per cent in 1986/87 and to 9.9 per cent in 1988/89 (see Table 2). The higher priority accorded to industry is understandable, but too great a reliance on import substitution industries with practically no attention to export promotion industries led to a misallocation of resources. To begin with, the import substitution industries were protected by both tariffs and quantitative import controls which tended to make inefficient factories look profitable in the seventies. Furthermore, when the foreign exchange situation became very tight, imports of raw materials and spare parts were slashed with disastrous consequences on the state economic enterprises. It is estimated that even as early as 1980/81 the average capacity

TABLE 2

Public Investment by Sector, 1962/63–1989/90

(In per cent of total)

	1962/63	*1985/86*	*1986/87*	*1987/88*[a]	*1988/89*[a]	*1989/90*[b]
Agriculture	13.0	12.0	9.2	12.8	9.9	11.2
Livestock & Fishery	—	2.8	2.8	1.9	2.7	2.7
Forestry	0.2	3.0	2.9	3.0	3.3	4.1
Mining	2.0	5.0	3.8	6.4	11.6	11.1
Processing & Manufacturing	4.9	28.9	24.1	20.1	18.0	18.7
Power	4.2	10.3	8.8	12.6	10.1	9.0
Construction	15.8	6.0	9.2	9.3	5.8	6.0
Transport & Communication	23.5	12.7	17.7	17.8	20.5	14.4
Trade	4.9	2.8	2.5	2.0	1.7	1.4
Social Services	4.5	9.2	8.8	7.1	6.6	6.9
Admin. Organizations	26.0	6.2	8.0	4.4	7.5	9.5
Other[c]	1.0	1.1	2.2	2.6	2.3	5.0
	100.0	100.0	100.0	100.0	100.0	100.0

[a] Provisional.

[b] Annual Plan for 1989/90.

[c] Financial Institutions and Town and City Development Committees.

SOURCES: Ministry of Planning and Finance, *Report to the Pyithu Hluttaw on the Financial, Economic and Social Conditions for 1988/89*, and *Review of the Financial, Economic and Social Conditions for 1989/90*.

utilization of industrial SEEs was about 70 per cent. This situation did not improve in subsequent years and even deteriorated during 1986–88 as imports were further reduced.

Investment in capital-intensive projects combined with a low capacity utilization rate will tend to make the incremental capital output ratio (ICOR) higher than need be. There are many methods of computing ICOR, each with its own problems of compilation and interpretation. Some of the issues relate to the use of appropriate deflaters for investment and output, the extent of the lags, and the influence of other factors besides capital. For example, weather conditions, availability of suitable labour and of management, credit, savings, openness of the economy, and terms of trade.[3] One easy way of compilation, which would provide a first approximation, is to divide the investment rate by the growth rate. Using this method and the data provided in Table 1, one notes that Myanmar's ICOR rose from 2.8 in 1962–65 to 5.0 in 1966–69, and still further to 8.6 in 1970–73, averaging 5.5 for 1962–73. In subsequent periods the ICOR fell to 2.3 in 1974, 3.2 in 1978–81, and 3.8 in 1982–85, averaging 3.1 for 1974–85. Myanmar's ICOR during this latter period compares rather favourably with those of its Asian neighbours whose ICOR in 1976–82 was as follows: Indonesia 2.3, Malaysia 3.7, Philippines 4.7, Singapore 4.3, Sri Lanka 3.4, and Thailand 3.7.[4] However, Myanmar's smaller ICOR is mainly due to its low investment rate. If one were to compute ICOR in Myanmar separately for the public and private sectors, one would obtain a different picture. Table 3 provides data on investment and output among public, co-operatives, and private sectors for the years 1984/85–1987/88. While the public sector usually accounted for three-quarters of total investment, it contributed only about 38 per cent of GDP over the same period. In relation to its own output, the public sector in 1987/88 invested 34 per cent, the co-operatives 6.8 per cent, and the private sector 6.3 per cent. Since the rates of growth of these sectors were 1.6 per cent, 9.9 per cent, and 1.7 per cent, respectively, the ICOR was 21 for the public sector, 0.7 for the co-operatives, and 5.5 for the private sector. The differences in ICORs arose in part because of the varying efficiencies and in part because of

TABLE 3
Investment and Output among Public, Co-operative, and Private Sectors, 1984/85–87/88
(In per cent of total)

	Output			*Investment*		
	Public	*Co-op*	*Private*	*Public*	*Co-op*	*Private*
1984/85	38.2	5.0	56.8	75.2	23.5	
1985/86	37.7	5.5	56.8	74.0	26.0	
1986/87	37.4	6.8	55.8	73.5	26.5	
1987/88[a]	37.2	7.2	55.6	75.9	3.0	21.1
1987/88[a] (million kyats)	23,303	4,546	34,812	7,916	308	2,198

[a] Provisional

SOURCES: Ministry of Planning and Finance, *Report to the Pyithu Hluttaw on the Financial, Economic and Social Conditions for 1988/89*, and *Review of the Financial, Economic and Social Conditions for 1989/90*.

the nature of each sector's investment. Public investment was concentrated more on transport and communication, construction, power, and industry (see Table 2), while the co-operatives were mainly in trading activities which do not require much investments, and the private sector in agriculture, light manufacturing and internal trade.

Fiscal Policy. The main fiscal problem has been that, excluding foreign loans and aids, the central government budget has been in deficit for many years (see Table 4). Revenues (tax and non-tax combined) have fallen from 17 per cent of GDP in 1981/82 to 10 per cent in 1987/88, and still further to 7 per cent in 1988/89. Although expenditures have been contained in nominal terms and even in real terms, the overall deficit has persisted because the economy has not been growing as expected. Government wages were frozen in the seventies and increased by only 10 per cent in 1981/82, rising significantly only in 1989/90. Since prices rose rapidly, real wages fell drastically, lowering work incentives and reducing government efficiency and revenue collections.

TABLE 4
Budgets of State Administrative Organizations, 1984/85–89/90
(In million kyats)

	Current Receipts	*Current Expenditure*	*Current Surp./Def.*	*Investment*	*Overall Surp./Def.*
1984/85[a]	7,370.0	5,293.2	2,079.8	1,841.4	238.4
1985/86[a]	7,300.5	5,606.2	1,694.3	2,051.9	−357.6
1986/87[a]	6,835.6	6,047.9	787.7	2,327.5	−1,539.8
1987/88[b]	6,674.3	5,927.1	747.2	2,158.9	−1,411.7
1988/89[b]	5,030.8	6,135.8	−1,105.0	1,746.9	−2,851.9
1989/90[c]	7,822.8	6,623.4	1,199.4	1,729.4	−530.0

Financing

	Foreign Loans and Aid	*Financial Account*	*Other*	*Total*
1984/85[a]	998.4	90.3	−1,327.1	−238.4
1985/86[a]	1,228.3	48.6	−919.3	357.6
1986/87[a]	1,586.4	−1.4	−45.2	1,539.8
1987/88[b]	1,284.8	−71.7	198.6	1,411.7
1988/89[b]	729.2	117.0	2,005.7	2,851.9
1989/90[c]	169.4	315.6	45.0	530.0

[a] Actuals
[b] Provisional
[c] Annual Plan for 1989/90

SOURCES: Ministry of Planning and Finance, *Report to the Pyithu Hluttaw on the Financial, Economic and Social Conditions for 1988/89*, and *Review of the Financial, Economic and Social Conditions for 1989/90.*

Another factor for the poor tax revenue performance was the shrinking size of the recorded private sector because of the growth of black-marketing and the expansion of the underground economy. The reductions in contributions from state economic enterprises resulted from lower profits as these enterprises could not get sufficient inputs and faced growing financial difficulties. Their contributions fell from K2,217 million in 1981/82 to K1,936 million in 1985/86, and still further to K1,676 million in 1988/89. The foreign exchange shortage reduced imports, with adverse consequences on custom duty collections which fell from K1,297 million in 1982/83 to K1,000 million in 1988/89.

Another example of misplaced fiscal policy, inherited by the socialist regime from the governments of the fifties, was the system of government procurement of rice and other agricultural products at prices well below international levels until September 1987 when these products, including rice, were decontrolled. The difference between the export price, less expenses, and the procurement price represented profits to the government trading corporations. While this system helped the fiscal situation, the low producer price adversely affected the production of rice and other crops. Rice procurement prices remained unchanged from 1977/78 (the price of higher grade paddy was raised slightly in 1980/81) until September 1987.

The central government deficits were financed mainly by foreign loans and aid until 1987/88, but beginning in 1988/89 loans from the banking system (which is the main component of "Other" in Table 4) have been an important source of finance.

Management of State Economic Enterprises. There are more than 50 state economic enterprises playing a major role in power, energy, mining, construction, manufacturing and processing, and external trade and internal distribution, especially during the past decade. About 60 per cent of public investment and about 45 per cent of total investment in the economy have been undertaken by the SEEs. Their investment programme and yearly output targets are determined by the government in the annual economic budget.

The SEEs have had financial difficulties for a long time and their operations since 1984/85 are presented in Table 5. The government, conscious of the need to run these enterprises efficiently, established official guidelines in 1975/76 giving them greater autonomy over administrative and financial matters and stipulating that they be operated on a commercial basis. They were expected to be self-financing in that surpluses of profitable SEEs would be channelled to deficit enterprises to finance their investment programmes. These guidelines, however, could not prevent a deterioration of their finances in 1982 and 1983 because of a weakening of export markets and a rapid rise in investment

TABLE 5

Operations of State Economic Enterprises, 1984/85–89/90

(In million kyats)

	1984/85	*1985/86*	*1986/87*	*1987/88*[a]	*1988/89*[a]	*1989/90*[b]
Current Receipts	22,533	22,335	21,539	18,296	19,562	24,595
Current Expenditure	22,829	22,503	20,626	18,996	21,567	25,406
Current Surp./Def.	– 296	– 168	913	– 700	–2,005	– 811
Capital Receipts	15	5	9	90	35	108
Capital Expenditure	4,489	4,299	3,877	3,826	3,892	2,961
Overall Surp./Def.	–5,066	–4,462	–2,955	–4,436	–5,862	–3,664
Financing						
Foreign Loans/Aid	1,524	1,719	1,682	1,615	1,727	—
Bank Financing	4,312	3,961	2,616	3,755	5,033	—
Other[c]	– 770	–1,218	–1,343	– 934	– 898	—

[a] Provisional

[b] Annual Plan for 1989/90

[c] Balancing item

SOURCES: Ministry of Planning and Finance, *Report to the Pyithu Hluttaw on the Financial, Economic and Social Conditions for 1988/89*, and *Review of the Financial, Economic and Social Conditions for 1989/90*.

expenditures. They continued to have financial difficulties in the eighties, as evidenced by the data in Table 5. There are SEEs with current surpluses, but for that sector as a whole, except for 1986/87, there were no savings to finance their investments during 1984–88.

About one-third of their overall deficits have been financed by foreign loans and aids and two-thirds by bank financing. This use of bank credit has led to inflationary pressures and balance of payments difficulties, not only for the period shown in the table but as far back as 1978. During the Plan period 1978–81, bank financing of state enterprises averaged about 40 per cent of money and about 30 per cent of domestic liquidity (money plus quasi-money). During 1982–85, bank financing increased to 46 per cent of money, while for 1986/87 it improved to 29 per cent of money and 16 per cent of domestic liquidity because of cutbacks in the investment programme.

Why were the SEEs unsuccessful? To begin with, despite the so-called autonomy given to SEEs, they were still very much controlled by the central government and decision-making was slow. Secondly, even though controls were exercised through operating ratios (the ratio of operating expenditures to operating revenues) to keep them below unity, a glaring defect was that financial costs were excluded. Thirdly, price adjustments were allowed but these were either too cumbersome or in some cases hid the inefficiency of the enterprise itself. Fourthly, some of the underlying investments of the SEEs were not viable, especially in certain import-substitution industries. Fifthly, the government itself, being under financial constraints, was unable to provide adequate capital. Sixthly, the quality of the management and of the workers was not good enough. Lastly, the macro-economic environment was not conducive to make profits. The shortage of foreign exchange meant that raw materials, spare parts and so forth, could not be imported and, more recently, the shortage of fuel oil further aggravated the utilization of capacity which fell to very low levels. Since workers could not be laid off, losses became greater. The average capacity utilization percentage for all industrial SEEs fell from 73.4 in 1981/82 to 67.9 in 1983/84 and must have fallen further in recent years.

Monetary and Pricing Policy. The banking system consists of the Union of Myanmar Bank, the Economic Bank, the Agricultural Bank, and the Foreign Trade Bank, all government-owned. All private commercial banks were nationalized in the sixties. The Union of Myanmar Bank is the central bank of the country. The Economic Bank lends mainly to the SEEs, the Agricultural Bank lends to agriculture, and the Foreign Trade Bank handles Myanmar's external transactions. The annual credit requirements are derived from the investment, production, procurement, and trading targets of the annual plans. As such, one might say that monetary policy in Myanmar has been only to serve the credit requirements of the public sector.

There has been no systematic analysis of the effect of monetary and credit aggregates on prices and balance of payments. However, when things got out of hand, the authorities used the technique of demonetization of the larger denomination currency notes to try to bring about a more sensible balance between money, output and prices. This weapon was used three times, once in 1964 and again in 1985 and 1987. The government used this weapon also to reduce black-marketing and to catch those who had evaded payment of income taxes by deducting estimated tax arrears from those with large holdings of currency. The first two demonetizations did not adversely affect the masses because holders of small amounts of notes were given new currency on a one-for-one basis. But at the third time no exchanges were permitted. Since small and medium-sized notes were also demonetized it had a disastrous effect on the poor people. Currency in circulation was reduced from K17.7 billion in June 1987 to K8.1 billion at the end of September 1987.

Table 6 provides data on money, credit, and prices for Myanmar for the period 1962–88. It will be noted that inflation in the first decade of the socialist regime was tolerable. Starting with the first Four-Year Plan, inflation was much higher, eased considerably in the second period, but deteriorated again in subsequent periods. The prices reported here are official ones. Free market prices rose much more rapidly and in 1989 they accelerated even faster. This occurred in part because of an increase

TABLE 6
Money, Quasi-Money, Credit and Prices, 1962–88
(Average annual percentage change)

	Money	*Money Plus Quasi Money*	*Domestic Credit*	*GDP Deflator*	*Consumer Prices*
1962–65	11.0	1.2	12.4	−2.8	3.2
1966–69	3.8	3.2	10.1	5.3	6.1
1970–73	17.6	12.3	16.3	8.3	7.8
1974–77	16.0	14.1	14.6	14.2	19.5
1978–81	12.9	17.3	19.8	3.0	0.1
1982–85	10.3[a]	11.2	17.2	1.9	5.7
1986–88[b]	−2.4[c]	2.1[d]	15.3[e]	10.3	17.4

[a] Three years' average.
[b] Average of two years, 1986 and nine months ending September 1987 for money, quasi money, and credit.
[c] Average of 41.4 per cent increase in 1986 and −46.2 per cent in 1987.
[d] Average of 31.3 per cent increase in 1986 and −27.1 per cent in 1987.
[e] Average of 33.2 per cent increase in 1986 and −2.7 per cent in 1987.

SOURCES: International Monetary Fund, *International Financial Statistics*, and *Yearbook, 1988*.

in the velocity of circulation of the remaining currency, and in part because of the activation of savings deposits and the further creation of money through bank loans to the government and to the SEEs.

Nominal interest rates have been lower than the rate of inflation, thus yielding negative real rates. The twelve-year savings certificates and savings bank accounts pay 10.9 per cent and 8.0 per cent, respectively, and are popular. Savings outstanding have increased, in part because of its tax-free nature, from K878 million in 1978 to K8,190 million in 1987. Lending rates to the SEEs range from 5 to 8 per cent per annum, to co-operatives from 8 to 9 per cent per annum, and to the private sector, including agriculture, from 8 to 12 per cent per annum. Only small personal loans, formerly handled by pawnshops, are charged 24 per cent per annum.

As regards pricing policy, reference has been made already to keeping the producer prices of rice and other agricultural products below the world market price, which tended to discourage agricultural production. The prices of imported goods were also kept low, but as the government distribution system could not adequately supply the needs of the people, there was black-marketing by those who got monthly rations from the government stores. Similarly, prices of utilities, government services, and goods produced domestically were generally kept lower than levels that would have cleared the market demand. These goods were also resold by those fortunate enough to get their hands on the limited supplies. Consequently, people devoted much of their energy to redistributing goods through a private network of petty traders and black marketeers, who undoubtedly performed a useful task, but their capacities for work should have been channelled into producing goods. Thus, as a result of the government controlling prices and its inability to supply goods adequately, distortions existed everywhere. The present government in late 1988 and early 1989 took steps to eliminate some of the distortions by raising the prices of goods and services to market levels — for example, gasoline, bus-fares, air fares, train fares, electricity and water charges, wages of government workers, and by freeing internal and external trade.

Balance of Payments and Exchange Rate Policy. Myanmar's balance of payments has been dominated by transactions on trade account. There were trade surpluses in the fifties and in the early sixties, but beginning in 1964 there have been trade deficits which have gotten larger each year, reflecting the inability of the economy to export sufficient quantities of goods to pay for the growing needs of investment. In the fifties, exports were about 18 per cent of gross domestic product and even during 1962–65 they were still about 16 per cent of GDP. Beginning in 1966, when it declined to 12 per cent of GDP, things got worse and by 1975 exports reached a low of 4.3 per cent of GDP. There was some recovery in subsequent years, reaching 8.1 per cent in 1980 and 1981, helped in part by the infusion of ODA assistance into high-yielding projects. But from 1982 onwards things deteriorated again and new lows were reached, namely, 3.7 per cent of GDP in 1986 and averaging 2.2 per cent in 1987 and 1988. The very low figures in the last two years reflect in part the uncertainties arising from the decontrol of the rice trade without changing the exchange rate, and in part the political difficulties. The decline in the unit value of exports from 1984 to 1988 by some 30 per cent was also an important contributing factor. But the major blame for the declining trend of exports must be borne by the mismanagement of the economy and the SEEs, the lack of incentives to work hard and produce more for the export of traditional commodities such as rice, teak, and pulses, the policy of establishing import-substituting industries without sufficient priority given for the import of raw materials and spare parts, and embarking on new investment projects without sufficient domestic financial resources.

With this poor export performance, it is not surprising that there were huge trade and balance of payments deficits on current account, as shown in Table 7. Although imports were cut, beginning in 1982, the tide could not be stemmed. In fact, this severe cut in imports had adverse effects on domestic output and increased inflationary pressures.

TABLE 7
International Trade, Payments and Reserves, 1962–88
(Averages in million US$)

	Exports	*Imports*	*Current Account*	*Capital Account*	*Reserves Change*	*End Res. % Imports*
1962–65	248.3	222.8	– 4.1	89.6	85.5	39.2
1966–69	138.1	157.8	– 34.9	–16.4	– 51.3	27.0
1970–73	128.7	167.4	– 52.8	23.9	– 28.9	64.7
1974–77	185.5	250.8	– 55.2	67.8	12.6	37.6
1978–81	399.2	719.6	–308.4	434.7	126.3	27.8
1982–85	368.2	687.2	–316.5	120.9	–195.6	12.0
1986–88	215.0	272.0	–256.0	301.6	45.6	31.7

SOURCES: International Monetary Fund, *International Financial Statistics*, and *Yearbook, 1988*; Ministry of Planning and Finance, *Report to the Pyithu Hluttaw on the Financial, Economic and Social Conditions for 1988/89*, and *Review of the Financial, Economic and Social Conditions for 1989/90.*

Besides the trade account, the need to service the ever growing external debt, estimated to have reached US$4 billion in 1988, was also a strain on the balance of payments. It has been estimated that in recent years, debt servicing has amounted to as much as three-quarters of export earnings.

Foreign exchange reserves have fluctuated, partly in response to changes in export earnings, and partly to government decisions to borrow abroad from international banks to finance the current account deficit. Occasionally, as in the 1978–81 period, it reflected an inflow of foreign aid. Although the ratio of gross foreign exchange reserves, including gold holdings at national valuations, to imports are shown in Table 7, it is difficult to interpret these statistics because of variations in the size of imports and because there is considerable *de facto* window-dressing in the figures. Both the Union of Myanmar Bank and the Foreign Trade Bank have huge liabilities abroad in the form of overdrafts, swap, and other arrangements. In fact, beginning in 1982, the banking system has had a negative net foreign asset position, which amounted to K1,317 million at the end of 1985, and a negative K717 million in September 1987.

A few years ago, the socialist government decided that it should try to get a reduction of its external debt owed to governments by applying to the United Nations for the "least developed country" status on the basis that its per capita GDP was below US$356 (average of 1983–85), that its manufacturing share was 10 per cent or less of GDP, and that its literacy rate was 20 per cent or less. This designation was granted by the United Nations on 11 December 1987, but the Japanese Government while agreeing to reduce the debt owed by Myanmar did not allow the Myanmar Government to stop making the payments. Instead, the debt servicing payments had to be put into a special Japanese account to be used for further aid to Myanmar in future years. In other words, it was more like a roll-over at best and the cash drain on the debt account would continue until new aid projects could be agreed upon and fresh disbursements made.

As with most countries, Myanmar has been reluctant to use the exchange rate to solve its balance of payments difficulties.

Instead, it has relied on trade and exchange controls to prevent domestic demand from spilling over into more imports. Consequently, a flourishing black market in foreign exchange is reported to have developed at about seven times the official rate. Goods are smuggled in and out across the Thai border, and this parallel economy has acted like a safety valve for more than a decade.

Under the Bretton Woods system until 1971, the kyat was pegged to gold at a fixed rate of K4.716 to US$1. Soon after the SDR (special drawing right from the International Monetary Fund) was created, Myanmar was the first country to be pegged to it and, consequently, the value of the kyat appreciated in terms of other currencies whenever the dollar depreciated *vis-à-vis* the SDR which, of course, aggravated Myanmar's balance of payments problem. Minor adjustments in the external value of the kyat were made in the seventies, the last in 1977 when its value was fixed at K8.5085 to one SDR. It remains unchanged at that rate in 1989. Over the years, and especially in 1988 and 1989, the kyat has become overvalued in that domestic wholesale prices of agricultural commodities, especially rice, are well above world market prices. Thus, there is a need to adjust the exchange rate. How this might be done and to what level is taken up in the next section.

Stock-taking, Restructuring, and Economic Programming, 1989–92

The country was at an economic standstill when the present military government under General Saw Maung came into power in September 1988, but by the third quarter of 1989 it had taken a number of initiatives in the economic field. It has welcomed foreign investment, given fishing and timber extraction leases to foreigners, formed joint ventures with domestic businesses, liberalized domestic and foreign trade to the private sector, raised government wages, increased the price of gasoline and transport services, and adjusted upwards the charges for water and electricity.

Colonel Abel, the Minister of Planning and Finance, and concurrently the Minister for Trade, has said that " . . . according to talks held with economists both within and without the country and with officials concerned of Asian countries in which the economy is specially developing, it is known that the economic policy laid down in the country today is on the right path. . . . "[5] While this is broadly correct, the new orientation needs to be carefully monitored so that the full potential of the economy may be realized. Undoubtedly, this is not an easy task.

The present government has continued the practice of preparing annual economic plans and the one for 1989/90 is presented in Table 8, together with the results of some earlier years for output, investment, and trade. Some of the foreign press have indicated that Myanmar's efforts at an economic recovery have failed to impress foreign investors.[6] They have, however, recognized some of the positive steps taken, such as the lowering of tax rates. More adventurous foreign investors such as the Daewoo Corporation of Korea have continued to invest in Myanmar, in textiles and a department store, for example. Another article has mentioned that the government is struggling to lift Myanmar's economy and that the increasing rate of inflation, especially rising rice prices, underscores its difficulties. It points to the raising of public sector wages by as much as 350 per cent for the lower scales, 200 per cent for the middle scales, and about 30 per cent for the higher scales as one of the causes of further inflation, although this connection has been denied by a Foreign Ministry spokesman.[7]

From Table 8, it will be noted that the main adjustment in 1989/90 is to come from a reduction of investment, but that consumption in total and on a per capita basis is targetted to rise slightly. Exports in quantum terms are expected to rise by 59 per cent but this will be difficult to realize even considering that 1988/89 is a low base, because the 1989/90 target is still about 30 per cent higher than the figure in 1986/87 which was a good export year before the political troubles. Imports are to increase by only 1 per cent in real terms, which will make it difficult for the output target to be achieved, but given the foreign exchange position and the small prospects of foreign aid increasing in the near future, this target probably had to be adopted.

TABLE 8

Selected Economic Targets for 1989/90 and Results for 1985/86–1988/89

(In million kyats at 1985/86 producer prices)

	1985/86	*1986/87*	*1987/88*[a]	1988/89[a]	1989/90[b]	
					Value	% Growth
Net Output	55,889	55,397	53,047	53,156	54,958	3.4
Imports	4,802	3,913	3,925	3,289	3,324	1.0
Exports	2,566	3,068	2,496	2,775	4,412	59.0
Net Available for use	58,225	56,242	54,476	53,670	53,870	0.4
Consumption	49,532	49,053	47,590	46,197	47,185	2.1
Investment	8,649	8,272	7,473	6,717	6,655	−0.9
			(In kyats)			
Per Capita						
Net Output	1,509	1,464	1,374	1,351	1,370	1.4
Consumption	1,335	1,296	1,233	1,174	1,176	0.2
Investment	233	219	194	171	166	−2.9
Net Output per worker	3,701	3,573	3,355	3,315	3,347	1.0

[a] Provisional

[b] Annual Plan for 1989/90

SOURCES: Ministry of Planning and Finance, *Review of the Financial, Economic and Social Conditions for 1989/90.*

Stock-taking and Restructuring

What do we mean by stock-taking and why is it important? Stock-taking is getting a handle on all things that have gone right and wrong, especially in the last few years, with a view to making appropriate changes to improve the economic situation. One must take stock of structure, organization, and the method of managing the economy. Structure includes infrastructure as well as the allocation of resources among various sectors, such as agriculture, industry, transport and communications, and trade. It covers the provision of technical education and training to both management and labour. It also encompasses the extent to which the economy will be open or closed from the world economy.

By organization, one means how efficiently the government is run and how well organized it is to be able to respond to changing economic conditions, domestically and abroad. It is only when the government and the private sector work in unison, as for example, in Japan, that an economy can function at its full potential. It also includes whether labour and management can work together in harmony or whether there are strikes and walk-outs by labour, and whether business is enlightened enough to invest for the long haul rather than to make quick profits.

Managing the economy can be carried out in a number of ways. There is the extreme socialist way which relies greatly on planning and a quantification of everything without sufficient attention being paid to costs and the feasibility of projects. At the other extreme is the *laissez-faire* approach which relies completely on the market to allocate resources in the belief that the "consumer is king". In between, there are various combinations of socialism and capitalism. But whatever the mix, as mentioned earlier, it is most important to have a pragmatic approach and not be wedded to "isms". Policies and measures which work in other countries should be tried, but with a watchful eye to make necessary adaptations. The impact of changes in the world economy will continue to have an important bearing on the economic well-being of the Myanmar people. How the authorities react to these changes and make suitable policy adjustments can make a difference between achieving economic progress and forever facing financial difficulties as in the past.

So much for conceptual generalities. Concretely, the authorities must make lists of import requirements linked to different levels of output growth and different possibilities of financing it, namely, national savings, export earnings, and foreign assistance. These lists would be compiled with a view to importing machinery, spare parts, and raw materials to make the factories operate at full capacity, or to significantly raise rates of utilization. Transport and communications, and other sectors including agriculture, fisheries, and forestry all need to be reviewed from this point of view. Since Myanmar has been stagnating for a long period, there will be a financing gap. Policy measures to close the gap would be an important ingredient in an economic programme, which will be discussed later. Some observations on structure, organization, and management of certain sectors is given below.

Investment. From the point of view of achieving growth, it may be considered desirable to have more investment. But in Myanmar's present financial situation that is not possible, and hence the decision to reduce investment by 0.9 per cent in 1989/90 (see Table 8) is a good one. But what is not clear is the breakdown between starting new projects and completing existing ones begun earlier. Needless to say, priority should be given to the latter category. Equally important is the division between fixed capital and working capital. Fixed capital means creating more productive capacity, whether through new projects or by completing existing projects. Working capital means having more supplies of raw materials, machinery, and spare parts to make the existing capacity more productive. Working capital also means having foreign exchange reserves to provide flexibility in carrying out an economic programme in case of a shortfall in national savings, export earnings, or external financial assistance.

As mentioned already, the net foreign assets of the banking system have been negative for many years. However, gross reserves including gold have been positive but they have fallen from US$239.2 million in 1981 to US$35.1 million in the third quarter of 1987. Since then, they have recovered to US$89.2 million at the end of 1988 and increased to US$159.0 million by June 1989, or about 30 per cent of projected imports for 1989/90. However, given the temporary nature of the boost in reserves from advance sales of forestry and fishing rights, and the fact that imports are still low compared to those in 1986/87 and 1987/88 (see Table 8), not to mention that Myanmar has stopped servicing its external debt of some US$4 billion, the level of reserves must be considered low especially in comparison to the peak level of US$271.8 million in 1980. It is obvious that the government is trying to have some room to manoeuvre, but should the reserve level reach US$200 million, it would be preferable to bring in more imports.

The composition of investment in the public and private sectors needs to be kept under review. The policy should be to gradually reduce the importance of public investment, except in needed infrastructure. Foreign and domestic private investment will expand and the long-range target should be to have 50 per cent of total investment carried out by the private sector (foreign and domestic), as was the case in the early fifties.

The allocation of public investment by type of activity, such as agriculture, industry, power, transport and communications, is crucial to getting the "most bang for the buck". It is well known that the incremental capital–output ratios are smaller in agriculture, livestock and fishery, than in mining, transport and communications. Industry is generally in between although there are heavy industries requiring a lot of capital. It is gratifying that more investible funds are being allocated to agriculture for 1989/90 (see Table 2), but it is still below the level in 1962/63 and furthermore, the output contribution of that sector is rather important. Investment in industry, though below peak levels, is still dominated by the desire to produce import-substituting goods. Industrialization is desirable, but it should be export-oriented.

Public Finance. In the budgets for State Administrative Organizations (see Table 4) the overall deficit is expected to fall from K2.9 billion in 1988/89 to K0.5 billion in the current year. This would be achieved by holding down the increase in current expenditures, despite the pay increases, and by reducing investment expenditures. The holding down of current expenditures must reflect in part the non-inclusion of interest payments on a portion of government debt abroad. At the same time, current receipts are slated to rise by K2.8 billion, a whopping 55 per cent increase but only 17 per cent above the 1987/88 current receipts.

It is uncertain whether revenues will reach the targetted levels. Undoubtedly, it is within the realm of possibility because of inflation and the fact that these figures are in current prices. Furthermore, with the liberalization of the economy to the private sector the tax base will be larger. The border trade, so far with China being legalized, is bringing in more customs duties, and will be legalized shortly with Thailand. Finally, as mentioned by Finance Minister Colonel Abel, "By reducing the rate of taxes a little each, there will be more tax payers, there will be more incentive to engage in plying businesses thereby increasing earnings, tax payers will willingly pay taxes because the tax burden will be light thereby increasing revenues. Moreover, there will be less tax evasions".[8] While lower income taxes, business profits tax, and taxes on foreigners will have the desired effect, it will take time to yield results, and hence the revenue forecasts for 1989/90 might be slightly optimistic. If that is so then the category "other financing" which consists mainly of domestic borrowing from the banking system may be much larger than the K45 million shown in Table 4.

A key policy question for the authorities is if a larger deficit in 1989/90 were to add undue inflationary pressure on the economy, what steps they would be prepared to take besides the efforts already mentioned in the *Review of the Financial, Economic and Social Conditions of 1989/90.* For example, would interest rates be raised to attract more savings, or would investment be cut further, or would more efforts be made to secure external financial assistance? One avenue categorically ruled out by the present government is another demonetization of currency notes.

State Economic Enterprises. All the operations of the state economic enterprises should be reviewed from the following points of view: 1) What are the main reasons that they are not profitable — for example, macro-economic conditions such as the non-availability of fuel and other inputs, inefficient management, lack of skilled labour, low worker productivity, inadequate capitalization, wrong investment decision from the outset, and so forth? Depending on the answers, one can decide whether to rationalize their operations, go into joint ventures with foreign or domestic businesses, privatize them or even shut them down. 2) Which state economic enterprises should be maintained for non-economic considerations, namely, national security or for long-range economic considerations such as that they would act as catalysts for the establishment of private sector businesses, or because they are natural monopolies and hence should not be privatized? However, even in such cases, one has to develop tests to ensure that the losses are reasonable. 3) Even if the state economic enterprise is making a profit, a determination has to be made whether it could run more efficiently by a joint venture or by the private sector alone. This review will take many years, but a start has to be made in laying the foundation for proper decisions.

Banking System. So far, banking has been reserved for the state for political reasons and because of a feeling that the present banking system can adequately serve the needs of the Myanmar economy. There is a natural aversion to foreign ownership of banks in most developing countries. Even Thailand opened its doors to this sector only gradually and there are limitations in most developing countries on the operations of foreign banks. In the Myanmar context, domestic banking could still be handled by the state, but to facilitate foreign trade and foreign investment it might be beneficial to open the banking business to foreigners or at least to have joint ventures with one or more foreign banks.

Exchange Rate System. At present the kyat is pegged to the SDR, which in and of itself does not assure the stability of the currency as the kyat cannot be defended because of a shortage of foreign exchange. Many observers feel that the kyat should be devalued to promote exports and limit imports, but the authorities are reluctant to do so because of the fear of further inflationary pressures.

However, one has to distinguish between a structural change in prices which align domestic prices to international prices at a new realistic rate of exchange which is then defended, and a continuing wage, price, and exchange depreciation spiral. Admittedly, in some developing countries, especially in Latin America this has occurred. However, if the exchange rate reform is combined with a set of other measures including an infusion of foreign assistance, then the spiral will not occur.

It is for the authorities to decide whether they wish to change the exchange rate or not. But the benefits of having realistic exchange rates have been demonstrated by the conditions of border trade with China. At first, in late 1988 private traders could retain only 60 per cent of the foreign exchange earned to bring in the imports, while 40 per cent had to be surrendered to the state at the official rate. This was changed to 100 per cent retention in 1989 and consequently, there has been a tremendous increase in the flow of goods, and customs duty collections have risen. It is expected that border trade with Thailand will also be legalized in the near future.

The key question, in the absence of a straightforward adjustment of the exchange rate, is how the principles of border trade should be applied to sea-borne trade so as to get a realistic effective exchange rate? This will not be easy because border trade is essentially barter trade. For sea-borne trade, the government in the third quarter of 1989 decided to allow exporters shipping by sea to open a foreign currency account with the Foreign Trade Bank to which 60 per cent of the value would be credited. They could then use this account to import goods. This may help promote exports if the paper work at the Foreign Trade Bank does not unduly delay the import of goods. Some of the paper work may be transferred to the new Myanmar Investment and Commercial Bank to be opened soon to provide banking services to foreign investors and joint venture concerns.

Another way would be to have a dual rate exchange system as a transitional device. The official rate for government transactions would be a more appreciated rate, not necessarily the current rate, and there would be a depreciated rate for private sector transactions. Government exports and foreign aid would be channelled through at the government rate while state economic enterprises would transact foreign trade at the depreciated rate, as would tourists and the remittances of Myanmar people working abroad.

Another possibility is to abandon the pegging of the currency to the SDR and instead fix the rate with reference to a composite currency basket, as is done by many developing countries including Malaysia and Thailand. Thailand has managed this system reasonably well and would be able to provide expertise to operate it. Alternatively, the kyat could be floated under a managed system as in India, Indonesia, Korea, Singapore, and Sri Lanka.

Apart from the system is the question of the level at which the kyat should be fixed or floated. Certainly, one does not need to accept the current black-market rate *vis-à-vis* the U.S. dollar as the equilibrium rate. A rate in the neighbourhood of one-half to one-third the current black market rate might be chosen. Before taking a decision, one has to make an elaborate comparison of local prices and wages in Myanmar with those in Thailand and other neighbouring countries. A further advantage of an exchange rate adjustment is that it would encourage the inflow of foreign investment.

Economic Programming and External Assistance

The purpose of this section is to highlight some of the things which will have to be carried out over the next four years or so in the financial and non-financial fields; hence, the use of the term "economic programming". External assistance is crucial because there is no way that Myanmar can do it alone. The sooner that Myanmar can work out programmes with the International Monetary Fund (IMF) and the World Bank, the better for the country. The main advantage of using the Fund and the Bank is that they are able to mobilize external assistance from donor governments and international banks, and also facilitate the inflow of private equity investment.

The International Monetary Fund uses a financial programming exercise to ensure that a member country receiving financial assistance would be able to improve its balance of payments and achieve a viable position over the medium term, defined as three to five years. It is not the purpose here to go into the economic rationale, the need for, the justification, and *modus operandi* by which IMF programmes are established,[9] nor dwell on the co-ordination between the IMF and the World Bank in helping member countries in situations similar to that of Myanmar.

The elements of an economic programme are given below. Some of the points have already been made in the previous sub-section on stock-taking and restructuring.

1. A decision must be made about the optimum mix between the state and private sectors. As already mentioned, an investment mix of 50–50 which existed in the fifties might be appropriate. However, this may be changed in the light of 1) the need to continue investing in infrastructure related to agriculture and other quick-yielding sectors, and 2) the difficulty that the private sector will have in gathering sufficient venture capital after two and a half decades of inactivity. Nevertheless, it is clear that the state must invest much less than before. State output will also have to be reduced. This could come automatically when the review of SEEs mentioned earlier is carried out and some of the SEEs are privatized.
2. How can the country be changed from "a nation of petty traders", selling unused rations in the market to supplement personal incomes, to "a nation of productive workers"? One supposes that a flooding of goods in Myanmar will automatically eliminate these middlemen. But this may not happen.
3. How can the efficiency of government workers be improved and moral standards both within the government and outside be raised? The raising of government wages is a good start, but unless the recent rise in prices can be halted, there could be a further round of wage–price increases. The government is selling some rice at K6 per pyi or at about one-quarter to one-fifth the open market price. The key to stopping further inflation is a bumper rice crop in 1989/90.
4. Energy supplies, especially gasoline, are crucial. To what

extent can production of crude oil be increased? Already in 1988 and 1989 Myanmar had to import oil from abroad. The Ministry of Mines has been discussing with international oil companies on further exploration, but even if agreements can be signed it will take many years before the energy situation improves. Therefore, crude oil may still have to be imported in the coming years.

5. An overhaul of the tax system is needed to ensure that government revenues increase when the economy expands. Only then can the overall deficits be reduced.
6. The banking system has to be overhauled.
7. The exchange rate system will have to be changed, as mentioned previously.
8. There will be credit ceilings in any programme agreed upon with the IMF. This is necessary because in the past several years excessive credit expansion to the SEEs and to the central government has increased money and domestic liquidity and caused inflation. However, too restrictive a credit plan could jeopardize economic recovery. There is also a need to provide adequate credit to the private sector by cutting back credit to the SEEs and to the government.
9. Myanmar needs to tackle its external debt problem and begin servicing it again. Some options are debt rescheduling and debt reduction as in the case of Mexico. Debt equity swaps could also be explored. Most of Myanmar's debt is to governments and hence they may be more generous if the government adopts a courageous and comprehensive economic reform programme.
10. The amount of external assistance also depends on a country's domestic effort. Hence, there is great urgency to raise the national savings rate through higher interest rates and an expansion of financial services.
11. Finally, the annual economic programme should be monitored monthly and quarterly. Appropriate policy changes must be made in the light of domestic developments and trends in the world economy. Myanmar is well endowed with natural resources and if economic adjustment and stabilization pro-

grammes are well designed and implemented for a period of about four years, the country would be able to correct the mistakes of the past few decades and lay the foundations for solid economic growth and perhaps catch up with some of its more prosperous Asian neighbours.

Concluding Observations

The approach taken in this chapter is that one has to understand the past and the present in order to meaningfully plan the economic future. In this task, one should not be wedded to "isms", be it capitalistic or socialistic. What counts most is a pragmatic assessment of past failures and successes, reasons for the results, and lessons to be learned so that the same mistakes are not made again.

While the fortunes of a country are greatly dependent on natural resources, sound economic management and perhaps a little bit of luck are equally important. There are two components of sound economic management. One is the ability to have a correct vision of things which are happening and to have a realistic appreciation of what can be achieved in a given time span. The other is to literally manage the implementation of the economic policies adopted. The first component is tricky and equally difficult for policy-makers under either a capitalist or socialist system. The second component is perhaps somewhat easier in a capitalist system because of the assistance of the market which is always giving signals to the authorities. But, of course, this assumes that markets are functioning reasonably well and that the authorities will pay attention to market signals.

The views expressed here are based in part on the author's experience with other developing countries, but obviously he could be wrong either in the analysis or in the recommendations. What is needed is a dialogue among policy-makers and economists to arrive at a viable economic policy package for both the short run and the long run. It will take many years, maybe even longer than the four years indicated here to put Myanmar on a sound economic footing because there are deep-seated problems in all sectors of the economy. As noted here, the present government has taken a large number of good economic policy decisions, but more needs to be done.

Sometimes, economists are asked to prioritize the solution of economic problems, especially when they are so many as in the case of Myanmar. This is difficult to do because problems are usually inter-related, and the solution of a given problem requires at least some progress in solving other problems. In the financial field, the increasing deficits of the state economic enterprises is perhaps the most urgent problem, which can be gradually resolved by the suggestions made. In the real or output sector, the problem is how to get the private businesses and farmers to produce efficiently. Price decontrol and other policy measures encouraging private investment have been announced, but more help may be needed from the government. The international trade and payments field has many urgent problems which are being tackled, but there are still many remaining which have to be given immediate attention.

Myanmar's rate of economic progress will be negligible unless it can succeed in getting assistance from abroad. For this reason, the co-operation of the International Monetary Fund and the World Bank is a *sine qua non*. The inflow of foreign capital is linked to many factors, including domestic financial stability, handling of the debt overhang, and how efficient the government is in processing applications for foreign investment, besides the basic incentives provided to attract such investment.

When all is said and done, there is hope for the Myanmar economy because it has rich natural resources and its people can be very hard working provided the proper incentives are given by the authorities.

NOTES

1. For details on planning and performance during 1948–62, see chaper on Burma by U Tun Wai in Cranley Onslow, ed., *Asian Economic Development* (London: Wiedenfeld and Nicolson, 1965).
2. Kazushi Hashimoto, "Economic Development Issues in Burma", in *Challenge*

of Asian Developing Countries: Issues and Analysis, edited by S. Ichimura (APO, 1988).

3. For the effect of some of these variables on ICOR, see U Tun Wai, "Study of ICOR in Developing Countries", *Savings and Development* 9, no. 3 (1985).
4. Evelyn M. Go and Jungsoo Lee, "Foreign Capital, Balance of Payments and External Debt in Developing Asia", *Challenge of Asian Developing Countries: Issues and Analysis*, edited by S. Ichimura (APO, 1988).
5. *Working People's Daily*, 13 July 1989.
6. See *Asian Wall Street Journal*, 20 June 1989.
7. *Asian Wall Street Journal*, 13 June 1989.
8. *Working People's Daily*, 23 March 1989.
9. There is extensive literature on the subject put out by the IMF. Some references are: IMF Institute, *Financial Policy Workshops: The Case of Kenya* (Washington D.C., 1981); International Monetary Fund, *Theoretical Aspects of the Design of Fund-Supported Adjustment Programs*, Occasional Paper No. 55 (Washington D.C., 1987); International Monetary Fund, *Beyond Adjustment: The Asian Experience*, edited by Paul Streeten; and *IMF Survey Supplement on the Fund* (Washington D.C., August 1989).

REFERENCES

Asian Development Bank. *Asian Development Outlook*. Manila, 1989.

Ichimura, S. *Challenge of Asian Developing Countries: Issues and Analysis*. Tokyo: Asian Productivity Organization, 1988.

Ministry of Planning and Finance. *Report to the Pyithu Hluttaw*. Rangoon, various issues.

______. *Review of the Financial, Economic and Social Conditions for 1989/90*. Yangon, 1989.

Steinberg, D.I. *Burma's Road toward Development*. Boulder: Westview Press, 1981.

U Tun Wai. *Role of Foreign Capital in Southeast Asian Countries*. Research Notes and Discussion Paper No. 68. Singapore: Institute of Southeast Asian Studies, 1989.

Union of Myanmar. *The Union of Burma Foreign Investment Law*. Yangon, November 1988.

Walinsky, L.J. *Economic Development in Burma 1951–1960*. New York: Twentieth Century Fund, 1962.

3

MONETARY AND FISCAL POLICIES FOR DEVELOPMENT

MYAT THEIN

Introduction

It is a well known fact that before the economic collapse of the mid-1980s, the Burmese economy went through two distinct sub-periods, each roughly a decade long, of stagnation and development. The first, stretching from 1962/63 to 1973/74, was a period of stagnation and decline. The second, stretching from 1974/75 to 1985/86, saw recovery and growth. Then, beset with perennial balance of payments deficits, burdened with ever increasing external debt, and ailing with creeping inflation, economic growth abruptly slowed down.

In the context of that development this chapter will first consider the development of financial institutions and monetary policy from a historical perspective; secondly, analyse the fiscal aspects of development in the eighties; and thirdly, explore the possibilities for the effective use of monetary and fiscal policies for development in the 1990s.

The main thrust is directed towards the consideration of appropriate monetary and fiscal policies for development in the 1990s. The first two sections may, therefore, be looked upon as preliminary and necessary steps for achieving that objective. It is hoped that the study will be of use to future governments in charting out their own monetary and fiscal policies for development.

The Development of Financial Institutions and Monetary Policy in Historical Perspective

It is not the intention of this section to give an exhaustive historical account of either the development of financial institutions or of budgetary policy. The intention, rather, is to look back briefly into the major developments in the past so as to have a sort of road map in our search for a prosperous future.

In the context of developing countries, the development of new financial institutions and the strengthening of existing ones constitute an important aspect of monetary policy. Looking at the development of financial institutions in Burma from that point of view, three distinct phases can be identified. The first phase, between 1948 to 1963, saw the development of financial institutions along the lines of market or capitalist economies. The second phase, stretching from 1963 to 1976, witnessed the eventual realization of a mono-bank system (in 1969) along socialist lines. The third phase, from 1976 to the present, saw the rationalization of that mono-bank system into one which is better suited to a developing economy such as Burma.

The development of the banking system in independent Burma began with the creation of the Union Bank of Burma (UBB*) as the central bank of Burma in 1948. Under the Union Bank of Burma Act of 1947, UBB* took over the central banking functions of the Rangoon Branch of the Reserve Bank of India which has served as the central bank in Burma since 1935. But Burma's currency system was still managed by the Burma Currency Board in London. Thus, it was only in 1952 that UBB* was bestowed the full prerogative of a central bank with the new Union Bank of Burma Act (1952).

Under this new Act, the UBB* took over the sole right of note issue and other traditional central banking functions from the Burma Currency Board and established a flexible currency system with the legal obligation to hold international reserves of 25 per cent of the currency in circulation and demand deposits. Following the advice of central bank authorities, the Act also gave UBB* wide powers of inspection and licensing over commercial banks, thereby making it responsible for fostering the growth of the banking sector.[1]

In accordance with the specific needs of the agricultural and industrial sectors, the state Agricultural Bank and the Industrial Development Bank were established in 1953 and 1961 respectively. Four new commercial banks, namely, the Burmese Economic Bank, the Union of Burma Co-operative Bank, the State Commercial Bank and the Rangoon Bank also came into being. Thus, the banking sector, consisting in 1948 of 20 commercial banks of which 18 were foreign-owned, came to have by 1963, 25 commercial banks, of which 14 were foreign-owned.

In 1953, the Eight-Year Plan, also known as the KTA plan, was launched. And from 1954 onwards UBB* began granting long-term loans for economic development by purchasing debentures issued by state enterprises and guaranteed by the government. The UBB* also purchased three-month Treasury Bills and two-year and five-year Treasury Bonds from the government.

Between 1952/53 and 1955/56 the money supply more than doubled. This was due to the fiscal policy of the government which financed its capital formation largely through money creation. As a result, inflationary pressures set in. However, until the end of 1955 when there was still relatively ample foreign exchange reserves, these pressures could be relieved by the government through the liberalization of private imports. This move, which reduced the foreign exchange reserves, had the added advantage (in so far as controlling inflation is concerned) of reducing money supply and excess demand. Nevertheless, continued deficit financing eventually led to price increases.[2]

The central bank authorities began to use the reserve requirements of commercial banks as an instrument of monetary policy in August 1957. In order to restrain credit expansion the reserve requirements of commercial banks were raised from 8 to 16 per cent for demand deposits and from 3 to 6 per cent for time deposits. Had this trend continued, it might even have been possible eventually for UBB* to use such monetary instruments for open market operations in a by now fairly well developed financial market. But it was not to be so.

In accordance with the ideology and general policy objectives of the new government which came to power in March 1962, all the banks in Burma were nationalized in February 1963. Then in May 1964 newly designed notes and coins were issued after the demonetization of 100 kyat and 50 kyat notes. Not long after, the pay scales of many bank personnel were revised downward and the system of accounting and interest rates on loans and deposits were changed to conform with the one used by the State Commercial Bank.[3] Then, from 1965 the government set out to transform the financial structure along socialist lines into a monobank system. This was accomplished in November 1969 under the People's Bank of the Union of Burma Act, 1967.

The People's Bank of Burma, as the only bank in Burma, functioned not only as a central bank but also engaged in commercial, industrial, savings, insurance and financing operations through specialized divisions.

For a decade from 1962, Burma did not have an officially declared economic plan. There may, of course, have been an unofficial plan.[4] Nevertheless, the overriding influence over the course of development during that decade was the government's policies of "Burmanization", nationalization and self-reliance.

As most scholars have observed, these policies led to the poor performance of the economy.[5] Nationalization of trade, industry and important segments of the economy, as it turned out, proved to be more of a burden (at least on State finances) than a blessing: they failed to make a significant contribution in the mobilization of domestic resources for investment. With rampant inefficiencies and gross misallocation of resources, exports and imports declined, per capita income remained unchanged or even declined slightly, and the economy became almost self-reliant in an impoverished form.

By 1972 foreign exchange reserves had sunk to an all-time low of some US$52 million and in the same year the requirement for the limitation of currency and demand deposits to 25 per cent of international reserves was abolished by the government.

In the midst of rising social and political unrests and disturbances resulting from the poor performance of the economy, the government began to modify its policy stances and the twenty-year long-term plan (TYP), 1974/75 to 1993/94, was launched. Among the important changes in the mid-1970s was the reorganization of the People's Bank of 1 April 1976, under the 1975 Bank Law.

This new banking set-up, organized on a functional basis, consisted of the Union of Burma Bank (UB*B) as the central bank and three specialized banks under its supervision. The three specialized banks are the Myanmar Economic Bank (MEB), the Myanmar Agricultural Bank (MAB) and the Myanmar Foreign Trade Bank (MFTB). The insurance function was transferred to the newly created Myanmar Insurance Corporation (MIC) outside the banking system.

The UB*B, as the central bank, may advise the Ministry of Planning and Finance on the fiscal and monetary implications of the government's internal and external financial operations. It may be noted, however, that in Burma all major decisions on monetary matters, such as the issue of currencies, credit expansion, interest rates, foreign borrowing, exchange rate, demonetization and so on are made not by the Minister of Planning and Finance or even the Prime Minister, but by the ruling oligarchy in which the Prime Minister may or may not be included.

The MEB, as the state commercial bank, finances the activities of the state economic enterprises (SEEs), the co-operative sector and registered private enterprises. The MAB which lends through a system of village banks, provides seasonal finance for crops as well as medium and long-term loans for agricultural development. The MFTB, acting on behalf of the UB*B, conduct all foreign exchange transactions arising out of external trade as well as non-trade activities of the State. Exchange control is, however, administered by the Exchange Control Board through MFTB in accordance with instructions from the Ministry of Planning and Finance.[6]

Since 1976, the MEB and the MAB have expanded their branches and increased their volume of transactions. Between 1976/77 and 1983/84 loans and advances of the MEB increased tenfold, from 1,739 million kyats to 27,454 million kyats. Of this, the major portion was taken up by the public sector whose share increased from 28.7 per cent in 1976/77 to 95.6 per cent in 1983/84. As for MAB, its volume of transactions doubled during the same period, from 250.6 million kyats in 1976/77 to 531.7 million kyats in 1983/84. Apparently, the economy was increasingly being monetized. Taking the ratio of money (broadly defined as currency in circulation, demand, savings, and time deposits — M_2) to gross domestic product (GDP) as a rough index of the degree of monetization or financial deepening, it increased from about 23 per cent in 1976/77 to about 37 per cent in 1984/85. However, the ratio in 1984/85, comparable to that of the Republic of Korea during the same period, was chiefly due to loans and advances made to state economic enterprises. Therefore, whether or not it represents the degree of monetization in the case of Burma is a matter which must be given much thought.

For a decade from 1975 the economy enjoyed a respectable rate of growth. Between 1974/75 and 1986/87 real GDP increased at an average rate of about 6 per cent per annum. As the rate of population growth was approximately 2 per cent per annum, this meant that per capita income also increased during that period.

From the fiscal-monetary point of view, three of the major developments which contributed to economic growth during that period were the introduction of a Commodities and Services Tax (CST) in 1975/76, the establishment of the Export Price Equalization Fund (EPEF) in August 1976, and the increase in the rate of interest on savings deposits in November 1977. CST simplified the existing tax structure and broadened the base of indirect domestic taxation. EPEF, an alternative measure to exchange rate adjustment, was designed to promote exports by transferring a portion of export earning surpluses to those exporters whose products had become unprofitable. The remaining portion, if any, had to be transferred to the budget as government revenue. EPEF was seen by the authorities as a temporary measure and not as a desirable instrument of economic management in the longer term. CST, together with EPEF was said to have "raised the share of Union Government revenue in GDP from less than 10 per cent in previous years to almost 14 per cent in 1977/78".[7] As exports did not increase appreciably during the period being considered, apparently EPEF succeeded more in raising revenue than in promoting exports. As regards the third major development, that of increasing the rate of interest on savings deposits from 6 per cent to 8 per cent, it led to a tremendous increase in savings, as most Burmans had by then forgotten the 1964 demonetization. Between 1976/77 and 1987/88 savings increased on the average by 28.33 per cent per annum. See Tables 1 and 2 and Figures 1 and 2 for changes in personal savings.

On the negative side were the demonetization of 50 kyat and 100 kyat notes in November 1985 and the demonetization of 25 kyat and 75 kyat notes in September 1987. That the latter demonetization in particular had inflamed the general discontent of the populace was immediately obvious. What was not so

TABLE 1
Personal Savings (1962/63–1975/76)
(End March)

Year	*Kyats (in million)*	*Annual Growth Rate*
1962/63	180	—
1963/64	244	35.6
1964/65	375	53.7
1965/66	340	−10.3
1966/67	332	− 2.4
1967/68	340	2.4
1968/69	333	− 2.1
1969/70	340	2.1
1970/71	355	4.4
1971/72	412	16.1
1972/73	418	1.5
1973/74	418	0
1974/75	440	5.3
1975/76	456	3.6

r = 5.01%
where r = average annual rate of increase.

SOURCE: Ministry of Planning and Finance, Burma, *Report to the Pyithu Hluttaw*, various issues.

TABLE 2
Personal Savings (1976/77–1987/88)
(End September)

Year	*Kyats (in million)*	*Annual Growth Rate*
1976/77	502	10.1
1977/78	878	74.9
1978/79	1,309	49.1
1979/80	1,939	48.1
1980/81	2,728	40.7
1981/82	3,579	31.2
1982/83	4,410	23.2
1983/84	5,632	27.7
1984/85	6,380	13.3
1985/86	7,331	14.9
1986/87	8,190	11.7
1987/88	8,288	1.2

r = 28.33%
where r = average annual rate of increase.

SOURCE: Ministry of Planning and Finance, Burma, *Report to the Pyithu Hluttaw*, various issues.

obvious was the extent to which they had destroyed the "banking habits" of the households and arrested the development of the financial sector.

It should be mentioned that the UB*B and indeed the whole banking set-up is not an independent entity like, for example, the Federal Bank and the commercial banks in the United States. In theory, of course, the UB*B in consultation with the Ministry of Planning and Finance and sometimes with the International Monetary Fund (under Stand-by Arrangements) may draw a credit plan and prescribe a credit ceiling. It may also prepare a cash plan and project the "permissable" level of money supply that may be injected into the economy in the coming year. Above all, the UB*B, in its advisory role, may advise the government on monetary matters as and when needed.

In practice, however, as it has evolved over the years, the credit plans and cash plans merely accommodate the public sector investment programme (capital budget) which plays the dominant

FIGURE 1
Public Savings (1963/64–1975/76)

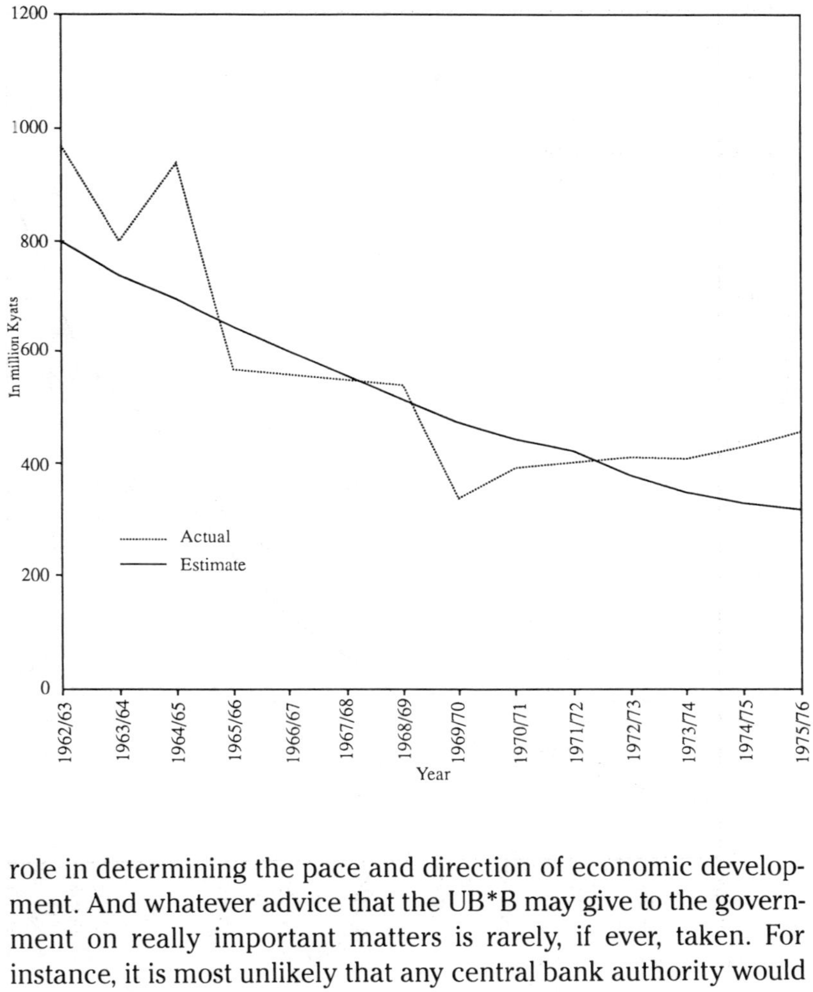

role in determining the pace and direction of economic development. And whatever advice that the UB*B may give to the government on really important matters is rarely, if ever, taken. For instance, it is most unlikely that any central bank authority would have suggested the issuance of 15, 45 and 90 kyat notes. The financial system, based as it is almost solely on transactions with cash (instead of with cheques), is bad enough: primitive, cumbersome and utterly lacking in banking services. Thus, one must conclude that the central bank authorities have little authority. Apart from routine day-to-day operations, they could, to some

FIGURE 2
Personal Saving (1976/77–1986/87)

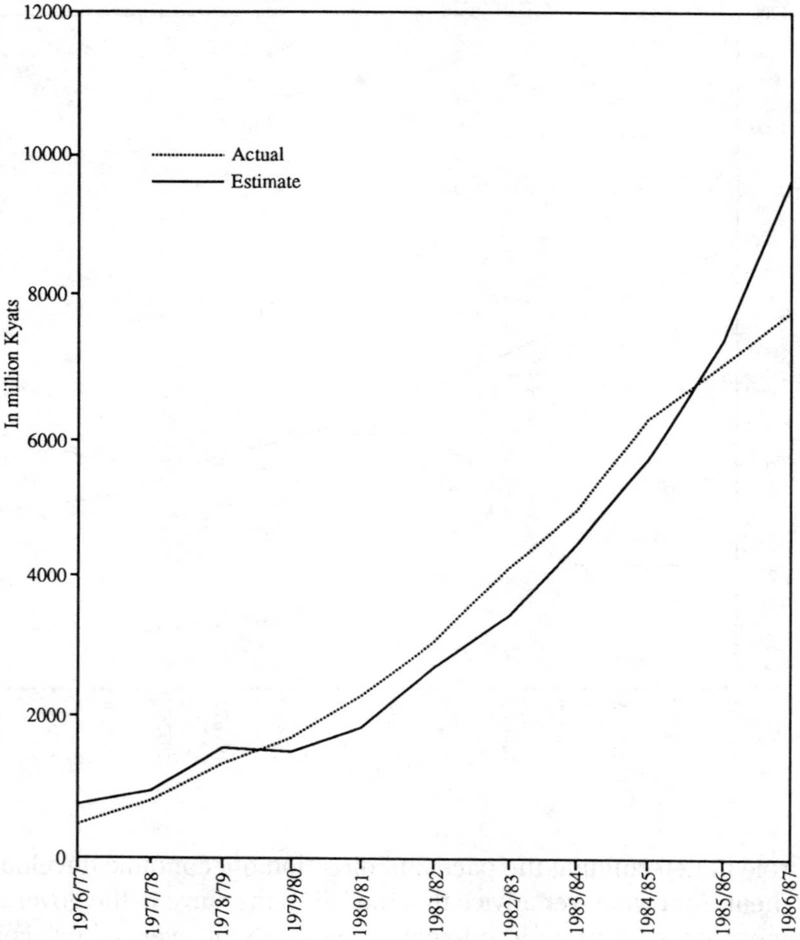

extent, select trainees for studies abroad or recruit new blood. But these fall far short of developing the financial sector.

The financial sector, as it stood near the end of the 1980s, was in certain respects even less developed than it was before the 1963 nationalizations. Taking the currency ratio, defined as the ratio of currency to the narrow definition of money (M_1), as a proxy of financial development, it is noteworthy that it was 70.3 per cent in 1987 whereas it was even less, at 63.05 per cent, in 1962. In other words, in terms of the complexity of financial structure and the diversity of financial instruments available, the financial sector in Burma in 1987 was even less developed than it was in 1962.

Looking back over the years, it seems that since the early sixties, the financial sector in Burma has been developing in the manner of what in the literature has been referred to as "demand-following",[8] that is, in accordance with the demand for financial services generated by the growth of the real sector. As scholars in this field have noted, however, there is another way, especially in the early stages of development, by which the financial sector could develop. And that is, "channelling scarce resources from (small) savers to (large) investors according to relative rates of return. The financial sector precedes and induces real growth" in the manner of a "supply-leading" relationship between the two developments.[9]

This is the way that the financial sector in Burma should develop. In this way it could not only alleviate the problems of external imbalance, budgetary deficits and inflation that now afflict the economy (to be considered in the next section), but could also promote real growth. This will not be easy. The deliberate establishment of a wide array of financial institutions providing a variety of financial instruments is a task, perhaps, beyond that of the government alone. But then, given the "open-door" policy that future governments are likely to follow, it should not be impossible.

Fiscal Aspects of Development in the 1980s

The purpose of this section is to analyse the fiscal aspects of development in the 1980s. It will begin with an analytical framework commonly employed by economists. This framework, based on the absorption approach, starts with a simple proposition that a balance of payments deficit on the current account arises whenever absorption (consumption and investment) is greater than domestic output. Using the usual notations for national income identities we can derive the above proposition, which is,

$$M - X = A - Y \qquad (1)$$

from the national income identity

$$Y = C + I + X - M$$

where:

Y = Gross Domestic Product
C = $(C_g + C_p)$ = Consumption
I = $(I_g + I_p)$ = Investment
A = $(C + I)$ = Absorption
X = Exports
M = Imports
g = Public sector
p = Private sector

Given that M − X is positive, or the current account to be in deficit, equation (1) tells us that as a nation we are consuming and investing more than we are producing.[10] This is obvious. But starting from this basic position we can go on the less obvious aspects of the interrelationships among macro-economic variables.

First, since the difference between output and consumption equals saving, $(Y - C = S)$, we can show that

$$M - X = I - S \qquad (2)$$

Equation (2) expresses the current account of the balance of payments in terms of domestic investment and domestic saving. It thereby highlights the possible causal relationship between current account deficit and the gap between domestic investment and saving.

For the purposes of our analysis we may split investment and savings into their private and public components and elaborate equation (2) into

$$M - X = (I_p - S_p) + (I_g - S_g) \qquad (3)$$

Furthermore, since by definition public expenditure, G, equals $(C_g + I_g)$, and public savings, S_g, equals $(T - C_g)$ where T is current tax and non-tax revenue, equation (3) may be transformed into

$$M - X = (I_p - S_p) + (G - T) \qquad (4)$$

Given that the private sector net balance $(I_p - S_p)$ is constant, it may be possible to establish empirically, the causal relationship between the public sector deficit and the current account deficit. And to the extent that it is public sector deficits which cause the current account deficits in the balance of payments, fiscal measures would take an overriding importance in the context of balance of payments adjustment.

Equation (4) may be further transformed to show the relationship between fiscal variables and the overall balance of payments. Subtracting capital movements, CM, from both sides of equation (4) gives

$$M - X - CM = (I_p - S_p) + (G - T) - CM \qquad (5)$$

The left hand side of equation (5) shows the overall balance of payments outcome, which is by definition equal to the change in net foreign assets, Δ NFA. The right hand side of the equation shows the net domestic financing of the public and private sectors. In so far as the causal relationship in equation (4) can be established, it follows that domestically financed public sector deficit is the appropriate fiscal target for influencing the overall balance of payments position.

Then again, since the financing of the "formal" private sector is relatively unimportant in Burma, the focus will be on the financing of public sector deficits in order also to determine its inflationary impact. Denoting the public sector deficit by $D_g = (G - T)$ we can show that

$$D_g = F_g + \Delta M_g + \Delta B_g \qquad (7)$$

where

F_g = foreign financing to the public sector.

ΔM_g = government borrowings from the central bank and other banks plus use of its idle cash balances which change money supply.

ΔB_g = net increase in domestic government borrowing from outside the banking system.

The inflationary impact of public sector deficits on the economy depends largely on ΔM_g. Resort to F_g or ΔB_g, on the other hand, means increasing public indebtedness and will thus represent a drag on future standards of living.

Finally, using the familiar monetary survey identity, we may examine to what extent ΔM_g contributed to the increase in overall money supply, using Burmese data. Now, let us look at the Burmese data.

Table 3 shows GDP and its uses for the years 1980/81 to 1987/88. As may be seen from the table, the difference between imports and exports, (M – X), has been positive throughout the eighties. It has fluctuated around 2,000 million kyats or 1,500 million kyats, the exception being 1982/83 when it reached a peak of 3,310 million kyats. The exception was due to the 1982 world-wide recession on the one hand, and to the increasing momentum of investment projects (requiring imports) on the other. Apart from that exceptional year, imports fell together with exports, leaving the size of the deficit almost unchanged. The fall in exports was due largely to the fall in the prices of export products or in the unit value of exports. Be that as it may, for the analysis at hand, the important questions regarding the deficits are what causes them, what have they caused and how may they be managed.

Table 4 shows more deficits. But note that exports and imports in Table 4 do not exactly match those in Table 3. This is due to the slight differences in the system of recording, including that of recording imports on a c.i.f. basis in one and f.o.b. in the other. These differences, however, do not affect the rough magnitudes of the trade deficits. These deficits, it may be seen, are larger than the current account deficits. This is because grants, which average about 500 to 700 million kyats annually, are included in the current account balance. The current account balance, including grants, shows the gap that is needed to be financed through borrowing or some other means. The current account balance, exclusive of grants, on the other hand, shows the true

TABLE 3
Gross Domestic Product in Current Prices
(In million kyats)

	1980/81	*1981/82*	*1982/83*	*1983/84*	*1984/85*	*1985/86*	*1986/87*	*1987/88 (provisional)*
GDP	38,609.1	42,879.2	46,810.5	49,823.3	53,597.1	55,989.3	59,028.1	66,369.4
Total Imports (c.i.f.)	4,635.0	5,611.3	6,313.6	5,197.3	5,041.2	4,802.0	3,936.1	4,065.7
Total Exports (f.o.b.)	3,176.4	3,432.3	3,003.3	3,372.6	3,133.1	2,566.1	2,418.5	1,655.2
Trade balance	−1,458.6	−2,179.0	−3,310.3	−1,824.7	−1,908.1	−2,235.9	−1,517.6	−2,410.5
Total consumption	31,774.5	35,217.9	39,746.6	42,685.5	47,395.6	49,531.9	53,066.6	60,966.6
Total investment	7,228.3	8,634.8	10,043.7	9,057.1	8,476.8	8,649.5	8,617.6	8,567.1
Stock changes	+1,064.9	+1,205.5	+ 330.5	− 94.6	− 367.2	+ 43.8	−1,138.5	− 754.1

SOURCES: Ministry of Planning and Finance, Burma, *Report to the Pyithu Hluttaw, 1988/89* and preceding issues; and *Review of the Financial, Economic and Social Conditions for 1989/90*.

TABLE 4

Selected Balance of Payments Indicators (1980/81 to 1987/88)

(In million kyats)

	1980/81	*1981/82*	*1982/83*	*1983/84*	*1984/85*	*1985/86*	*1986/87*	*1987/88 (provisional)*
Merchandise exports (f.o.b.)	3,180.0	3,462.1	2,891.4	3,291.7	3,056.8	2,672.6	2,180.0	1,658.2
Merchandise imports (f.o.b.)	−4,602.7	−5,951.4	−6,869.9	−4,895.3	−4,816.9	−4,700.9	−3,755.0	−3,392.0
Trade Balance	−1,422.7	−2,489.3	−3,978.5	−1,603.6	−1,759.1	−2,028.3	−1,575.0	−1,733.8
Current Account Balance (including grants)	− 895.9	−2,289.4	−3,645.3	−1,337.9	−1,412.8	−1,686.9	−1,113.3	−1,113.3
Current Account Deficit as a percentage of GDP	2.32	5.34	7.79	2.69	2.64	3.01	1.89	1.68
Gross International Reserve	1,894.7	1,586.5	622.6	874.1	489.0	430.3	310.1	429.8
(In months of imports)	4.9	3.2	1.1	2.1	1.2	1.1	1.0	1.5

SOURCES: Ministry of Planning and Finance, Burma, *Report to the Pyithu Hluttaw, 1988/89* and preceding issues; and *Review of the Financial, Economic and Social Conditions for 1989/90.*

position of the gap between domestic absorption and output.

Looking at the trends in the current account balance, it may be seen that the deficits, as expected, peaked in 1982/83 when Burma had to draw twice on the Compensatory Financing Facility. It was also forced to reverse the long-held policy of maintaining high levels of international reserves; its international reserves was drawn down to almost one month's worth of imports. The current account deficit then was 3,645.3 million kyats, or 7.7 per cent of GDP. Since then, it has gradually been scaled down to 1,113 million kyats, or 1.7 per cent of GDP. Nevertheless, external financing continued to be important, as may be seen from Table 5.

Table 5 presents the other side of the current account deficit (equation 2). It also shows the private and public components of the investment-savings gap (equation 3). It may be seen from the bottom row that external financing after peaking in 1982/83 continued to constitute 25 per cent or one-fourth of gross investment.[11] That this, coupled with the unprofitability of most public investments, has led directly to rising external indebtedness and debt service burden is now a well known fact (see Table 6). Note that the reduction in the deficits was being achieved not through an increase in domestic savings but by cutting back on investments. While domestic savings remained more or less around 6,000 million kyats (although its share in GDP decreased from around 13 or 14 per cent to 10 per cent), that of investment declined in both absolute and relative terms. It declined from around 10,000 million kyats, or 22 per cent of GDP in 1982/83, to about 8,000 million kyats, or 13 per cent of GDP in 1987/88.

In the context of the Burmese economy, it should be understood that these outcomes were primarily due to deliberate actions by the government to promote development within the framework of the TYP. In this connection, note in particular the fact that the excess of savings over investment in the private sector had in large part been offsetting the large public sector investment–savings gap.

The above, then, may be seen as an aggregate fiscal response, in an *ex-post* sense, to the balance of payments problem. For policy purposes, however, it is necessary to know the functional

TABLE 5
Investment and Savings, 1980/81–1987/88
(In million kyats at current prices)

	1980/81	*1981/82*	*1982/83*	*1983/84*	*1984/85*	*1985/86*	*1986/87*	*1987/88*
Gross Investment	8,293	9,841	10,375	8,962	8,110	8,693	7,478	7,813
(as % of GDP)	(21.5)	(23.0)	(22.2)	(18.0)	(15.1)	(15.5)	(12.7)	(12.9)
Fixed Investment	7,228	8,635	10,044	9,057	8,477	8,649	8,617	8,567
(as % of GDP)	(18.7)	(20.1)	(21.3)	(18.2)	(15.8)	(15.5)	(14.7)	(14.1)
Public	5,613	6,941	8,288	7,252	6,582	6,600	6,566	6,381
Private	1,615	1,694	1,756	1,805	1,895	2,049	2,051	2,186
Change in stock	+1,065	+1,206	+ 330	− 95	− 367	+ 44	−1,139	− 754
National Savings	6,722	7,438	6,795	6,875	6,044	6,090	5,728	6,375
(as % of GDP)	(17.4)	(17.3)	(14.5)	(14.7)	(11.3)	(10.9)	(9.8)	(10.5)
Domestic Savings	6,772	7,478	6,957	7,006	6,161	6,338	6,030	5,479
(as % of GDP)	(17.5)	(17.4)	(14.9)	(14.1)	(11.5)	(11.3)	(10.3)	(9.0)
Public*	1,641	1,564	2,444	2,075	1,343	1,083	1,131	− 109
Private	5,131	5,914	4,513	4,931	4,818	5,255	4,899	5,588
Net Payment of Factor Income	− 160	− 168	− 347	− 510	− 517	− 581	− 658	− 520
(as % of gross investment)	(18.9)	(24.4)	(34.5)	(23.3)	(25.5)	(29.9)	(23.4)	(18.4)
Nominal GDP	38,609	42,879	46,811	49,823	53,597	55,989	58,759	60,660

* Difference between current revenue and current expenditure.

SOURCES: Ministry of Planning and Finance, Burma, *Report to the Pyithu Hluttaw, 1988/89* and preceding years.

TABLE 6

Selected Indicators of External Medium and Long-Term Public Debt, 1981/82–1986/87

Item	*1981/82*	*1982/83*	*1983/84*	*1984/85*	*1985/86*	*1986/87*
			(In million kyat)			
Total Debt Outstanding (end of period)	12,941	15,996	18,489	19,757	22,241	23,705
Concessional Loans	9,887	12,448	14,771	16,379	19,272	—
Non-concessional Loans	2,629	2,995	3,021	2,740	2,467	—
Total Debt Service Payments	1,055	1,055	1,395	1,480	1,787	2,076
Interest	383	419	545	553	596	655
Amortization	664	637	850	919	1,191	1,421
			(In per cent)			
Total Debt Service						
Total Current Receipts	25.6	29.7	34.4	38.4	52.5	60.5
Exports of Goods and Services	26.1	31.0	37.6	42.6	58.1	66.8
Concessional Loans/Total Debt	79.0	80.6	83.0	85.7	88.6	—
Outstanding Debt/GDP	30.2	34.2	37.1	36.9	39.7	40.4

SOURCE: IMF, *Burma: Recent Economic Developments*, 20 May 1987.

relationships between the fiscal deficit and the balance of payments deficit in terms of equation (4) of the analytical framework outlined above. Hence, following Milne, the equation $(M - X) = \alpha + \beta (G - T)$ was formulated using annual data for the period 1975/76 to 1987/88.[12] The results are as shown in Table 7.

In equations (1) and (2) the current account balance was regressed on the fiscal balance. The difference between the two equations is that in the latter, the log function was used. As may be seen from the results shown in the table, although the values of β are significantly different from zero at the 95 per cent level, neither equation suggests causality. In equations (3) and (4) the trade balance was regressed on the fiscal balance. Again, equation (4) was regressed with log transformed variables. In both the equations the results are very good, particularly that of equation (4). Coefficient β on the public balance is significantly different from zero at the 99 per cent level, the explanatory power is very high, and the existence of an empirical relationship between trade balance and public balance implies causality. According to equation (4), a one unit change in the fiscal balance is likely to cause a 0.87 unit change in the trade balance.

Therefore, as indicated in the analytical framework outlined above, in the context of balance of payments adjustment, the focus should be on fiscal measures. This will be discussed later. For the moment, let us consider further the impact of fiscal deficits on monetary developments (Table 8).

TABLE 7
Statistical Relationship between Current Account and Fiscal Balance

Equation	*Coefficients* α *(1)*	β *(2)*	$\bar{R}^2$ *(3)*	*D.W.* *(4)*	*N* *(5)*	*t– ratios* $\beta=0$ *(6)*	$\beta=1$ *(7)*
(1)	–544.60	0.2329	0.24	1.44	13	2.19	7.21
(2)	2.3633	0.5873	0.30	1.78	12	2.41	1.69
(3)	–173.62	0.3826	0.80	2.02	13	6.95	11.22
(4)	0.2099	0.8707	0.91	1.94	12	10.55	1.56

TABLE 8

Monetary Analysis, 1979/80–1986/87

	Change in 1979/80 to 1980/81	*Change in 1980/81 to 1981/82*	*Change in 1981/82 to 1982/83*	*Change in 1982/83 to 1983/84*	*Change in 1983/84 to 1984/85*	*Change in 1984/85 to 1985/86*	*Change in 1985/86 to 1986/87*	*Comulative change in 1979/80 to 1986/87*
Broad Money Supply (M_2)	1,594	1,922	1,662	2,390	2,428	7,512	4,743	22,351
Factors								
1. Net Foreign Assets	455	−415	−1,176	162	−471	−521	121	−1,845
2. Total Domestic Credit	1,873	2,700	2,164	2,406	3,302	18,376	−619	30,222
(a) Net Claims on Public Sector	1,895	2,602	2,226	2,369	3,228	17,165	−742	28,743
in which: Loans to SEEs	(4,027)	(4,990)	(4,742)	(4,605)	(5,204)	(5,825)	(3,862)	(33,000)
(b) Net Claims on Private Sector	−2	98	−62	37	74	1,211	123	1,479
3. Other Liabilities	−754	−363	−679	−178	−303	−10,343	5,241	−6,026
	1,594	1,922	1,622	2,390	2,528	7,512	4,743	22,351
4. Net Claims on Public Sector as % of Total Domestic Credit	(86.8)	(88.5)	(90.5)	(91.0)	(92.2)	(92.7)	(92.3)	

SOURCE: Table 9.

Between 1979/80 and 1986/87 money supply broadly defined, or M_2, increased at the rate of about 15 per cent per annum, except the period March 1985 to March 1986 when it shot up at the rate of 38.1 per cent. During the same period M_1, or narrow money supply, including currency in circulation and demand deposits, increased at an even higher rate of 56.2 per cent.[13] As may be seen from Table 8, this increase was mainly due to increases in net claims of the public sector, which grew from 84.5 per cent of total domestic credit in 1980/81 to 92.3 per cent in 1986/87. In short, the increase in money supply was mainly caused by the fiscal deficits. The increase in money supply would have been astronomical but for the fact that the government was also financing its deficits with foreign loans (Table 9).

Before considering Table 10, however, it should be noted that in spite of the tremendous increases in money supply, the rise in the general level of prices as represented by the consumer price index (CPI) was not very much, at least until 1986. Although the money supply (both M_1 and M_2) doubled between 1981/82 and 1985/86 prices increased by only 29 per cent, or by about 6 per cent per year (see Table 10). Thus, it may be concluded that the inflationary pressures generated by the budgetary deficits were being offset by the tremendous increases in personal savings noted in the preceding section. Yearly increases in CPI became serious only after the increases in personal savings slackened off from 1985/86 onwards, just when imports were also being reduced.

Table 11 shows structural changes in public sector finance, comprising the Union government, local authorities and state economic enterprises. As expected, the deficits peaked in 1982/83, at least in percentage, at 11.6 per cent of GDP, and then fell to about 10 per cent by 1987/88. In other ways too, 1982/83 was a landmark year. Both total receipts and total expenditures continued their climb up to 1982/83. From then onwards it was mostly downhill for both the series. The years 1985/86 and 1986/87 were exceptional as both registered marginal increases over the preceding years.

Concentrating first on the revenue side, it may be seen that tax revenue which constitutes two-thirds of total revenue, has

TABLE 9

Monetary Survey, 1978/79–1986/87

(In million kyat)

	1978/79	*1979/80*	*1980/81*	*1981/82*	*1982/83*	*1983/84*	*1984/85*	*1985/86*	*1986/87*
Monetary Aggregates									
1. Currency in Circulation	6,397	7,317	8,275	9,163	9,781	11,248	12,571	15,240	17,035
2. Demand Deposit	563	648	671	822	970	994	1,161	6,208	7,188
Narrow Money Supply (M_1)	6,942	7,965	8,946	9,985	10,751	12,242	13,732	21,448	24,223
3. Quasi Money	1,075	1,654	2,267	3,150	4,046	4,945	5,983	6,779	7,747
4. Broad Money Supply (M_2)	8,017	9,619	11,213	13,135	14,797	17,187	19,715	27,227	31,970
Factors									
1. Net Foreign Assets	415	1,148	1,603	1,188	12	174	−294	−818	−697
2. Total Domestic Credit	8,822	10,643	12,536	15,236	17,400	19,806	23,108	41,484	40,865
(a) Net Claims on Public Sector	7,194	8,990	10,885	13,487	15,713	19,082	21,310	38,475	37,733
in which: Loans to SEEs	(4,393)	(7,672)	(11,699)	(16,689)	(21,431)	(26,081)	(31,285)	(37,110)	(40,972)
(b) Net Claims on Private Sector	1,728	1,658	1,651	1,749	1,687	1,724	1,798	3,009	3,132
3. Other Liabilities	−1,320	−2,172	−2,926	−3,289	−2,615	−2,793	−3,096	−13,439	−8,198
4. Broad Money Supply (M_2)	8,017	9,619	11,213	13,135	14,797	17,187	19,715	27,227	31,970

SOURCE: Union of Burma Bank.

TABLE 10
Changes in Money Supply and CPI

Year	M_1	*Growth Rate*	M_2	*Growth Rate*	*CPI*	*Growth Rate*
1978/79	6,942		8,017		106.08	
1979/80	7,956	14.7	9,619	19.98	107.16	1.02
1980/81	8,946	12.3	11,213	16.37	107.46	0.28
1981/82	9,925	11.6	13,135	17.14	112.00	4.23
1982/83	10,751	7.7	14,797	12.65	118.29	5.62
1983/84	12,242	13.9	17,187	16.15	124.02	4.84
1984/85	13,732	12.2	19,715	14.71	132.47	6.81
1985/86	21,148	56.2	27,227	38.1	144.67	9.21
1986/87	24,223	12.9	31,970	17.4	178.76	21.05

SOURCES: Union of Burma Bank, and Central Statistical Organization.

remained more or less stagnant since 1981/82, although its share in GDP has fallen from about 15 per cent in 1981/82 to slightly less than 7 per cent by 1987/88. Of course, the fact that it fell, even in relative terms, is a reflection not only of the low elasticity and buoyancy of the tax system as a whole, but also the inherently unstable nature of a system which relies heavily on indirect taxes such as CST and customs duties. The two together constitute about 80 per cent or more of the total tax revenue during the period of study (see Table 12). The fact that CST, by far the major component of the two, in particular has stagnated or declined in the last few years has made new thinking on tax policy imperative.

Total receipts also fell because of the decline in its lesser component, namely, non-tax revenue and particularly contributions from the SEEs, which on the average accounted for more than 80 per cent of that component. In this connection, it should be mentioned that the government did make some efforts in 1982/83, such as adjustments in the pricing of products of some SEEs, tightening of bank credits, and so on. But these punitive measures were hardly enough to offset the well-known amalgam of negative factors that afflict the SEEs, namely, bureaucratic overstaffing, high overhead costs, and below capacity utilization as a result of the shortage of imported inputs and spare parts.[14]

TABLE 11

Structural Changes in Public Sector Finance

(In million kyat)

Particulars	*1980/81*	*1981/82*	*1982/83*	*1983/84*	*1984/85*	*1985/86*	*1986/87*	*1987/88*
1. Receipts[1]	5,722	6,231	7,247	7,057	6,636	6,689	7,179	5,718
Tax Revenue	3,711	4,257	4,602	4,602	4,601	4,622	4,375	4,373
Direct Tax	182	194	239	266	313	368	472	480
Indirect Tax	3,529	4,063	4,363	4,336	4,288	4,254	3,903	3,893
Non-tax Revenue	2,011	1,674	2,645	2,455	2,035	2,067	2,804	1,445
Contributions from SEEs	(1,712)	(2,217)	(1,954)	(2,062)	(2,071)	(1,936)	(1,540)	(1,422)
Others	299	−543	691	393	−36	131	1,264	23
2. Expenditure	9,384	11,166	12,658	11,918	11,671	12,004	12,369	11,955
Current Expenditure	4,081	4,667	4,803	4,982	5,293	5,606	6,048	5,827
Capital Expenditure	5,303	6,499	7,855	6,936	6,378	6,398	6,321	6,128
Overall Deficit (−)/ Surplus (+)	−3,662	−4,935	−5,411	−4,861	−5,035	−5,315	−5,190	−6,237
3. Financing								
Foreign Loans	1,710	2,587	3,078	2,280	2,020	2,304	2,596	2,278
Domestic Borrowing	+1,952	+2,348	+2,333	+2,581	+3,015	+3,011	+2,594	+3,959
				(In % of GDP)				
4. Receipts	14.8	14.5	15.5	14.2	12.4	12.0	12.2	9.4
5. Of which Tax Revenue	9.61	14.79	9.8	9.23	8.58	8.25	7.41	6.59
6. Expenditure	24.3	26.0	27.0	23.9	21.8	21.4	21.1	19.7

[1] Including grants.

SOURCES: Ministry of Planning and Finance, Burma, *Report to the Pyithu Hluttaw, 1988/89*, and preceding issues, and *Review of the Financial, Economic and Social Conditions for 1989/90*.

TABLE 12

Composition of Tax Revenues and Expenditure Shares

(In million kyat)

	1980/81	*1981/82*	*1982/83*	*1983/84*	*1984/85*	*1985/86*	*1986/87*	*1987/88*
Commodity & Services Tax	2,358.2	2,545.7	2,630.3	2,736.0	2,759.5	2,799.6	2,496.6	2,204.6
As % of total	(63.55)	(59.3)	(57.16)	(59.45)	(61.58)	(60.57)	(57.06)	(50.41)
Income Tax & Profit Tax	182.0	194.5	234.1	266.1	235.6	256.9	472.5	480.0
As % of total	(4.9)	(4.57)	(5.2)	(3.78)	(5.26)	(5.56)	(10.8)	(10.98)
Custom duties	846.1	1,014.2	1,297.1	1,143.6	1,050.0	1,060.0	949.4	986.5
As % of total	(22.8)	(23.82)	(28.19)	(24.85)	(23.43)	(22.93)	(21.7)	(22.36)
Tax on the use of state properties	181.0	199.4	192.2	252.8	216.0	225.9	230.5	489.9
Others	143.3	203.1	243.1	203.6	219.7	234.6	226.2	212.4
Total	3,710.6	4,256.9	4,601.8	4,602.1	4,480.8	4,621.9	4,375.2	4,373.2
Current Expenditure as % of Total Expenditure	43.5	41.8	37.9	41.8	45.4	46.7	48.9	48.7
Capital Expenditure as % of Total Expenditure	56.5	58.2	62.1	58.2	54.6	53.3	51.1	51.3
SEEs Capital Expenditure	4,013.9	5,142	5,848.5	4,956.3	4,489.4	4,298.8	3,876.5	3,826.2
As % of Total Capital Expenditure	75.7	79.1	74.5	71.5	70.4	67.2	61.3	62.4

SOURCE: Ministry of Planning and Finance, Burma.

On the expenditure side, it may be seen that, excepting 1987/88, current expenditures increased throughout even while total receipts were going down, thereby dwindling the size of public sector savings. More importantly, it may be noted that capital expenditures constitute some 50 to 60 per cent of total expenditure. Of this, the lion's share or about two-thirds was used by the SEEs. Given the fact that most of them were running at well below capacity for want of imported inputs, it seems rather foolhardy to press on with more of the same.

For the purposes at hand, the SEEs have been identified as the major source of fiscal deficits or what may also be called "fiscal disequilibrium". Prior to that, links have been established between external imbalance and fiscal deficits on the one hand, and fiscal deficits and external debt on the other. And although a link between fiscal deficits and inflation have not been found, there can be no doubt that it would have caused inflation had it not been for the tremendous increase in personal savings and also foreign financing. Thus, appropriate monetary and fiscal policies will have to be determined that will revive the economy and put it back on the path of sustained growth.

Monetary and Fiscal Policies for the 1990s

In the context of the Burmese economy, it is somewhat irrelevant and certainly premature to speak of fine-tuning the economy (in the conventional sense) with an appropriate mix of monetary and fiscal policies. While the interrelationship between the two in the usual macro-economic context is acknowledged, in the present case, their relationship can only be considered to the extent that both must work in unison to achieve high rates of savings and efficient allocation of resources. It may be noted, therefore, that high tax ratios may not be compatible with high rates of financial savings. Furthermore, since the ability of financial institutions to entice financial savings depends on their allocative efficiency, budgetary allocations may have to give way, to some extent, to financial intermediation. Bearing these in mind, monetary and fiscal policies may each be considered separately.

According to Mckinnon and Shaw, the major aim of monetary policy should be to promote the development of capital and financial markets rather than to focus on short-term stabilization.[15] A number of studies support this view. According to a recent study on domestic savings and financial development in Asian countries, "Countries with higher levels and faster growth in M_2/GDP (that is, financial development) tended also to have higher saving, investment, and real rates of economic growth".[16] In an even more recent study on financial development and economic growth, the author stated that, "Concentrating on LDCs, I also found that those countries with a higher-than-average growth rate of GNP (or GDP) are rather strongly associated with a supply-leading phenomenon when the currency ratio is used as a proxy of financial development".[17] The same study also found the LDCs (less developed countries) to have a supply-leading causality pattern more frequently than a demand-following pattern.

None of the studies mentioned above disproved the importance of stabilization measures or programmes. What they imply is that as far as monetary policy is concerned much more emphasis must be given to the matter of financial development. This is especially so in a country such as Burma, which is financially as well as economically very underdeveloped. An awareness of this, as well as the fact that future governments are likely to choose a development strategy in favour of greater private-sector participation has led to the proposition of a supply-leading type of financial development described earlier. And having advocated such a development it now remains for us to suggest policies and measures to bring it about.

For this we can draw not only from our own findings and an insider's knowledge of the true situation in the country but also from the experiences of other Asian countries as provided by two studies.[18] The findings here and that of the above-mentioned studies indicate that significant reforms will be needed to promote financial development in Burma (as in some of the South Asian countries) so that the financial sector may perform the functions of attracting domestic savings and allocating funds in the most efficient manner.

For the forward-looking type of supply-leading financial development that has been advocated here, this would imply:

1. expanding the coverage of depository institutions so as to tap the full potential of rural savings (the network of MAB branches at present simply act as conduits for disbursing credit and little or no attempt has been made to mobilize rural savings);
2. increasing the supply and variety of financial assets like bonds, shares, debentures, mortgages, and so forth so as to induce those who hold their savings in the form of land, real estate, jewelry and so on, to hold their savings in the form of income-yielding financial assets;
3. providing higher real rates of return for savers and/or allowing more freedom in allocating funds and setting rates in accordance with market conditions (the tremendous increases in personal savings noted earlier have lost momentum now that real deposit rates have become negative);
4. promoting the establishment of new financial institutions so as to tap "small savings" in urban areas and to provide increased competition which can lead to cost-effective operations and long-term efficiency gains;
5. promoting the "banking habit" of the people, especially by trying to overcome the people's distrust and dislike of bureaucratic procedures and by encouraging the adoption of technical advances in financial services;
6. shifting the financing of SEEs to a strictly commercial basis so as to force them to become viable; and
7. uplifting the skills of bank personnel and changing their outlook (there will soon be a dearth of skilled personnel in the top posts as experienced hands reach retirement).

The effectiveness of the above measures in enhancing financial development in Burma depends chiefly on how far the government is willing to go as regards the participation of private enterprise in the financial sector.

In this connection it may be mentioned that even Sri Lanka, supposedly an inward-looking country like Burma, allowed a number of foreign banks to set up branches in the late 1970s, thereby creating competition for deposits with domestic banks. "As a result, a wider range of financial instruments and services became available and the domestic savings rate began to increase".[19] At the other extreme, the Republic of Korea denationalized its commercial banks in the early 1980s to allow greater scope for market forces and to reduce government controls over the financial system. Somewhere between Sri Lanka and the Republic of Korea is Thailand. Private commercial banks dominate the financial sector in Thailand in terms of the proportion of savings they mobilize and the credit they extend. Thus, private enterprise participation is common in the financial sector to a greater or lesser degree. For the supply-leading type of financial development that is being advocated here private enterprise participation would be even more important.

The financial sector is not an island. If it is to operate on market principles, a sound macro-economic environment must be created, a matter which monetary policy alone cannot achieve.

Fiscal policy, on the other hand, must be directed towards the gradual reduction and final elimination of chronic deficits. Achieving stabilization in Burma will depend chiefly on the ability of the government to manage a tight fiscal policy.

In this regard, it should be acknowledged that the question of which taxes to increase, and by how much, what expenditures to cut, by how much, and so on, depends much on the preferences and prejudices of the political masters and on their "political will" to override vested interests. As Richard Goode has stated succinctly, "Budgeting is part of politics; it can never be a purely technical exercise".[20]

Another factor that must be accepted *a priori* concerns the matter of public sector current expenditures. Following the pay hike for all government servants in April 1989, these expenditures are likely to increase by an unprecedented amount. The wage bill in the public sector is estimated to increase on the average by about 2.7 to 3 times, or by 170 to 200 per cent. Assuming that the wage component constitutes roughly a third of current expenditures, an increase in the former would translate into a 90 or 100 per cent increase in the total current expenditures. Moreover, the increase in current expenditures will not be confined to the increase in the total wage bill alone. It will also increase by the amount of the "inflation factor" as real current expenditures have somehow to be maintained at their already low levels. Thus, current expenditures will be doubled.

The choice is therefore left of either raising revenues or cutting down capital expenditures. In either case, Draconian measures will be necessary.

To consider the matter of raising revenues first, the present government amended in March 1989 the income and profit tax law and the income tax rules. It is estimated that revenue from income tax is not likely to increase by much as the minimum level of income liable for taxation has been raised from 10,000 kyats per annum to 15,000 kyats per annum. In other words, the income tax base will remain more or less unchanged.

The axe will fall on the profit tax, and therein lies the danger. As anyone who is fairly well acquainted with public finance knows, heavy taxation of profits could adversely affect growth. Already, there are indications of private enterprises scaling down their businesses and going "underground", that is, to the informal sector. It is difficult to estimate to what extent tax evasions of that sort will affect government revenue.

On the other hand, taxes on the profits of foreign enterprises which constitute a large portion of the total tax revenue in a number of developing countries will not amount to much in the case of Burma, at least in the immediate future. This is because the Foreign Investment Law of Burma allows a tax holiday of at least three years and other tax exemptions as an incentive to attract direct foreign investment, although much controversy exists as to the effectiveness of such measures.

In sum, government revenues from taxes will fall far short of what is needed if drastic cuts in capital expenditures are ruled out (for the moment). The tax ratio of about 7 per cent of GDP in Burma is, by international standards, on the low side. It should be increased to between 10 and 12 per cent of GDP. However, a major finding of a recent study "that high tax ratios may adversely affect growth" should also be noted.[21] Thus, while tax revenues must be increased, careful thinking is needed in the choice of the income tax base, progressivity of the tax rates and the incentive effects of tax exemptions. The general objective should be to have a tax system which is fairly elastic with respect to changes in income and which do not unduly penalize work effort and entrepreneurship.

Even assuming that tax revenues could be raised to some 10 or 12 per cent of GDP, and further assuming that non-tax revenue would also increase proportionately, it will still not be enough to cover the total expenditure of the public sector of over 20 per cent of GDP. Hence, capital expenditures must be cut by some 4 to 6 per cent of GDP. Furthermore, as capital expenditures on public services such as health, education and so on are essential and (as evidenced by over-crowded hospitals and schools) can hardly be reduced, most of the trimming must be done on the capital expenditures of the SEEs.

Many of the SEEs, as indicated earlier, are running at well below capacity. This reflects in significant measure the over-extension of the public sector and the failure of the government to adequately shoulder the burdens of the SEEs. A reduction in their capital expenditures, if it is carried out rationally, should therefore not adversely affect growth. An even more attractive option would be to privatize some of the SEEs in the manufacturing sector. How and in what manner is, however, beyond the scope of the present study.

Conclusion

The present study set out to consider the development of the financial institutions and monetary policy from a historical perspective. It found the present financial sector in Burma to be less developed in many respects than the one which existed before the 1963 nationalizations. Next, the study attempted to analyse the fiscal-related problems of external and internal imbalances. It found the fiscal deficits to have been largely responsible for the twin problems of external imbalance and external indebtedness.

It further found the over-extension of the public sector particularly in the area of SEEs to have in turn been chiefly responsible for the fiscal deficits.

Based on the above findings, the study proposed a "supply-leading" type of financial development as the single most important aspect of monetary policy for development. The scope for using traditional monetary instruments in the immediate future is heavily constrained by the underdevelopment of the financial structure. As regards fiscal policy, the study argued for a tax reform (entailing a moderate increase in tax revenues) on the one hand and for drastic cuts in the capital expenditures of SEEs on the other.

Needless to say, apart from adjustment costs or pains, the choices that must be made and the complicated process of efficiently managing an economy as required by the proposed changes will not be easy. On the other hand, there can also be no doubt about the urgency of the need for financial development and for reductions in the fiscal deficits. Whatever the policy package that may eventually be considered there can be no escape from the adjustment costs or pains entailed by the hard choices that must be made.

NOTES

1. U Tun Wai (1962), p. 211.
2. For more details of financial and monetary trends in the 1950s, see K.S. Mali (1960) and U Tun Wai (1962).
3. These actions of the government certainly led to the deterioration of banking habits and the flight of trained personnel and skilled workers. However, it is difficult to determine to what extent these contributed to the stagnation and decline of the 1960s.
4. According to Carol Goldstein, U Ba Nyein, then economic adviser to the government, was said to have mentioned about the existence of an economic plan drawn up in 1967. See Carol Goldstein, "Human Errors", *Far Eastern Economic Review* 63, no. 1 (2 January 1969): 13–14.
5. See Hill and Jayasuriya (1986).
6. For more details of the growth and development of the existing financial system, see Union of Burma Bank, *A Collection of Papers Prepared by the Research and Training Department* (Rangoon, 1985), Vol. 1 and 2.
7. U Maung Maung Hla, *A Collection of Papers Prepared by the Research and Training Department* (Union of Burma Bank, 1985), Vol. 1, p. 10.

8. H. Patrick (1966).
9. Woo S. Jung (1986), p. 333.
10. Unless otherwise stated, it is assumed (for the sake of simplicity in exposition) that the trade balance (M − X) is equal to the current account balance.
11. Denoting external financing by E_f,
    $E_f = M - X$
    and therefore,
    $(I_g + I_p) - (S_g + S_p) = E_f$
12. Milne's paper was not available but his approach was learnt through Kelly (1982). According to Kelly, the approach by Milne assumes that the private sector deficit/surplus is essentially constant and that changes in the balance of payments reflect primarily changes in the government deficit.
13. The demonetization of 50 and 100 kyat notes in November 1985 did not seriously affect the increase in money supply as most of it was refunded by March 1986.
14. In fact, many of the SEEs in the manufacturing sector were defective at birth in the sense that they had long gestation periods and cost overruns (The Council of People's Inspectors, 1975).
15. Ronald I. Mckinnon (1973); and Edward S. Shaw (1973).
16. W.E. James et al. (1987), p. 79.
17. Woo S. Jung (1986), p. 34.
18. W.E. James et al. (1987); and Graham J. Abbott (1984).
19. W.E. James et al. (1987), p. 90.
20. R. Goode (1984), p. 39.
21. Keith Marsden (1983).

REFERENCES

Abbott, Graham J. "National Saving and Financial Development in Asian Developing Countries". In *Asian Development Review* 2 (1984): 1–22.

Aghelvi, Bijan B., Moshin S. Khan, P.R. Narvekar, and Brock K. Short. "Monetary Policy in Selected Asian Countries". INST/85 –iv/I.B 1(b). Washington D.C., 1985.

Central Statistical Organisation, Burma. *Quarterly Bulletin of Statistics*, Rangoon, 1988, and preceding years.

Ministry of Planning and Finance, Burma. *Report to the Pyithu Hluttaw on the Financial, Economic and Social Conditions of the Socialist Republic of the Union of Burma*. Rangoon, 1974/75 and preceding years.

———. *Review of the Financial, Economic and Social Conditions for 1989/90*. Rangoon. 1989.

Daw Khin Kyi Kyi, Daw Myint Myint Tin, U Hla Phyu Chit, and Daw Khin Mar Kyu. "Financial Structure and the Effectiveness of Monetary Policy (Burma)". (In Burmese.) Rangoon, 1986.

Daw Khin Ohn Thant, Daw Khin Nyo Nyo, U Sein Win, U Khin Aung, U Saw Maung Hla, and Daw Aye Aye Thant. "Domestic Resource Mobilization". (In Burmese). November, 1986.

Goode, R. *Government Finance in Developing Countries*. Washington D.C., The Brookings Institution, 1984.

Hill, Hal, and S. Jayasuriya. *An Inward-looking Economy in Transition: Economic Development in Burma since the 1960s*. Occasional Paper No. 80. Singapore: Institute of Southeast Asian Studies, 1986.

International Monetary Fund. *Burma: Recent Economic Developments*. Washington D.C., 20 May 1987.

———. *Current Issues in Fiscal Policy*. INST/85-IV/I.B. 1(d).

James, W.E., Seiji Naya, and Gerald M. Meir. *Asian Development*. University of Wisconsin Press, 1987.

Kelly, Margaret R. "Fiscal Adjustment and Fund-Supported Programs, 1971–80". *Staff Papers* 29, no. 4 (December 1982): 561–602.

Mali, K.S. "Financing Economic Development of Burma Since Independence". Ph.D. dissertation, Indiana University, June 1960.

Marsden, Keith. "Taxes and Growth". *Finance and Development* 20, no. 3 (September 1983): 40–43.

Mckinnon, Ronald I. *Money and Capital in Economic Development*. Washington D.C.: The Brookings Institution, 1973.

Patrick, H. "Financial Development and Economic Growth in Underdeveloped Countries". *Economic Development and Cultural Change* 14 (January 1966): 174–89.

Shaw, Edward S. *Financial Deepening in Economic Development*. Oxford: Oxford University Press, 1973.

The Council of People's Inspectors. *Report to the Fourth Meeting of the First Pyithu Hluttaw* (in Burmese). Rangoon, 23 August 1975.

U Tun Wai. *Burma's Currency and Credit*, revised edition. New Delhi: Orient Longmans Ltd., 1962.

———. *Financial Intermediaries and National Savings in Developing Countries*. New York: Praeger Publishers, 1972.

Union of Burma Bank. *A Collection of Papers Prepared by the Research and Training Department*, Vol. 1. Rangoon, September 1985.

______. *A Collection of Papers Prepared by the Research and Training Department*, Vol. 2. Rangoon, September 1985.

Woo S. Jung. "Financial Development and Economic Growth: International Evidence". *Economic Development and Cultural Change* 34 (January 1986): 333–46.

4

AGRICULTURAL POLICY REFORMS AND AGRICULTURAL DEVELOPMENT IN MYANMAR

MYA THAN and NOBUYOSHI NISHIZAWA

Introduction

There is no need to stress the importance of the agricultural sector in the Myanmar economy. The rise and fall of the sector decides the performance of the national economy and the fate of nearly 80 per cent of the population. Therefore, it is no wonder that any reform in this sector attracts much attention. Many reforms have been carried out in the agricultural sector since the Revolutionary Council took over power in 1962. These reforms have mainly been concerned with land tenure, credit, and marketing. The objective of this chapter is to analyse these reforms in relation to agricultural development in Myanmar since 1962. The period of study is divided into three sub-periods: a period of stagnation (1962–73), a period of recovery (1974–82), and a period of decline (1983 onward), in terms of performance in paddy production.

The chapter analyses reforms in land tenure and ownership, credit policy, marketing and pricing policies of agricultural products, technology, and rural institutions for each period. In the final section, the findings are summarized and some suggestions are offered for further reforms in order to achieve development objectives in the rapidly changing economic environment in this region. Included also is a brief discussion on the outlook for Myanmar's agricultural products.

Agricultural Policy Reforms in the Period of Stagnancy (1962–73)

Land Policy and Institutional Reforms

Soon after the Revolutionary Council came to power in March 1962, an agricultural development programme, which aimed at abolishing landlordism and improving the social and economic conditions of the peasantry, was launched. Its objectives were as follows:

1. to increase agricultural production through raising productivity;
2. to introduce scientific methods in agriculture;
3. to improve the agrarian system (structure);
4. to improve the social conditions in rural areas; and
5. to organize the peasantry throughout the country.[1]

The first Tenancy Law was decreed in 1963 by which the right of tenancy of land was vested in Agrarian Committees composed of farmers at the village level. Two years later, the Tenancy Law of 1965 abolished tenancy, which was the most progressive step in the agrarian history of Myanmar. This law affected about five million acres, which comprised about a quarter of the total cultivated area in Myanmar. In practice, however, tenancy was not totally eliminated, at least not until 1971 when the official data on tenancy was released by the government in the *Report to the People*.[2] Some scholars have found that tenancy still existed even after 1971.[3] The Farmers' Rights Protection Law of 1963 protected the rights of all cultivators; for instance, no one could confiscate or seize any of the farmer's means of production such as land, livestock, farm implements and agricultural produce as payment for debts. It is interesting to note that although the "Burmese Way to Socialism" aimed to nationalize all "productive forces", the agricultural sector was left almost intact. This policy reform confirmed again that the state is the ultimate owner of the land and it gives cultivators "the right to work" on the land as individuals. However, they were prohibited to buy, sell or mortgage it. Because of this policy, there was further land fragmentation and lack of improvement of the land. In the redistribution of land, the Agrarian Committee tended to give priority to the poorest person in the village, thus affecting productivity since very often he did not have the requisite skills nor sufficient capital, including seed, draught cattle, and farm implements. The land policy, in effect, stressed equity rather than productivity. This reform, in essence, represented a continuation of the land reforms of the 1950s and its main thrust was to break up the landowner–tenant relationship in order to create a new government–owner–cultivator relationship and, at the same time, to strengthen government control over farmers.[4]

As far as the agricultural credit policy was concerned, the amount of credit made available during the Revolutionary Council government was much more than that of the previous governments. It increased from K48 million in 1962/63 to K167 million in 1973/74. The government raised agricultural credit from K12 per acre in 1962/63 to K25 in 1963/64 while its interest rates were lowered from 12 per cent to 9 per cent per annum. However, in 1972, only 1.8 million rural households out of 4.4 million had real access to official credit.[5] Although it somewhat relieved the dependence of the farmers on more expensive private sources of credit, the lending rate of K25 covered only about 11 per cent of the cost of cultivation in 1972/73.[6] The consequence was that farmers continued to look to unofficial sources to meet their credit needs. Moreover, since credit was distributed on a per acre basis, farmers with larger land holdings benefited from this system. The credit system emphasized equity rather than efficiency, and agricultural loans were granted on the basis of need rather than on the basis of productivity. Some economists have gone as far as to state that agricultural production, especially paddy production, had fallen since the implementation of the new credit scheme.[7] These evaluations indicate that the government's credit system was not as effective as had been expected.

It would also seem that the government's policy on investment was made less effective because of competing priorities. Although, on paper, it recognized the role of the agricultural sector in contributing to the national economy and aimed to bring improvements to the rural sector, in practice, it gave priority to the heavy industry, manufacturing, and transport sectors rather than the agricultural sector. Public investment in the agricultural sector, in fact, dropped from 13 per cent in 1962/63 to 8.5 per cent in 1973/74, while that of the processing and manufacturing sector increased from 4.9 per cent in 1962/63 to 29.8 per cent in 1973/74.

During this period, the village administration system was also changed. The Village Councils under the previous administration were replaced by the Village Security and Administrative Committees (SACs) which were appointed by the Township SACs. However, the functions of the Village SAC remained the same as those of the Council except that it took direct responsibility for social and economic affairs. The SAC had direct responsibility for the economic planning of the village, such as the number of acres to be brought under cultivation, the amount of paddy to be sold, and so forth. Most of its committee members were at the same time members of the Agrarian Committee which decided the agrarian affairs of the village and implemented the government's agrarian policy at the village level. Government control was thus strengthened in the rural sector through a wide range of measures limiting the transfer and use of land, the distribution of farm inputs and supply of credit.

Marketing Policy Reform

Before 1962, the official procurement of rice by the government was carried out by the State Agricultural Marketing Board (SAMB), created in 1946. Its objectives were 1) to assume all rice export marketing functions which had previously been performed by alien groups such as the British, the Chinese, and the Indians; 2) to provide revenue for development plans by profiting from the difference between the purchase price given to farmers and the export price received for rice; 3) to provide a guaranteed price and the stability necessary to encourage cultivators to expand their paddy acreage; and 4) to stabilize the entire economy, and especially urban wages, by holding down rice prices.[8] They bought paddy from millers, middlemen, co-operatives and the farmers. The SAMB purchased between two and two and a half million tons of paddy a year from 1950 to 1962. The government purchase price was kept constant from 1948/49 to 1960/61 (Table 1). This system kept inflation rates at low levels and greatly increased the government's involvement in the domestic market for paddy by providing rice at a subsidized price for urban and rice-deficit areas all over the country. It also contributed greatly to capital formation. However, while there were other contributory factors such as national unrest, lack of proper land reforms and an appropriate credit system, the marketing system — especially the procurement price system — brought about a stagnation in agricultural development.

Soon after the Revolutionary Council took over power, the SAMB changed its name to the Union of Burma Agricultural and Marketing Board (UBAMB) in January 1963. However, the functions remained unchanged. Then in July 1963, the trading of eleven essential commodities, including rice, wheat, and vegetables was nationalized. Thus, the workload of the UBAMB increased five or sixfold since it bought, distributed, and exported not only rice but also other "controlled" crops. The UBAMB established depots for buying paddy directly from the farmers and the procurement of paddy became a government monopoly. By 1964, as part of the nationalization of all trade and commerce, private trade in rice in the domestic market was officially prohibited and all paddy had to be sold to Trade Corporation No. 1, although the official procurement system was said to be a "voluntary" one. The Corporation was the successor to the UBAMB. It was again renamed as the Agricultural and Farm Produce Trade Corporation (AFPTC) in 1974, and later became known as the Myanmar Agricultural Products Agency in 1989. Some "controlled" crops such as groundnut, sesamum, onions, potatoes, garlic, chillies, and a few pulses were released later. The export of paddy was mainly

TABLE 1
Net Output in Agriculture and Paddy Production, 1962/63–1988/89*

Year	*Agricultural Output (million kyats)*	*Paddy Area (thousand acres)*	*Paddy Production (million baskets)*	*Paddy Production (thousand tons)*	*Paddy Production per caput (ton)*	*Paddy Yield (baskets per acre)*	*Population (million)*	*Rice Export (thousand tons)*
1962/63	2965	11952	367	7544	.325	31.16	23.2	1521
1963/64	3014	12475	373	7720	.326	31.94	23.7	1445
1964/65	3255	12624	408	8373	.346	30.95	24.2	1176
1965/66	3106	12391	386	7928	.320	33.16	24.8	989
1966/67	2904	12328	318	6531	.258	32.22	25.3	624
1967/68	3287	12193	372	7647	.295	28.50	25.9	336
1968/69	3326	12402	385	7896	.299	32.02	26.4	345
1969/70	3449	12243	383	7859	.291	33.15	27.0	528
1970/71	3710	12294	391	8033	.291	32.92	27.6	639
1971/72	3777	12300	392	8046	.284	33.28	28.3	596
1972/73	3480	12014	353	7241	.251	31.51	28.9	204
1973/74	3826	12575	413	8466	.287	34.19	29.5	196
1974/75	3757	12793	411	8583	.288	34.09	29.8	166
1975/76	3955	12858	441	9207	.303	35.51	30.4	419
1976/77	4169	12547	447	9319	.301	36.80	31.0	646
1977/78	4377	12690	454	9462	.299	37.73	31.6	637
1978/79	4697	12957	505	10528	.326	40.75	32.3	187
1979/80	4956	12420	501	10448	.318	45.62	32.9	759
1980/81	5497	12668	638	13317	.396	53.82	33.6	673

TABLE 1 (*cont'd*)

Net Output in Agriculture and Paddy Production, 1962/63–1988/89*

Year	*Agricultural Output (million kyats)*	*Paddy Area (thousand acres)*	*Paddy Production (million baskets)*	*Paddy Production (thousand tons)*	*Paddy Production per caput (ton)*	*Paddy Yield (baskets per acre)*	*Population (million)*	*Rice Export (thousand tons)*
1981/82	5928	12610	678	13923	.406	57.06	34.3	674
1982/83	6293	12064	689	14146	.404	61.10	35.0	683
1983/84	6625	11938	685	14287	.400	59.48	35.7	874
1984/85	6908	12151	683	14255	.392	60.09	36.4	622
1985/86	7077	12114	686	14317	.386	59.58	37.1	582
1986/87	7125	11968	677	14126	.373	58.72	37.9	597
1987/88	6780[1]	11531	654	13636	.353	59.00	38.6	303
1988/89	6789[2]	11802	650	13553	.344	56.88	39.4	49

* Net output in production of crops and livestock in 1969/70 constant prices.

[1] Revised provisional.

[2] Provisional.

SOURCES: Ministry of Planning and Finance, *Report to the Pyithu Hluttaw*, various issues; and *Review of the Financial and Social Conditions for 1989/90*; Central Statistical Organization, *Selected Monthly Economic Indicators*, various issues.

carried out by the SAMB until 1963 and from that time on it was monopolized by the UBAMB and then by Trade Corporation No. 1.

The objectives of the marketing policy of this period were 1) to assure stable prices for both producers and consumers, 2) to provide revenue needed for development plans, and 3) to stabilize the economy. These aims were not different from those of the SAMB period except that the Revolutionary Council government had more control over the marketing of agricultural products than its predecessors. In practice, the economic significance of the SAMB, the UBAMB, and Trade Corporation No. 1 was that it was a means of (progressive) taxation of the agricultural sector, although it was asserted that their role was to replace the middlemen in the paddy trade. However, in 1972/73, local co-operatives were given the responsibility for the procurement and distribution of rice. The bad weather contributed to the decline in production during this year and, as a result, farmers, traders, households, and even local authorities started hoarding paddy. This led to rice shortages in the towns and the situation became chaotic. This in turn sparked the workers' riots in Rangoon in 1974.

As far as the agricultural price policy is concerned there was no significant change except in 1973/74 when the government increased prices based, unlike in previous cases, on the cost of cultivation. The government controlled the prices of paddy, wheat, maize, cotton, kenaf, jute, rubber, sugar-cane, Virginia tobacco and some beans and pulses and set the procurement prices of "controlled" crops nationally regardless of geographical location, varying only according to the type or grade of each crop. Paddy price was kept low and constant for a long time and the export price was approximately two times higher than the government procurement price (Table 2). This was the result of the pricing policy of the Revolutionary Council which was, in essence, the continuation of the price policy of the previous governments. The rationale was that the government, by keeping paddy price low, could make profits for capital accumulation, and it would be able to supply urban dwellers and labourers with cheap staple food, and thus control the rate of inflation. One could say that the price policy of that period was consumer-biased and a kind of welfare

TABLE 2
Prices of Paddy/Rice
(In kyat per ton)

Year	*Retail*		*Procurement*		*Ratio of Export Price/ Government Price*	*Export Price*
	Govt.	*Free Market*	*Govt.*	*Free Market*		
1962/63	222	378	149	166	2.973154	443
1963/64	222	395	149	159	3.000000	447
1964/65	229	357	149	155	3.167785	472
1965/66	229	499	149	147	3.248322	484
1966/67	251	1400	163	165	3.196319	521
1967/68	265	1300	172	209	3.360465	578
1968/69	265	900	172	528	4.087209	703
1969/70	311	568	172	244	3.877907	667
1970/71	311	628	172	281	2.703488	465
1971/72	311	1038	172	538	2.436047	419
1972/73	427	1109	204	582	2.509804	512
1973/74	640	1344	431	729	1.916473	826
1974/75	710	1368	431	744	3.733179	1609
1975/76	804	1283	431	679	4.074246	1756
1976/77	870	1123	431	579	2.684455	1157
1977/78	894	1368	431	732	3.185615	1373
1978/79	935	1674	446	1132	3.226457	1439
1979/80	935	1176	446	1211	3.349776	1494
1980/81	935	1647	472	1253	3.190678	1506
1981/82	894	1289	472	1833	4.978814	2350
1982/83	894	1500	472	1986	5.317797	2510
1983/84	894	1834	472	2291	3.750000	1770
1984/85	894	2022	472	2444	3.341102	1577
1985/86	894	2126	472	2521	2.790254	1317
1986/87	894	2139	472	2597	3.010593	1421
1987/88	894	5747	472	2879	1.737288	820
1988/89	3998	9406	472	3834	2.978814	1406

SOURCE: Ministry of Planning and Finance, *Report to the Pyithu Hluttaw*, various issues; and *Review of the Financial and Social Conditions for 1989/90*; and Central Statistical Organization, *Selected Monthly Economic Indicators*, various issues.

policy measure. This price policy obviously has depressed the incentives of farmers to grow paddy.

Distribution of rice from 1948 to 1963 had been carried out by private enterprises and the method of distribution had been through the operation of market forces. This task was taken over by the People's Stores and Cooperatives during the 1963/64–1973/74 period.

Policy Reform in Technology in Agriculture

One of the components of the agricultural policy of the government was to introduce scientific methods in agriculture in order to raise productivity and production. It is true that the government spent more and more on irrigation, chemical inputs and better quality seeds, among other things. The irrigation ratio, for example, increased from 7.4 per cent in 1962/63 to 12 per cent in 1973/74. Notwithstanding this, its impact on paddy production was not significant because the percentage of irrigated area under paddy with respect to total irrigated area in fact fell from 80 to 75 during the period and almost all of the paddy areas in lower Burma, which are considered to be the "rice bowl of Myanmar", are rain-fed. Similarly, fertilizer utilization went up from 21 thousand tons in 1962/63 to 120 thousand tons in 1973/74. Since the ratio of paddy price to fertilizer price was very unfavourable (Burma's 0.12 against Thailand's 0.32 and Ceylon's 0.72 in 1971), farmers were reluctant to use them. Although the introduction of high yielding variety (HYV) seeds were introduced only in 1970/71, their share in the total production of rice grew from 11 per cent to 16 per cent within three years. However, there were limitations in applying HYVs in paddy production. Farmers needed more fertilizer and labour to cultivate it. The cost of hired labour was very high and continually increased because of the labour shortages in the rural area. Accordingly, the marginal returns from cultivating HYVs then were very small and farmers were therefore reluctant to use HYVs. Some studies have found that farmers used less hired labour during the early 1970s. Some farmers switched from the transplanting method of cultivation to the less labour-intensive low-yielding broadcasting method because of higher labour cost. Tractor utilization was encouraged by the government, but its contribution to total paddy production was minimal, because farmers used tractor power for the second crop when more labour was needed within a short period. In short, the majority of farmers still used primitive techniques in paddy cultivation and there was no co-ordination among price systems of agricultural crops and their chemical inputs and wage policy. The policy on the introduction of new technology in the agricultural sector during the period, 1962/63–1973/74, was thus less effective than desired in spite of the government's efforts.

Policy Reforms and Performance in the Agricultural Sector

This section will deal with the impact of policy reforms on the performance of the agricultural sector for the period between 1962/63 and 1973/74. For the purpose of this chapter, the performance of paddy output will be used to represent the performance of the whole sector. This is because rice is still a very dominant crop in Myanmar agriculture as it comprises about 60 per cent of total GDP in the agricultural sector, its sown area covers more than half of the total sown area, its contribution to foreign exchange used to be about half of total foreign earnings, and its production, marketing and distribution involved about two-thirds of the labour force employed. Its performance is shown in Table 1.

As far as the sown area of paddy is concerned, this caught up with its pre-war level only in 1962/63. It is important to note that the pre-war sown area covered only "Burma proper" excluding the sown areas in some states and frontier areas whereas post-war figures cover the entire Union. The paddy acreage steadily grew until 1964/65 when the government's agricultural policy started to take effect. Thus, soon after 1964/65, the sown area began to decline until 1967/68 when the ratio of the official price to the black market price was one of the lowest in the decade. Then the price increased in 1968/69 when the black market price rose because of the shortage of rice in the previous year. Generally speaking, it could be said that the area under paddy was directly related to the ratio of the government price and that of the black market for the period under study.

As for paddy production, the sown area and weather seemed to be decisive factors and the government's supply of modern inputs seemed to have little effect. Since the farmers' decision on how many acres of paddy should be cultivated depended on the difference between the official price and that of the black market, the production of paddy depended on government price policies in the sector. If one looks at production figures for the period, one finds that it varied from year to year and that per capita production fell towards the early 1970s. In other words, agricultural growth gradually slowed down during the 1960s and it barely increased in the early 1970s. Government procurement as a percentage of production declined drastically. Production fell because of bad weather and the hoarding of rice by traders, farmers, individuals as well as the authorities caused shortages of rice in the country which in turn led to serious social unrest in the cities. Furthermore, the volume of rice exports fell from 1,521 thousand tons in 1962/63 to 104 thousand tons in 1973/74 as a result of the decline in the procurement/production ratio. This resulted in the stagnation of the whole economy. It is obvious that this was caused by the disincentives created by the government's land policy and the marketing policy introduced during the same period. Khin Maung Kyi and associates[9] found that the position of farmers in Lower Burma up to 1974 worsened and even farm labourers were better off than the farmers.[10]

Policy Reforms in the Period of Recovery (1974–82)

Land Policy and Institutional Reforms

The most important landmark during this period was the introduction of the new constitution which declared Burma as the Socialist Republic of the Union of Burma. The Constitution of 1974 states clearly that the State is the ultimate owner of all natural resources and also of land; and it shall develop, extract, exploit and utilize the natural resources. Another important landmark was the launching of the Second Four-Year Plan (FYP) in 1974, which was in essence the starting point of the Twenty-Year Plan (TYP). It consisted of general planning guidelines which were actually a liberal version of the "Burmese Way to Socialism". Although it was approved in 1972, its actual implementation was started only in 1974/75. The third landmark was the introduction of Official Development Assistance (ODA) as well as other financial inflows for higher investment. In short, although Burma did not give up its "socialist" economic policies, pragmatic policy measures had to be carried out because of the severity of the economic decline during the period from 1962/63 to 1973/74. These helped the stagnant economy to recover.

Several changes took place in the agencies responsible for granting credit to farmers up to 1973/74. From 1974/75, Trade Corporation No. 1 (later the AFPTC) took over the function and the granting of K35 per acre as part of the advance paddy purchase programme. Then in 1977/78, the rate was increased to K70 per acre, which was again raised to K140 for the HYV areas from 1981/82. (Since 1978/79, all agricultural loans have been issued through the Myanmar Agricultural Bank.) As agricultural credit increased year after year, the credit needs of the farmers also increased. Since institutional credit did not cover the cash part of the cultivation cost, farmers turned to unofficial sources of credit and as a result, farmers' indebtness was as acute as in previous times.[11] More importantly, the basic concept of priority of equity over efficiency did not change.

There was an improvement in agricultural investment during this period as a result of a policy shift in the government's development strategy. The ruling party recognized the role of the sector and approved the highest priority to be given to agriculture in future development plans. Government capital expenditure increased from 8.1 per cent in 1974/75 to 11.1 per cent in 1982/83. This shift in investment policy played an important role in agricultural development during the period 1974/75 to 1982/83.

Although the land policy remained intact, many institutional changes occurred. Firstly, Village Council members were elected along with those at township level, divisional/state level and national level (for the national assembly known as the Pyithu Hluttaw). These Village Councils replaced the SACs and they took care of not only administrative matters, but also of economic, social, and judicial affairs. Moreover, local Peasants Councils (later Peasant Asiayones) were formed and all these institutions at the village level co-operated and were involved in the implementation of the economic plan, especially in the agricultual sector. Athough it seemed that there was a decentralization of administrative power to the village level, stronger government control was none the less visible in the rural areas. Research and extension services to educate the farmers in the use of modern technology by the Agricultural and Rural Development Corporation (later Agricultural Corporation) were also expanded.

Marketing Policy Reform

With the beginning of the 1974/75 season, the government implemented a new procurement system which was actually a "compulsory delivery system". According to this system, a quota of paddy which had to be sold at a fixed price to the government depot was set for each farmer according to the size of his holding for paddy, the yield per acre, his family size and the amount of paddy to be paid to hired labour. The remaining part of the harvest could be sold within the township. This was actually a form of progressive taxation which favoured the small farmer with poor performance. In other words, this was yet again a policy of equity rather than of improving productivity. Moreover, the state applied, during this period, an advance purchase system which is similar to the "pindaung" system, by which lenders extended credit to the farmers in cash for which farmers had to pay back in crops. Trade Corporation No. 1 (later AFPTC) purchased paddy from the farmers with advance payment through its depots all over the country from 1974/75. State-procured paddy was milled by about 45 state-owned mills and by about 800 private mills under contract with the AFPTC. An additional 850 privately owned rice mills milled rice only for the domestic consumption of the farmers and were forbidden to mill paddy brought in by anyone other than the producers themselves.[12] However, rice found its way to the black market through direct sale or through private rice mills. Rice found in the black market were mostly from the large farmers. Small farmers, on the other hand, sometimes had to sell part of their *wunza* (the part of the production kept for home consumption) to the AFPTC to fulfil their quota and later were forced to buy rice for their own consumption at the black-market price, which was about twice the price of what they sold to the state. Since 1979/80, the AFPTC has provided incentives for the sale of rice above the quota. Those who sold extra rice could buy some goods at the state shops at the official price which was much cheaper than the free market price. These incentives plus a good harvest helped the AFPTC to buy more paddy during this period. However, it was found that the amount of procured paddy was inversely related to the gap between the official procurement price and the black market price. This means that the wider the gap between these two prices, the lesser the amount of government procurement.

In 1974/75 the government raised the procurement price of paddy to more than twice that of the 1972/73 price to correct the imbalance that had been perpetuated for more than twenty years. The prices of other crops were adjusted too. This price increase received enthusiastic response from paddy farmers and their sown acreage increased along with production and procurement. The paddy price was increased again in 1979/80 and in 1980/81 as the government felt that the incentives created by the price hike in 1974 had declined in importace after 1977/78. From the 1980 season onwards, the procurement price was kept constant. It is important to note that while the official price had gone up, the free market price had also gone up. However, the government measure to increase the procurement price reflected the pragmatic change in government policy, which used economic incentives rather than physical control in directing the economy to achieve the planned targets.

The distribution of rice for internal consumption was carried out by local co-operatives which replaced the People's Stores. Co-operatives were more flexible and easier to manage than the People's Stores. In practice, the amount of rice for distribution in each and every State/Division was calculated by the Ministry of Trade, with the approval of the Cabinet. Then the respective People's Council at each level set the amount to be distributed within their administrative areas. In a normal year, the usual per capita quota for those above 12 years of age was set at 6 pyis (2.13 kg) and for those under 12 it was 3 pyis (1.65 kg). The amount of rice distributed in 1974/75 was 0.8 million tons and this increased to 1.75 million tons in 1982/83.

Policy Reform in Agricultural Technology

There was a technical breakthrough during these years, especially in rice production in the mid-1970s. This came from the government's strategy to raise productivity through a "Green Revolution" by using improved seeds (HYVs) and fertilizers. Because of the government drive to use more fertizers combined with HYVs, the utilization of these modern inputs increased annually, resulting in higher yields. Thus, production increases during this period could be attributed to yield increases rather than area increases as there was little or no extension in cropped area. Mya Than found in his previous work that all four forms of productivity had improved since 1974/75, and of these, the highest contribution to growth came from the land-saving type of technology.[13] Actually, this preference for the land-saving type of technology began to emerge in 1975/76 when a pilot production programme was launched in a township in Lower Burma. This programme was expanded into the "Whole Township Special Rice Production Programme". By 1982/83, 82 townships were involved in this programme under which more than half of the paddy area was covered by HYVs, and fertilizer utilization grew about four times from 1974/75 to 1982/83. Due to this breakthrough in technology, the yield per acre of paddy increased from 34 baskets in 1974/75 to 61 baskets in 1982/83 (see Table 1).

Policy Reforms and the Performance of the Agricultural Sector

Before the mid-1970s, agriculture was at the mercy of the weather. However, the performance of the sector after 1974/75 was the best in the history of the country. The production of paddy increased from 8,448,000 tons in 1974/75 to 14,146,000 tons in 1982/83 (Table 1). The agricultural sector's average annual growth rate of 6.7 per cent during 1974/75 to 1982/83 was the major contributor to the national economy. This was made possible through policy reforms in marketing, distribution, technology and institutions. Let us see how these changes affected the development of the sector.

The good performance of paddy production up to 1977/78 was due to good weather and the increase in procurement was the result of the price increase in 1974/75 and the introduction of the "compulsory delivery with advance payment" procurement system, along with administrative pressure. This in turn helped to increase the export of rice from 0.2 million tons in 1974/75 to 0.6 million tons in 1976/77. However, in 1977/78, the procurement of rice fell again because of a rise in the free market price, although production increased. In 1978/79, some improvements in the procurement policy was introduced (namely, the prices for quality seeds were raised) and was extended to 166 townships for buying paddy. This resulted in increased procurement and hence more exports. The procurement of paddy rose from 185 million tons in 1978/79 to 206 million tons in 1981/82 and the average of the ratio of procurement to production during this period was about 33 per cent, the best in the decade.

Paddy production increases from 1978/79 were undoubtedly the result of the "Green Revolution", or rather, yield increase. In this particular year, more rice was procured than the target, most probably because of Government Order No. 4/78 of 16 September 1978. According to this order, those farmers who did not follow the instructions concerning the area of paddy to be cultivated and the amount of paddy to be sold to the government would be punished in the form of the withdrawal of the right to hold land.

The government price hikes in 1978/79 and in 1980/81 did not seem to have any effect since free market prices were more than two or three times that of the official prices.

What was the impact of these changes to the farmers? The price hike in 1974/75 which was about three times that of the last two decades obviously favoured the farmers. According to Mya Than's research entitled "Economic and Technological Changes of Sampled Farmers in Lower Burma (1972/73–1975/76)", the government procurement price acted as an incentive and was beneficial to farmers in terms of production as well as gross income.[14] At the same time, the cost of living increased by 250 per cent. Although the government distributed rice through co-operatives, the prices of other essential consumer goods were higher than those before 1973. This was one of the reasons that caused a series of labour unrests in 1974.

After 1976, the picture was not rosy for farmers, especially those with small holdings. Since the prices of essential consumer goods had also increased, real income did not rise. Sometimes, in a case of bad harvest, small farmers had to sell all of their harvests including the *wunza* to the government because the quota was set very high, at a flat rate for them. Thus, in the long run only those farmers with large holdings (that is, above 10 acres) benefited from the system for they had enough surplus to sell in the free market, after selling their quota to the government. Since those farmers operating farms of less than 5 acres comprised about one-quarter of all farmers, it is easy to estimate the size of the problem. However, it is important to note that export performance was better in this period.

What was the impact of the policy changes on rural sector development? Mya Than has attempted to answer this question elsewhere, in the article "Little Change in Rural Burma: A Case Study of a Burmese Village (1960–80)".

> An overall assessment of the governments in rural transformation in Mayin in the context of different rural development programmes under the three successive governments — all of which shared the common goal of a modern, prosperous, socialist society, could, perhaps, be summed up in the following terms:

- if the aim of the governments in rural transformation was to integrate the rural economy with the national economy, then in the case of Mayin the programmes were a partial success;
- if the aim of the governments was to fufill the basic needs of the rural population, then again it could be said that Mayin has borne witness to some progress;
- if the aim was to increase and to create more employment opportunities then, thus far, Mayin's has been an unsuccessful story.[15]

In this case, Mayin, a village in Lower Burma, definitely represented the general situation in the rural areas during the period of study.

Policy Reforms in the Period of Decline (1983 onwards)

Land Policy and Institutional Reforms

As far as land policy is concerned, there was no change in this period. All policies affecting the agricultural sector remained unchanged until September 1987 when the now defunct ruling party, the Burma Socialist Program Party (BSPP), held an Emergency Congress to initiate an economic reform forced by the steadily worsening economic situation since the beginning of the Fourth FYP, that is, since 1982/83.

Although agricultural loans had been fluctuating since 1982/83, a new loan was created for the farmers. It was meant for buying carts which are very useful for rural transportation. This loan was started in 1982/83 and it increased year after year although the repayments of the loans were very poor and indeed have been declining since 1984/85. The same trend of repayments was also found in the case of loans for purchasing draught cattle which are important not only because they are a means of production but also a mode of transportation. These loans were started in 1978/79 and increased sharply from 1983/84 onwards.

There were two important measures in tax reforms which were carried out during the period. The Water and Embankments

Tax Law was introduced in 1982/83. This was the first time in history that a tax system was introduced as a system in its own right. Previously, it had been included in the agricultural land tax. It was aimed at sharing the government's burden for the cost of construction of new water management projects and their maintenance. A second taxation system was introduced in 1987 according to which agricultural taxes, including a sales tax, should be paid in kind. Although it lasted only one year, the government collected 85.4 million baskets of paddy in 1988/89,[16] which is equivalent to about K770 million at the official price, or about K1,708 million at the free market price. It is interesting to note that agricultural revenue collected in 1978/79 was only K46 million. Before 1974/75, land revenue was collected by the Internal Revenue Department through the Agrarian Committees. However, since 1974/75, this responsibility had been taken over by the Village People's Councils.

During this period, an important change took place in rural administration. In September 1988, the army took over power after the political upheavals all over the country. Its ruling body, the State Law and Order Restoration Committee (SLORC) formed LORCs at various levels of administration, such as state/division level, township level, and village level in place of the existing People's Councils. The function of the Village LORC is almost the same as that of the SAC.

Marketing Policy Reform

The role of co-operatives in the procurement of agricultural products became more and more pronounced in this period. Since 1977/78, the co-operatives had purchased, transported, processed, stored and distributed paddy for home consumption in the townships where the AFPTC did not purchase paddy. This was because there were no marketable surpluses of paddy in these townships. The amount of paddy procured by the co-operatives went up from .57 million tons in 1978/79 to 2.04 million tons in 1982/83, and then to 2.41 million tons in 1984/85. This was also part of the strategy to increase the co-operatives' involvement in the country's economy, in line with the Twenty-Year Plan. But the amount procured by the co-operatives in 1984/85 was only about one per cent of the total procurement by the state. Before 1986, surpluses above the quota were supposed to be sold to the state, but in practice, they were sold on the black market where the price was at least two to three times higher.

A most radical reform in marketing policy was introduced in September 1987 when the government lifted 21-year-old restrictions on the free trade of paddy, maize and seven varieties of beans and pulses. This "carrot" was followed by two "sticks". A few days after this announcement, the demonetization of all currency notes of K25 and above was carried out without reimbursement. Soon after this, the government announced that farmers should pay agricultural taxes in kind. These measures were followed by an even more radical one in February 1988, when the government announced that it would allow private business and co-operatives to export rice, relaxing its 25-year-old monopoly (a carrot again!). The government was forced to implement all these radical measures as the procurement situation had become very serious after the 1985/86 season. Then, after the SLORC came into power in late 1988, these radical reforms were considered as failures and the old centralized procurement system was re-introduced. However, as far as both internal and external trade were concerned, the SLORC decided to give up its monopoly on all goods except teak, petroleum, natural gas, pearls and gems.

The procurement price of paddy since 1980/81 did not change until 1988. The SLORC government increased the procurement price after re-introducing the former procurement system. But the fall in paddy production since 1985/86 and the deregulation of marketing in 1987 raised the free-market price to five to seven times more than the official price. The free-market retail price of rice also jumped from about K1,800 per ton in 1983/84 to about K9,000 per ton in 1988/89, while the government retail price remained unchanged at K894 per ton.

Internal distribution was still carried out by the co-operatives. Since the procurement of paddy fell from 2.43 million tons in rice equivalent in 1983/84 to 1.1 million tons in 1988/89, the internal distribution of rice and rice exports also fell from 1.75 million tons and 0.67 million ton to 0.61 and 0.05 million ton respectively during the same period.

Policy Reform in Agricultural Technology

The utilization of fertilizer by paddy fell gradually from 332 thousand metric tons in 1983/84 to 192 thousand metric tons in 1988/89. The situation was the same with the utilization of pesticides. This was because of the "cut back" in the import of inputs as a result of foreign currency shortage arising from the fall in rice exports. This has become a vicious cycle. Three major irrigation projects in the paddy sector, assisted by the Asian Development Bank (ADB) and the International Bank for Reconstruction and Development (IBRD), the Sedawgyi and Kinta Dams, and Phase 2 of the Lower Burma Paddy Land Development Project, together providing irrigation to more than 100,000 hectares (about 250,000 acres of land) were completed in 1986–87.[17] In spite of this, the per capita cultivated area growth rate fell behind the population growth rate, most probably for lack of financial support. In short, although the government policy to modernize the sector was still intact, the application of modern inputs was limited because of financial constraints.

Policy Reforms and Performance of the Agricultural Sector after 1983

After 1983 the effects of the "Whole Township Special Production Programme" seemed to reach "saturation point" as the momentum of growth slowed down. The agricultural sector's growth rate of 6.6 per cent during the period 1973–83 slowed down to 2.1 per cent in the period 1983–88. The production of paddy declined from 14,146,000 tons in 1982/83 to 13,338,000 tons in 1988/89. This was mainly due to the decline in yield per acre which fell from 61.1 baskets to 56.88 baskets. The cultivated area under paddy also declined during the period, probably because there were no incentives, while prices of other cash crops were very attractive resulting perhaps in some crop substitution.

The impact of the marketing policy, including agricultural prices, may be explained in terms of the procurement of paddy. The ratio of the procurement of paddy to production decreased from 28.6 per cent in 1983/84 to 14.9 per cent in 1986/87. Then it fell drastically to 0.35 per cent in 1987/88 when the government relaxed its monopoly on the domestic marketing of paddy and some crops. Moreover, the government's demonetization of currency notes forced the farmers to hoard paddy. Government procurement price was kept constant throughout this period until 1987 while free market prices varied between five and six times that of the official price. However, the new tax system which forced farmers to pay land revenue and sales tax in kind helped procurement to increase to 85.4 million baskets of paddy in 1988/89. Since exports and internal distribution of rice depend on procurement, export performance since 1983/84 has been a total disaster. It decreased from 0.9 million tons to 0.6 million tons in 1985/86 and then to less than 50 thousand tons in 1988/89. Of course, some rice was being smuggled out of the country, although its amount was not known. Guyot estimated the volume of smuggled rice at 80,000 to one million tons per year, with 200,000 tons given as the most plausible figure.[18] The situation of the internal distribution of rice was even worse. In 1983/84, 1.75 million tons of rice were distributed, but fell to 1.56 million tons in 1986/87. This gave rise to social unrest throughout 1988. In 1988/89, the volume of rice distributed internally declined again to 0.61 million tons, resulting in an increase in the price of rice by at least four times during the first six months of 1988.

It is obvious that this situation favoured the farmers since the free market price was skyrocketing. However, it did not favour the urban population for even the official inflation rate (1978=100) had gone up from 119.83 in 1983/84 to 248.87 in February 1988. Some sources suggest that the true rate of inflation was as much as 500 per cent in the second half of 1988.[19] The government tried to defuse the worsening situation by increasing the salaries of the government servants in 1988, but it was not successful as expected.

The agricultural sector's performance over the years may well be summed up in Khin Maung Kyi's words: "The growth of agriculture which had done so well in the late seventies seems to be constrained by a general inefficiency of the economy as well as its own limitations".[20]

Summary and Conclusion

The findings from the previous sections may be summarized as follows. Firstly, general economic stagnation during the period 1962–73 caused by stagnation in the agricultural sector was due to the disincentives created by the land policy and the marketing policy (especially keeping the low prices for rice unchanged for more than two decades) and the position of farmers worsened during this time. In other words, the government's interventions in the agricultural sector seemed to hinder the development of the sector.

Secondly, the national economy recovered from the beginning of the Second FYP until 1982/83 as a result of the 6.6 per cent growth rate achieved in the agricutural sector during the 1973–83 period. This may be attributed mainly to the "Whole Township Special Paddy Production Programme" with more effective administrative pressure in procurement and to the "liberalization" of the "Burmese Way to Socialism". Although policy reforms during the period seemed to be in favour of the farmers, at least with respect to the terms of trade, real income did not rise and most of the benefits went to the farmers with large holdings.

Thirdly, in the period after 1983–84 the agricultural sector (especially paddy production) declined as a result of the slowing down of the "Green Revolution" effect, and the "carrot and stick" policy of the government in the marketing system. The terms of trade were in favour of the rural sector and urban social unrests occurred partly because of the rise in the free-market price of rice.

In sum, the government policy in resource allocation, land reform, marketing and pricing of agricultural products played a very important role in the development of the agricultural sector. In other words, *Myanmar farmers are very responsive to marketing policy and prices.* Therefore, the provision of favourable market and related marketing services acceptable to the farmers would be the most effective instruments for inducing an expansion of the sector. To meet these conditions, the state should assume the role of a regulatory institution whose objective would be to maintain income and price stability for the population without interfering in the day-to-day operation of free-market forces, both internal and external.

Finally, the findings indicate that if the government is serious about the development of the agricultural sector, it should concentrate on creating an effective and efficient economic infrastructure, for example, through improved transportation and irrigation, timely and appropriate provision of inputs, and credit for the farmers *based on their efficiency but at the same time not neglecting equity, rather than on equity considerations alone*, and effective provision of incentives through marketing.

Even if Myanmar succeeds in an expansion of agricultural sector production, it may face strong competition in rice exports from Thailand, the United States, Pakistan and, lately, Vietnam. Vietnam, which imported rice until early 1988, exported 97 thousand tons of rice in 1988 and expects to export 1.3 million tons in 1989, whereas Thailand and the United States expect to increase their exports up to 6 million tons and 2.8 million tons respectively in 1989.[21] Since the low quality of rice is a handicap for Myanmar, especially in the face of strong competition from Thailand and the United States, it should modernize its storage facilities and rice mills. As far as other crops such as maize, beans and pulses are concerned, the outlook for the 1990s is bright since demand for them in the neighbouring countries and Japan is still high.

However, many internal problems still need to be tackled so that Myanmar may come out again as an important exporting country in the very competitive international market in the 1990s. Even though the country is now making strenuous efforts to transform the "socialist" economy to a market-oriented one with the help of drastic changes in policies, people seem to be confused. Despite the policy changes in the agricultural sector which give farmers the freedom to sell, process, transport, and store agricultural produce, no significant effects of the policy have been seen so far. Instead, the prices of agricultural goods have risen considerably; in particular, the price of rice which is the staple food of a great majority of the people has doubled within a year. This is probably because of the lack of confidence in the new policies. It will, therefore, be necessary to eliminate such obstacles which hinder the full functions of the more free economy.

In line with liberalization measures, a clear export-oriented policy should be adopted to achieve higher economic growth. However, the emphasis should first be given to increasing production as well as the necessary steps to promote exports. To produce more surpluses, to meet internal as well as external demand, it is important to give farmers price incentives in the context of the liberalization policy, as it has been found that the price policy is one of the most important tools for the development of the agricultural sector. On the other hand, much attention should be paid to preventing high inflation which may aggravate the discontent among the urban dwellers.

Another important problem is the over-valuation of the domestic currency against the U.S. dollar. The government pegs the currency at around K6.50 to the dollar, while the black-market rate is about K70 to a dollar. This over-valuation of the domestic currency makes it harder for the country to export its products; thus, it is necessary to adjust the exchange rate.

In addition, it is necessary to improve the system of marketing agricultural products to make it more effective to meet the challenges of the 1990s. Irregular and late delivery of goods, which impairs the international competitiveness of agricultural products, is one of the factors hindering the growth of exports. To correct this, an overall improvement in buying, transporting, processing, distributing, and storing is essential and urgent. Although foreign trade has been open to co-operatives and private firms since October 1988, their participation has been very minimal. This is because the marketing system remains largely in the hands of the government; co-operatives and private firms should take over some of these marketing activities for export.

Myanmar is now on the way to a more open economy but needless to say, this does not ensure smooth economic growth automatically. Many constraints and obstacles still have to be eliminated for the further development of the Myanmar economy.

NOTES

1. Mya Than (1984).
2. Ministry of National Planning and Finance (MNPF) (1974).
3. Saito (1981).
4. Nishizawa (1985).
5. Ambler (1983).
6. Mya Than (1980).
7. Evans Yiyi Chit Maung (1972).
8. Ambler (1983), p. 19.
9. Khin Maung Kyi et al. (1982).
10. Ambler (1983).
11. Mya Than (1984).
12. Ambler (1983), p. 53.
13. Mya Than (1987).
14. Mya Than (1980).
15. Mya Than (1987).
16. *Working People's Daily*, 3 July 1989.
17. Vokes (1988).
18. Guyot (1989).
19. Vokes (1988).
20. Khin Maung Kyi (1985).
21. *Straits Times* (Singapore), 6 November 1989.

REFERENCES

Ambler, J.S. "Burma's Rice Economy under Military Rule". Unpublished paper, Cornell University, 1983.

Evans, Yiyi Chit-Maung. "Marketing of Export Crops in Burma and Thailand, 1948–1967: A comparative study, with special reference to rice marketing for the export trade". Ph.D. dissertation, microfilmed, McGill University, 1972.

Guyot, James F. "Burma in 1988: Perestroika with a Military Face". *Southeast Asian Affairs 1989*. Singapore: Institute of Southeast Asian Studies, 1989.

Khin Maung Kyi, "Modernization of Burmese Agriculture". *Southeast Asian Affairs 1982*, pp. 115–31. Singapore: Institute of Southeast Asian Studies, 1982.

______. "Political Economy of Agricultural Modernization in Burma". Unpublished paper, Singapore, 1985.

Ministry of National Planning and Finance, Burma. *Report to the People, 1974*. Rangoon, 1974.

Mya Than, "Agricultural Development in Burma". Paper presented at the UNITAR Conference on Alternative Strategies, New Delhi, 1980.

______. "Burma's Agricultural Development since 1962". *Unreal Growth*, edited by Ngho Manh-Lan. New Delhi: Industrial Publications (India), 1984.

______. "Little Change in Rural Burma". *SOJOURN* 2, no. 1 (February 1987).

______. "Growth Pattern of Burmese Agriculture: A Productivity Approach". Occasional Paper No. 81. Singapore: ISEAS, 1988.

Nishizawa, N. "Development Policy and the Economic Performance of (U) Ne Win's Administration" [Ne Win Seiken no Kaihatsu Seisaku to Keizai Jisseki]. Ajia Keizai. Tokyo: Institute of Developing Economies, 1985.

Saito, T. "Farm Household Economy under Paddy Delivery System in Contemporary Burma". *Developing Economies* 19, no. 4 (Tokyo, December 1981).

Vokes, R.W.A. "The Economy of Burma". *The Far East and Australasia*. London, 1988.

5

AN ECONOMIC ANALYSIS OF BURMESE RICE-PRICE POLICIES*

TIN SOE and BRIAN S. FISHER

Burma is predominantly an agricultural economy dominated by a single crop, rice.[1] Rice is a staple food as well as a major export item for Burma. Paddy production occupies about half of the total cultivated area and employs about 70 per cent of the Burmese work-force. Rice exports contributed between 40 and 50 per cent of total export earnings of Burma from the 1870s until 1965. Rice is also an important item, although the amount is unquantified, in internal illegal distribution and in the smuggling trade to Burma's neighbours, especially Bangladesh, India, China and Thailand.

Burmese agriculture has experienced many changes during the last century. The most dramatic of these changes was Burma's move from being a leading exporter of rice up to the early 1960s to being just self-sufficient since 1965–66.

In this chapter, an attempt is made to analyse the policies which have been at the centre of the change in Burma's agricultural prosperity. Attention is focused on the period 1948 to 1987. To provide some background, the trends in rice production, procurement, export and domestic use are examined. Then, the formulation and implementation of rice price policies and their impact on the above activities are analysed and discussed. In the conclusion, suggestions for further improvement in Burmese rice policy are made.

A Brief History of Burmese Agriculture

Until the mid-nineteenth century, Burma was a self-sufficient society based on subsistence (feudal) agriculture. Agriculture was commercialized during British colonial rule. The British annexed Burma in three phases following the three Anglo-Burmese Wars in 1824, 1852 and 1885. The Second Anglo-Burmese War was significant in relation to agricultural transformation because, after that war, the British annexed the whole of Lower Burma where the main arable land areas, including the fertile Delta Province and the Pegu Division, are located. In 1852, the population of Lower Burma was about 1.5 million and the area under rice cultivation was barely about 0.4 million hectares out of a total cropped area of about 0.6 million hectares.

Transformation into an export-oriented, commercialized agriculture by the British Administration in Burma started immediately after 1852. By 1890 the area of paddy sown had increased to 1.83 million hectares, with a population of 4.4 million in Lower Burma alone. The total area under rice in 1890 for the whole of Burma was 2.4 million hectares and the population was about 7.7 million. Rice production in 1890–91 was 2.4 million tons. About 0.98 million tons of this was exported. Despite the many side-effects of this rapid expansion, Burma had earned a reputation as the "No. 1 Rice Exporter" and as the "Rice Bowl of Asia" as early as 1890. By 1936–40, the average area of rice sown was 5.2 million hectares, with production of 4.9 million tons, of which 2.9 million tons were exported.

Much of Burma's agricultural infrastructure was destroyed during World War II and the Japanese Occupation (1941–45), resulting in a substantial decline in agricultural production. It is estimated that more than one-third of the agricultural infrastructure and working animals were destroyed during the period.[2] As a result of the disruption during and immediately after the war when Burma gained its independence from Britain in 1948, per person gross domestic product was less than two-thirds that of the late 1930s.[3]

Agricultural production in Burma was disrupted for two years after independence in 1948 due to civil war. Total agricultural output increased by 40.4 per cent from 1951 to 1960 (the period of the Eight-Year Plan, popularly known in Burma as the KTA Plan, or Pyidawtha Plan). At the end of this period agricultural production had just reached the pre-war level, although rice production was still only about 93 per cent of pre-war figures. Rice yields per hectare reached pre-war levels during the 1958/59 fiscal year but the targets for growth and production set by the Eight-Year Plan were not met. In spite of the importance of agriculture to the economy, it received only a modest proportion of the government's capital expenditure during the civilian governments (1948–57) and the military caretaker period (1958–60). Agriculture was neglected in favour of industrialization for more than a decade after independence. After 1962, the Revolutionary Government prepared to give priority to agricultural growth. However, this changed again after 1964/65 to an emphasis on industrial development.[4]

For the decade after 1962 the value of agricultural production as a percentage of gross domestic product (GDP) remained almost constant, the figures being 26 per cent in 1961/62 and 25.7 per cent in 1972/73. The earnings from agricultural exports (crops alone) fell from K1,071 million to K346 million during the same period.[5] Although total sown area increased by 10 per cent during the ten-year period following 1961/62, there were extensive crop failures in 1966–68 as a result of drought, and the area harvested in 1972/73 was only 1.6 per cent higher than that in 1961/62. This lack of growth again led to a shift in development priorities at the First Congress of the Burma Socialist Programme Party (BSPP) in 1971, where the priority was moved from a concentration on industry to the development of the primary sector. However, these changed priorities were implemented only slowly owing mainly to lack of finance. The percentage of public expenditure on capital works directed towards agriculture during the period after 1972 was little changed from the level in the previous decade.

During the Second Four-Year Plan period (1974–77), agricultural production increased by 3.6 per cent per annum. A number of years of favourable weather conditions were an important contribution to this outcome. Moreover, towards the end of 1977/78, the increased use of high-yielding varieties (HYVs) had a positive influence on yields. During the Third Four-Year Plan (1978–81), a target of 5.8 per cent increase per year in agriculture was set. Paddy was to expand by 4.2 per cent per annum. During this period a rate of growth of 6.7 per cent in the agricultural sector and 9.5 per cent in rice production was achieved. However, the progress was short-lived. The targeted growth rate of the agricultural sector set for 1986/87, the first year of the Fifth Four-Year Plan (1986/87 to 1989/90), was 2.5 per cent while the actual performance was 2.4 per cent. Overall, during the period since 1940, real agricultural output has increased by about 1 per cent.[6]

Trends in Area, Production, Procurement, Domestic Use and Exports of Rice

The production, procurement, distribution for domestic use[7] and export of rice have been under government control since 1962. Rice production is controlled by the government both through the land tenure system and land tilling right, and through the supply of agricultural inputs such as chemical fertilizer and the provision of credit and extension services. The procurement, distribution for domestic use and export of rice are directly controlled by the government as a sole selling agent. Data on sown area, production, procurement, export and domestic use of rice are shown in Table 1.

Sown Area and Production

The pre-war (1936/37 to 1940/41) average area sown with rice was 5.2 million hectares out of a total cropped area of 7.8 million hectares. This declined to 4.15 million hectares immediately after independence (1948–50), but increased gradually during the fifties and reached the pre-war levels again in 1964/65. Since then the

TABLE 1
Sown Area, Production, Yield Per Hectare, Procurement, Export and Domestic Use of Rice in Burma, 1890–1987

Year	*Sown area ('000 ha.)*	*Production ('000 mt)*	*Yield per ha. (kg)*	*Procurement ('000 mt)*	*Export ('000 mt)*	*Domestic Use ('000 mt)*
1890–91	2,385	2,352	980	n.a.	982	1,871
1911–15	4,220	3,118	739	n.a.	2,011	1,710
1936–40	5,193	4,904	944	1,180	2,894	1,653
1945–46	2,691	1,737	645	n.a.	n.a.	1,737
1946–47	3,404	2,454	721	1,446	848	1,333
1947–48	3,966	3,474	876	12,851	1,250	1,883
1948–49	4,187	3,432	820	1,260	1,049	1,192
1949–50	3,863	3,044	788	950	1,066	989
1950–51	3,919	3,591	916	1,949	1,284	1,157
1951–52	4,046	3,723	920	2,256	1,070	1,327
1952–53	4,287	3,882	906	2,422	1,038	1,422
1953–54	4,315	3,708	859	2,166	1,155	1,277
1954–55	4,216	3,755	891	1,893	1,505	1,125
1955–56	4,259	3,796	891	1,733	1,721	1,038
1956–57	4,310	4,175	969	1,937	1,858	1,159
1957–58	4,216	3,421	811	1,776	1,283	1,069
1958–59	4,191	4,377	1,044	2,472	1,458	1,460
1959–60	4,306	4,581	1,064	2,313	1,832	1,375
1960–61	4,323	4,543	1,051	2,636	1,435	1,554

TABLE 1 (*cont'd*)

Sown Area, Production, Yield Per Hectare, Procurement, Export and Domestic Use of Rice in Burma, 1890–87

Year	*Sown area ('000 ha.)*	*Production ('000 mt)*	*Yield per ha. (kg)*	*Procurement ('000 mt)*	*Export ('000 mt)*	*Domestic Use ('000 mt)*
1961–62	4,713	4,552	966	2,426	1,676	1,438
1962–63	4,960	4,834	975	2,070	1,521	1,657
1963–64	5,176	5,184	1,002	2,438	1,445	1,870
1964–65	5,240	5,165	1,081	2,443	1,176	2,245
1965–66	5,014	5,316	1,060	1,992	1,179	2,960
1966–67	4,989	4,380	878	1,294	705	1,838
1967–68	4,935	5,128	1,039	1,364	398	2,365
1968–69	5,019	5,294	1,055	1,908	399	2,448
1969–70	4,955	5,270	1,064	1,933	798	2,236
1970–71	4,975	5,387	1,083	1,442	874	2,270
1971–72	4,978	5,395	1,084	1,312	776	2,310
1972–73	4,862	4,857	999	786	309	2,274
1973–74	5,089	5,677	1,116	965	104	2,787
1974–75	5,177	5,665	1,094	1,684	227	2,719
1975–76	5,203	6,077	1,168	1,783	419	2,829
1976–77	5,078	6,149	1,211	1,878	538	2,806
1977–78	5,136	6,245	1,216	1,460	562	2,842
1978–79	5,243	6,842	1,305	2,469	187	3,328
1979–80	5,026	6,896	1,372	229	1,736	3,080

TABLE 1 (*cont'd*)
Sown Area, Production, Yield Per Hectare, Procurement, Export and Domestic Use of Rice in Burma, 1890–87

Year	*Sown area ('000 ha.)*	*Production ('000 mt)*	*Yield per ha. (kg)*	*Procurement ('000 mt)*	*Export ('000 mt)*	*Domestic Use ('000 mt)*
1980–81	5,256	8,789	1,672	2,738	673	4,058
1981–82	5,232	9,336	1,784	2,799	575	4,381
1982–83	5,006	9,321	1,862	2,639	683	4,319
1983–84	4,954	9,429	1,903	2,656	874	4,278
1984–85	5,042	9,408	1,866	2,385	622	4,393
1985–86	5,027	9,449	1,880	3,041	582	4,434
1986–87	5,111	9,323	1,824	2,344	601	4,361
Annual Compounded Rate of Growth						
1948/49–63/64	1.42	2.79	1.35	4.50	2.16	3.05
1964/65–86/87	−0.11	2.29	2.41	−0.19	−3.01	3.06
1948/49–86/87	0.53	2.66	2.13	1.65	−1.46	3.47

n.a. = not available.

SOURCES: Central Statistical Organization; Agricultural and Farm Produce Trade Corporation, HQ, Rangoon; *Statistical Yearbook*, 1965 and 1975 issues; Ministry of National Planning and Finance (MNPF), *Report to the Pyithu Hluttaw* (People's Assembly), various issues.

area sown with rice has shown little change. During the whole period from 1948/49 to 1986/87, the average annual increase in sown area was a modest 0.5 per cent.

Total production of rice has increased despite the little change in sown area in the last thirty years. For a brief period following independence, rice production fell to 3 million tons because of limitations in agricultural infrastructure and instability caused by civil war immediately after independence in 1948. Rice production increased gradually after 1950/51 and reached the pre-war level for the first time in 1962/63. Production then remained stable for more than a decade. The large increase in production which occurred in the early eighties was mainly due to good weather conditions and the strict supervision and emphasis given by the government to the cultivation of HYVs. The average annual increase in total rice production for the period 1948/49 to 1986/87, was about 3 per cent per annum (see Table 1).

Average yields per hectare, which had remained fairly stable at a low level of around 900 kg. until 1957/58, increased modestly to around 1,000 kg., which remained constant until 1974/75. Yields per hectare began to increase after 1975/76 because of the large-scale introduction of HYVs under the "Whole Township Special Paddy Production Programme". For example, it increased from 1,094 kg. in 1975/76 to 1,306 kg. in 1978/79, and further to 1,880 kg. in 1985/86 but declined to 1,824 kg. in 1986/87. Although yields nearly doubled during the 1975–85 decade compared with those of the long period between 1890 and 1960, yields are still below the levels achieved in neighbouring countries such as Thailand, Indonesia, and Malaysia. The area sown with HYVs contributed about 52 per cent of the total area sown with all varieties of rice in 1985/86. However, the average annual rate of growth in per hectare rice yield (2 per cent) was lower than that of total rice production (3 per cent). After 1981/82, the expansion in the area sown with HYVs slowed as a result of the lack of supply of modern inputs, insufficient water control and a lack of extension personnel.[8] Consequently, the rate of growth in yields slowed after 1981/82 until 1986/87 and this downward trend will most likely continue in the future unless the pace of technological change, the momentum of which was interrupted until 1981/82, can be re-energized again.

Procurement and Domestic Use

Until 1961/62, the official procurement of rice by the government was for the purpose of export and for maintaining a stock for emergency use.[9] The distribution for domestic consumption was operated by free market agents. All of these activities were brought under government control in 1962/63. Even private rice milling and inter- and intra-state transportation of rice were strictly controlled by the government. The official procurement data indicate that the average volume of rice procured by the government doubled from a little over 1 million tons to more than 2 million tons during the 1948–54 period, which was mainly due to increased export demand for rice created by the Korean War. Domestic procurement declined following the end of the Korean War in 1954 but still remained around 2 million tons a year until 1957/58. It peaked at 2.5 million tons in the next year and remained more or less stable until 1964/65. Thus, the official procurement of rice in Burma steadily increased and remained at a stable level of over 2 million tons a year for sixteen years from 1948/49 until 1963/64. During that period, government procured rice accounted for more than 40 per cent of production, and the average growth rate was also impressive at 4.5 per cent per annum. However, official procurement in relation to production declined consistently and continually from 1964/65 until 1986/87. The growth rate of official procurement during these 23 years since 1964/65 was negative (of −0.2 per cent per annum) while population increased at the rate of more than 2 per cent per annum.

The amount of rice available for domestic use increased from 1.2 million tons in 1948/49 to 4.4 million tons in 1986/87, the average annual increase rate being the highest (3.5 per cent) of all other activities. Reflecting the consistent increase in the amount available for domestic use, per person use of rice also increased consistently with the exception of a period in the early 1970s. However, the rate of growth in per person consumption was lower than that of total domestic availability. This was not only because population growth outpaced the growth in procurement but also because a considerable proportion of rice was diverted for illegal export to the neighbouring countries. Complete data on this illegal export are not available. However, the amounts are likely to be significant because rice is one of the major items used for payment in barter trade, both legal and illegal, which are apparently considerable in both volume and value terms. For instance, according to one independent source, the value of the recently opened border trade (both legal and illegal) between Burma and China alone was estimated at US$1.5 billion a year, and more than 2,000 selected items of merchandise were reported to be flooding the Burmese market (Economic Intelligence Unit, February 1989). Taking into account similar trade with Thailand, Bangladesh, India, Hong Kong, Penang, Malaysia, and other countries for which estimates were not available, the value and volume of trade, especially illegal trade since most of the trade with these countries were taking place illegally, would, no doubt, be remarkably large, perhaps much larger than the official volume and value of trade. Because this trade was undertaken mostly under the barter system, the major items of transaction from the Burmese side were basic food and raw materials, including rice, in exchange for manufactured goods and so one can imagine that the amount of rice diverted away from domestic consumption every year could not be inconsiderable. Thus, this diversion of rice to the illegal trade and the deficient price policies were the two major contributing factors to the consistent decline in the official procurement of rice in Burma after the mid-1960s.

Exports

The amount of rice legally exported is dependent on the amount of domestic procurement, the level of domestic use, and on external factors such as the world price. Despite the extremely fluctuating nature, Burma's rice exports were characterized by an impressive increasing trend during the period between 1948/49 and 1961/62. However, the combined effects of reduced exportable surplus because of an increase in domestic consumption, a decrease in official procurement, and the diversion of a considerable amount of rice to both the internal and external legal and illegal trade caused official exports to decline drastically after the mid-1960s (see Table 1) while the world market price of rice was consistently rising until 1982/83 (see Table 2). Exports reached an all-time low of 0.1 million tons in 1973/74. Despite a concerted official effort to raise rice exports, the volume reached its peak in 1983/84 at a little more than 0.7 million tons and then declined later to maintain at or around 0.6 million tons until 1986/87. During the forty-year period ending 1986/87, Burmese rice exports grew at a negative rate of 1.5 per cent per annum, with a positive rate of 2.2 per cent during the free-market economy phase of the 1948–64 period,[10] compared with a −3.01 per annum rate during the closed economy phase between 1964/65 and 1986/87.

TABLE 2
Rice Prices (Ngasein Variety), Burma, 1948–86
(In kyat per tonne)

	Procurement Prices			*Retail Prices*	
Year	*Govt.*	*Free Market*	*Export Prices*	*Govt.*	*Free Market*
1948/49	137	156	575	211	191
1949/50	137	159	731	211	289
1950/51	137	165	860	211	322
1951/52	137	158	706	211	296
1952/53	137	153	551	211	284
1953/54	137	151	469	211	286
1954/55	137	152	452	211	279
1955/56	137	156	435	211	290
1956/57	137	156	436	211	283
1957/58	137	156	429	211	275
1958/59	137	156	440	211	284
1959/60	137	162	428	211	298
1960/61	137	183	422	211	321
1961/62	144	151	432	222	358
1962/63	144	166	443	222	378
1963/64	144	159	447	222	395

TABLE 2 (*cont'd*)
Rice Prices (Ngasein Variety), Burma, 1948–86
(In kyat per tonne)

Year	Procurement Prices		Export Prices	Retail Prices	
	Govt.	Free Market		Govt.	Free Market
1964/65	144	155	472	229	357
1965/66	149	147	484	229	499
1966/67	163	165	521	251	1,400
1967/68	172	209	578	265	1,300
1968/69	172	528	703	265	900
1969/70	177	244	667	311	568
1970/71	177	281	465	311	628
1971/72	183	538	419	311	1,038
1972/73	210	582	512	427	1,109
1973/74	431	729	826	640	1,344
1974/75	431	744	1,609	710	1,368
1975/76	431	679	1,756	804	1,283
1976/77	431	579	1,157	870	1,123
1977/78	431	732	1,373	894	1,368
1978/79	446	1,132	1,439	935	1,674
1979/80	446	1,211	1,494	935	1,176
1980/81	472	1,253	1,506	935	1,647
1981/82	472	1,833	2,350	894	1,289
1982/83	472	1,986	2,510	894	1,500
1983/84	472	2,291	1,770	894	1,834
1984/85	472	2,444	1,577	894	2,022
1985/86	472	2,521	1,317	894	2,126
1986/87	472	2,597	1,421	894	2,225

SOURCES: Agricultural and Farm Produce Trade Corporation, Rangoon, Burma; Asian Development Bank (ADB), *Bank Staff Estimates (Burma): Report No. 2347-BA* (1975); MNPF, *Report to the Pyithu Hluttaw*, various issues; CSED, *Statistical Yearbook* 1955 and 1965; *U.N. Statistical Yearbook 1960*, and monthly bulletins, various issues.

Growth Rates

An interesting picture emerged when the rates of growth were comparatively viewed. The rates of growth indicate that the year 1963/64 could be taken as a demarcation line between the growing phase (say, Phase I), and the deteriorating phase (say, Phase II) if the whole period of forty years since independence is divided into two broad phases. Note that Phase I coincides with the "open and free market economy" period and Phase II the "closed and controlled economy" period respectively. As a contrast, the compound rates of growth of the activities for the two distinct phases are comparatively summarized below:

	Phase I (1948/49–63/64)	*Phase II (1964/65–86/87)*	*Overall (1948/49–86/87)*
Sown area	1.4	−0.1	0.5
Production	2.8	2.3	2.7
Procurement	4.5	−0.2	1.7
Yield per hectare	1.4	2.4	2.1
Export	2.2	−3.0	−1.5
Domestic use	3.1	3.1	3.5

These growth rates by phases reveal that the official claims that the production increase during Phase II was higher than that of Phase I, and that the decline in export during Phase II was due to increased domestic consumption were not true. As indicated by the figures above, all growth rates except yield per hectare during Phase I were remarkably higher than that of Phase II. The growth rate of procurement was impressively high during Phase I compared to a negative rate during Phase II. In sharp contrast, export growth in the two phases showed diametrically opposite trends since Phase II was characterized by a considerable negative rate of 3 per cent per annum while Phase I had a healthy positive rate of more than 2 per cent per annum. Surprisingly, the growth rates of domestic use were the same (3 per cent per annum each) for the two phases. Thus, increased domestic consumption was definitely not the only cause for the decline of exports and other consequences resulting from it. The remarkable rate of growth of official procurement of rice during Phase I (4.5 per cent per annum) compared to a negative rate (−0.2 per cent per annum) during Phase II was one of the main reasons for increased exports during Phase I, despite the then decreasing trend in world market rice prices. Only in the growth rate of yield per hectare did Phase II show a higher rate (2.4

per cent per annum) than that of Phase I (1.4 per cent per annum). Even this growth rate of yield per hectare was short-lived, as it declined rapidly after 1981–82. As will be seen later, it was the price policies and other factors but not increased domestic consumption alone that was responsible for such a pattern of development.

For the period as a whole, the growth rate of rice production was almost six times higher than that of sown area (2.7 per cent per annum compared with 0.5 per cent per annum). This no doubt was brought about by the increase in per hectare yield. The problem, however, was that the momentum gained in technological break-through in terms of introducing the HYVs during 1978/79 and 1982/83 could not be sustained and had to be aborted. The decreasing growth rate of land productivity since 1981/82 together with the low and decreasing rate of official procurement, the negative growth of exports, and a high rate of domestic consumption under an increasing population especially among the younger age group explained why the rice economy rapidly deteriorated within the two decades since 1966/67. This state of affairs can be explained mainly by the analysis of agricultural policies in general and rice price policy in particular.

An Overview of Burmese Agricultural Policies

Before analysing rice price policy, a brief description of the structure of the Burmese market and the institution important in the control of agriculture is provided as background. A central feature of Burma's economic policy since independence has been the government's control of domestic procurement and exports. Government procurement of rice until 1962 was mainly for export purposes. Domestic free trade prevailed at both the wholesale and retail levels until 1962 when farmers were completely free in their choice of crops and the markets in which they sold. Farmers' private land holding rights were also recognized and guaranteed by the government. Following the change of government in 1962, government control was extended to all activities. Beginning in 1963–64, crops cultivated throughout the nation were

FIGURE 1a

Sown Area, Production, and Yield Per Hectare of Rice, Burma, 1948–87

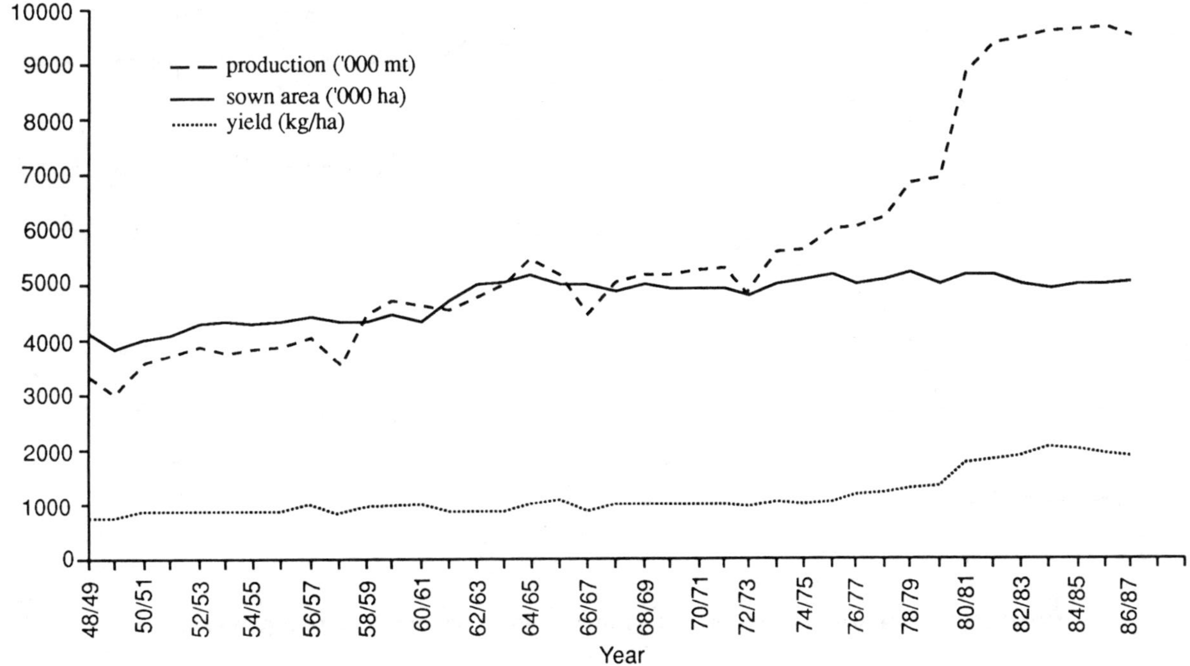

FIGURE 1b

Production, Procurement, Export, and Domestic Use of Rice, Burma, 1948–87

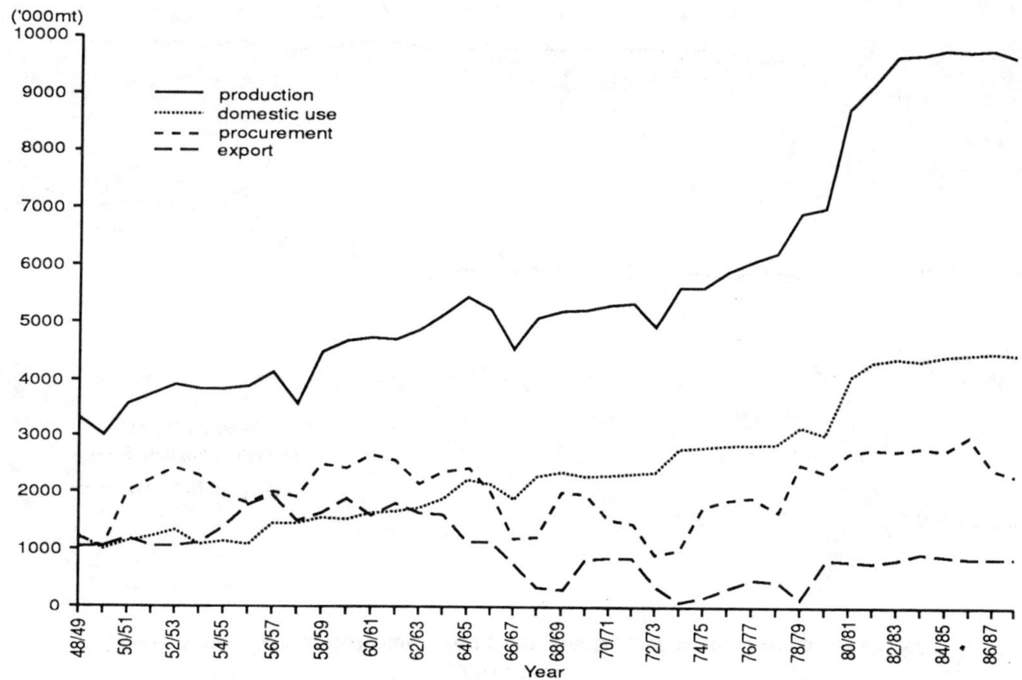

FIGURE 2a
Procurement Prices and Export Prices of Rice, Burma, 1948–86

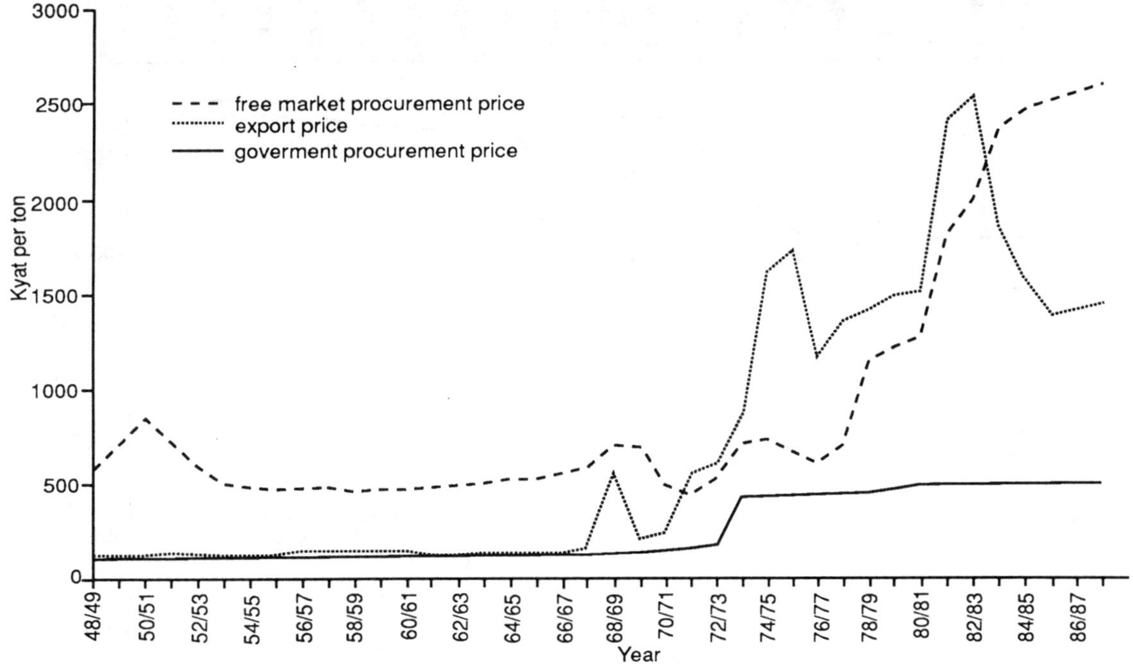

SOURCE: Table 2.

FIGURE 2b

Retail Prices of Rice (Ngasein Variety), Burma, 1948–86

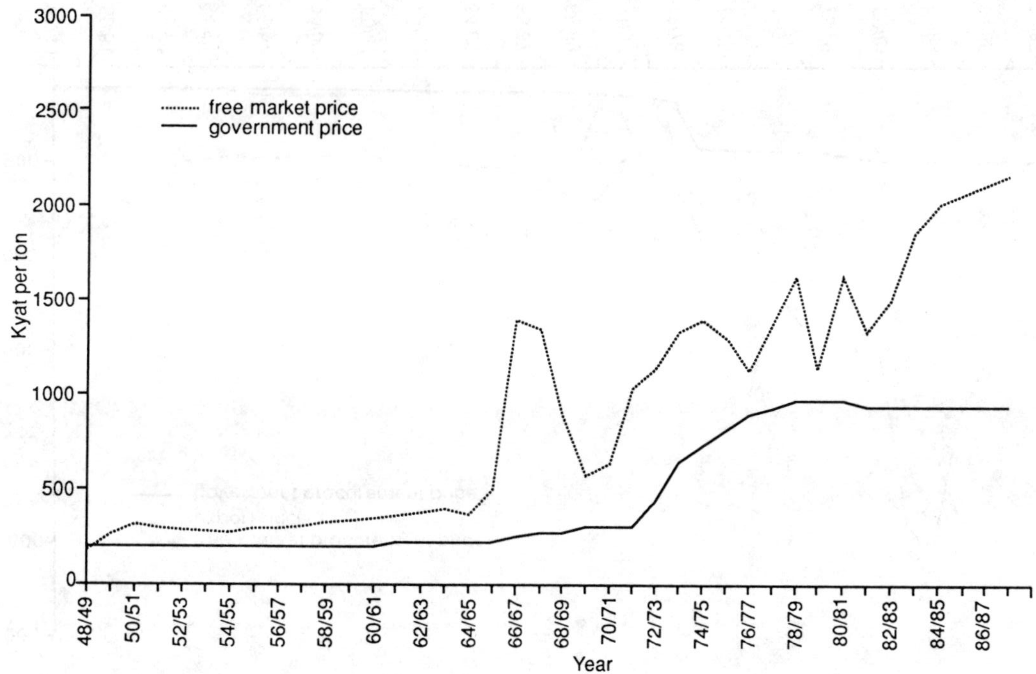

SOURCE: Table 2.

classified into two broad categories: "planned" or "controlled" crops and "non-planned" or "non-controlled" crops.[11] Cultivated areas were accordingly classified as "planned" and "non-planned" areas. In the first instance, 67 crop types were brought under control. After 1965, the number of "controlled" crops was reduced to 19 because of management problems. Rice is perceived as the most important of the "controlled" crops because of its importance as a staple food and as an export crop. Areas of "planned" crops can only be grown under supervision of the government agencies concerned. Priority for the provision of inputs, extension services and agricultural credits are given to farmers growing these crops. Farmers growing planned crops especially rice must supply a fixed amount of the product to the government at a fixed price. The quota of rice to be delivered to the government is determined mainly by the area sown and yield (see Table 3). Any residual above the compulsory delivery can be sold to the state procurement agency (Trade Corporation No. 1) which offers a price 33 per cent higher than the initial (procurement) quota price. Alternatively, farmers can sell the residual to the free market at prevailing market prices.

For "non-planned" crops farmers are given a free choice of what, how, and when to produce and sell. However, production of these crops cannot be carried out in the areas set aside for planned crops during the season when the planned crops are grown. In addition, the supply of inputs is not guaranteed by the government.

The distribution of both controlled and uncontrolled crops in the free market has led to a blurring of the distinction between the legal free market and the black market. The black market in which controlled products are traded, now constitutes a dominant part of the economy.

Rice Price Policies[12]

Objectives of Price Policy

Burma has a long history of price fixation by the government. Under the socialist economic planning system operating since

TABLE 3
Formula Table for Compulsory Delivery Quota of Paddy[a]

Sown Acres	*Yield Per Acre*	*Production*	*Compulsory Delivery Quota*	*Quota as % Production*
2	20	40	4	10
5	20	100	8	8
10	20	200	33	17
15	20	300	80	27
20	20	400	126	32
40	20	800	306	38
50	20	1,000	396	40
2	30	60	4	7
5	30	150	30	20
10	30	300	117	38
15	30	450	215	47
20	30	600	307	51
40	30	1,200	666	55
50	30	1,500	846	56
2	40	80	6	8
5	40	200	114	57
10	49	400	199	50
15	40	600	347	58
20	40	800	486	60
40	40	1,600	1,026	65
2	50	100	64	64
5	50	250	101	40
10	50	500	282	56
15	50	750	481	64
20	50	1,000	666	67
40	50	2,000	1,386	69
50	50	2,500	1,940	78

[a] Units are shown here in acres and baskets, as given in the original table. One basket of paddy equals 46 lbs or 20.9 kg. Delivery has to be made after deducting amounts for home consumption, seeds, payment for hired inputs and some allowance for wastage.

SOURCES: Agricultural Corporation, Rangoon.

1962, the main aims of the official price system has been to: a) maintain fair prices for both producers and consumers; b) efficiently allocate the available resources; and c) control the rate of inflation. Since rice has a dominant position in the economy, rice price policies are usually consistent with general economic policy. The main objectives of domestic rice price policies are to: a) guarantee minimum prices to growers while keeping retail prices low in order to maintain low costs of living; b) ensure a given pattern of income distribution and to provide a certain level of public revenue; c) act as a principal means of taxing the farm sector; and d) derive substantial revenue from the export of surpluses by keeping the domestic price low relative to export price.

Price Fixation

As a general rule, for the purposes of price fixation, commodities are classified into four categories: a) essential; b) necessity; c) semi-luxury; and d) luxury. Profit margins are fixed, depending on the category of the commodity, at a maximum of 5 per cent for essential items, 7 to 10 per cent for necessity items, 15 to 20 per cent for semi-luxury items, and flexible rates (usually 200 to 300 per cent) for luxury items. The official procurement price of rice is fixed after taking into account the estimated cost of production.

To justify the compulsory delivery system, the state supplies agricultural inputs at subsidized prices and agricultural credit at low interest rates. Furthermore, the shortage of peak season labour is partly met by organizing voluntary mass labour sponsored by party and council functionaries at various levels.

The Co-operative Sector

The co-operatives are allowed to fix the prices of both their own produce and those of the commodities in which they can legally trade. However, there is some regulation of the retail price of certain commodities such as rice. Profit margins are allowed to vary across regions depending on local conditions and overhead costs.

The Private Sector

In the private sector, prices are set by the market mechanism. Prices prevailing in neighbouring countries have a major influence on prices within Burma because of the extent of smuggling. It is difficult to evaluate the magnitude of this private illegal foreign trade. Some observers here have estimated that this trade was equivalent to about half the official export trade, that is, about US$60 to 70 million and possibly much more during the decade ending in 1975.[13] The trade has probably expanded in recent years given that official foreign trade has declined while the domestic market has expanded. It is estimated that about 70 per cent of the gross output enter into private and co-operative trade.[14] Since the share of the co-operatives either in production or trade is not more than 5 per cent, it is the private sector that is dominant in the Burmese economy. The sector is not officially encouraged but tolerated (and occasionally suppressed) by the government.

Official Procurement Prices

The official procurement prices are low when compared either with free market prices or with export prices (see Table 2). The government procurement price of paddy (ordinary Ngasein variety) was fixed at K137 per ton in 1948. The price remained constant until 1958. During the 1958–60 period, the then caretaker government introduced (in 1959) prices ranging from K137 to K149 per ton for various qualities of rice and delivery dates. Since that date there have been modest increases for ordinary grades and more generous ones for superior qualities. Beginning from 1980–81, the price was raised to K478 per ton and remained unchanged until 1986–87 (Table 2).

Regulations and Restrictions on Milling and Transportation

Milling and transportation of rice either by private traders and merchants or by farmers could be done freely until 1962. However, after 1962 private milling and transportation of rice was strictly regulated. Government agencies and corporations are primarily responsible for the milling and transportation of rice. No rice mill is allowed to mill private rice without permission. Priority must be given by private rice mills to government rice. Private traders have no legal rights to obtain permission for milling because they have no legal rights of procurement of paddy or marketing. Farmers wishing to mill their own rice for home consumption must also obtain permission. However, obtaining such permission is not easy and even if it is obtained it is often necessary to wait until the milling of government rice is finished. Most rice mills are old and inefficient and milling out-turns are generally low. Due to the shortage of spare parts and increasing costs of repairs, the milling of private rice attracts very high charges.

The private transportation of rice either domestically or for export is legally prohibited. In reality, however, since the official supply of rice fulfils only about one-third of domestic consumption, the remaining two-thirds is milled and transported by private traders.

The Level of Research

Following the introduction of the HYVs in the late 1960s, some research was encouraged by the government. However, this encouragement was confined to work on the technical and biological aspects of rice cultivation. During the period since 1962, only about 60 research papers related to socio-economic and agricultural development problems were completed.[15] Only three of those papers could be classified as dealing with the effectiveness of agricultural policies. Even these studies are rather more general than specific. As a consequence, many policy decisions have been made on the basis of incomplete information.

The Impact of Pricing Policies

Retail prices of rice for domestic consumers are fixed at a low level by the government in order to achieve the objectives mentioned above. The government's policy of maintaining retail prices of rice at levels well below international prices has meant that part of the margin between producer and international prices has flowed to domestic purchasers of rice as well as to the state's revenue through exports.

In the early 1950s sales of rice for domestic use (excluding farmers' repurchases of milled rice) was estimated to be about one-third of total rice production. The share taken by the domestic market gradually rose, and exceeded that of exports in 1966–68. Domestic consumption was stimulated after 1964 when retail prices of rice were equalized throughout the Union, regardless of the overhead costs, at levels prevailing in the delta. This policy was said to have cost the state some K70 million in subsidies in 1964/65 alone.[16] Since 1967, the government has given priority to supply for the home market. To the extent that it succeeds in holding down retail prices by subsidy or by diverting export supplies for local sale, it transfers income to urban consumers and reduces both farmers' and state resources for investment and the country's foreign exchange earnings. For example, the losses incurred by the state for such subsidized domestic supply of rice alone was enormous in later years; K96 million in 1980/81, K392 million in 1986/87, and K151 million in 1988/89 respectively.[17] The alternative of permitting a free market in grains to develop in the hope that it might stimulate production is officially considered to be unlikely to succeed and to be unacceptable politically.

Farmers pay an implicit tax representing the difference between export prices and procurement prices, plus processing, handling and transportation costs. During 1964–69 and after 1972, this implicit export tax generated substantial government revenues in the case of rice. Low pricing of agricultural commodities also allowed the distribution of cheap food to industrial workers who received low wages. This amounted to further subsidization of industry, and more generally, of the urban sector by agriculture. The uniform pricing system also benefited food deficient areas. To offset the effects of low rice prices to some extent, farmers received relatively cheap consumer goods through the co-operatives and security of tenure. In addition, they paid no rent for the land they cultivated and a low level of land tax.[18] However, the public and co-operative sectors failed to fulfil the demand for consumer goods by farmers at the prices set in recent years. This situation has encouraged the use of the black market.

For the period 1945–50 to 1986/87, the available data indicate that the free market producer price (that is, private procurement price) increased more than sixteen times compared with only 3.4 times in the case of the official procurement price. During the same period official retail prices for domestic consumption increased a little more than four times compared to nearly eight times in the case of the free market price. The divergence between the free market and the official prices provided farmers with a strong incentive to sell products outside the official system.

Pressures on Administered Prices

The official rice price policy operated fairly effectively during the 1948–61 period despite the low official procurement prices which remained unchanged for most of the period. During that time there was a consistent increase in rice production, procurement, domestic use and export. This enabled the government to maintain stability in the domestic retail prices of consumer goods.

During this period the volume of rice and the procurement price were not determined by a fixed formula as was the case after 1962/63. The volume procured was determined by considering the amount needed to fulfil the commitment made by the government under any bilateral or multilateral contracts for the sale of rice and the level of exports needed to earn the targeted level of foreign exchange. The main criteria considered in fixing the procurement price were the domestic cost of cultivation and the world price. In effect, the government encouraged growers by offering what amounted to a "minimum guaranteed price", by providing access to credit and by supplying certain inputs at subsidized prices. In addition, the government was able to keep wages low. These factors taken together meant that rice production was a profitable farm enterprise despite the low procurement prices. This, together with the freedom to sell residual production on the open market, and the encouragement provided by the provision of land-holding rights, motivated farmers to expand their production of rice and other crops.

However, pressure on the government's administered prices commenced with the change of policy after 1962/63. At first the change seemed conducive to the farm sector in general and to rice cultivation in particular.[19] Prior to 1966/67 farmers, particularly in the delta, had had little opportunity to obtain prices better than the official price because the domestic supply of rice had been in constant surplus. The first rice shortage in post-independence Burma occurred in the 1966–68 period as a result of both bad weather and problems in procurement and the distribution system. This rice shortage enabled paddy farmers for the first time to sell substantial quantities on the black market. The diversion of supplies away from authorized buying centres was exacerbated by rebel concentration in the main rice districts and the harassment of farmers prepared to sell to the state. Official deliveries at that time could thus frequently be made only in armed convoys. For a short time the government permitted farmers to barter rice for other goods but reverted to the system of monopoly rice-marketing again in May 1968. Rice and seven other basic food items were decontrolled for a brief period in 1977 and afterwards but the objectives of the trial were not realized. Official procurement declined further while illegal "black market" trade developed as a consequence of the unchanged official procurement price whereas the free market procurement price soared together with the world market price. In the domestic market, the government retail price of rice increased more than 50 per cent while the free market retail price increased only very insignificantly (see Table 2). Consequently, rice trade was again controlled by the government but the level of official procurement never recovered to that in 1964/65. This resulted in a decline in the level of official exports despite increasing world market prices.

The Impact of Official Prices on Production

As already mentioned, the "cost of production" has been one of the main criteria used for the determination of official procurement prices for rice and other "planned" crops. In the official calculation, the factors of production are generally priced using official prices with the assumption that there are adequate supplies available from the relevant government agencies. In reality, however, it is likely that government supplies fall far short of farmers' needs. It has been estimated that farmers had to depend on the black market for about a third of their needs for both production and consumption during the ten years up to 1975.[20] In view of the fact that the official export of rice and import of other commodities declined drastically after that date, together with a fall in domestic industrial production, farmers' dependence on the black market probably increased in later years. Available evidence reveals that farmers have had to depend on the free market for about half and, in some cases more than half, of their needs, depending on the locality and the type of crops grown.[21]

Dependence on the black market by growers for their household consumption needs was much heavier than for their production needs. In this respect, the official consumer price index (CPI) has many defects. No national price index is available. Those available for Rangoon are taken to represent the price trends for the country as a whole. The consumption weights utilized in the CPI for Rangoon are based on Trade Ministry reports which provide information on the quantity of items distributed in Rangoon through co-operatives. This does not take into account the leakage to the black market of an important portion of the goods supposed to be sold to consumers at official prices.[22] As a consequence it is not possible to establish the true extent of price increases. Price developments in other towns are not known as accurately as those for Rangoon, but it can be reasonably assumed that Rangoon is better supplied than most other towns. In December 1973, for instance, the price of rice, the staple food, was 50 per cent higher in Mandalay (the second largest city, located in Central Burma) and 60 to 70 per cent higher in Moulmein (the third largest city, located in southern Burma and famous for a flourishing black market trade) than in the Rangoon free market.[23] In 1986/87, the difference widened to about 2.5 to 3.5 times. Within Rangoon too, the retail price of an inferior quality of rice, ordinary Ngasein variety, in the black market in November 1986 was 2.5 times higher than the official price at the co-operative shops.[24]

For essential inputs such as gasoline and diesel oil, the price difference between Rangoon and other areas ranges between two and four times. The supply of these items is limited and priority is given to government departments and agencies and the population of Rangoon. It has been reported that other towns and rural areas in practice receive little more than 5 per cent of their needs from official sources.[25] It follows that both the officially calculated "cost of production" and the CPI do not reflect the actual cost of production and cost of living of the rural people. This, together with the additional input costs associated with the production of HYVs, has acted as a major disincentive to the farm population.

Shortcomings in the Compulsory Delivery System

The compulsory delivery formula was initially established with the intention of encouraging farmers to raise yields and expand production. However, under the system established an increase in yield per hectare (or an increase in farm size) is accompanied by a progressive rate of increase in the amount of the compulsory delivery quota after a threshold is reached. The effects of this system are illustrated in Table 3. In practice, the compulsory delivery formula acts as a definite disincentive to increase yields above a certain level and the system also discourages large land holders.

The second shortcoming of this formula is that policy-makers failed to envisage the possible effect on land fragmentation and its impact on production. The deterioration in farm sizes was slow until 1962 but after that date it was severe. For instance, the average size of paddy farms in the Irrawaddy Delta in 1953/54 was 4.2 hectares. This declined to 2.6 hectares in 1962/63 and further to 2.2 hectares in 1973/74.[26] For Burma as a whole, the proportion of farms under 2 hectares comprised only 6.2 per cent of the total sown area in 1953/54. This proportion increased to 25.1 per cent in 1986/87.[27]

Concluding Remarks and Suggestions

The official rice price policy in Burma could be deemed to have failed after 1962/63. It was observed that farmers suffered most as producers by receiving less for their produce at fixed official procurement prices and as consumers by paying much more in the free market for their needs. At their expense, urban consumers in general and consumers from rice-deficient regions in particular, benefited as a result of the price subsidies. When official procurement and export drastically declined and, as a consequence, official imports were curtailed, the privileges enjoyed by farmers in the period before 1962 were reduced dramatically. They also became the victims of the illegal black market in terms of paying higher prices for their consumption needs while their real incomes declined. At least until 1972 the government apparently gained as farmers responded positively to the official procurement prices. The implicit tax (revenue) for the government was large because of the big difference between the official procurement and export prices. However, government revenue fell as increasing numbers of farmers refused to sell their produce through the official channels.

Perhaps those who have benefited most from the official rice price policy since 1962 have been those operating in the black market. Operators in this market have taken advantage of the large differences between the official procurement price and the world price to attract supplies. A proportion of the rice obtained in this way was bartered for consumer goods smuggled from neighbouring countries while the rest was sold on the domestic market.

The policy objective of increasing total production by raising yields was moderately successful as a consequence of the introduction of HYVs rather than as a consequence of price policy. The official procurement price and compulsory delivery systems discouraged farmers from raising yields. Moreover, land fragmentation had a negative effect on yields.

It does not seem that partial measures, such as the changing of a few prices, have been sufficient to achieve the government's objectives. It was suggested by both private and official analysts almost twenty years ago that comprehensive changes were required. The IBRD in its report of 1975, for instance, recommended, among other things, that "a complete overhaul of the official price system, if not a sufficient condition, is a necessary one to do away with the present dual price system". It was further suggested then that in an economy largely privately operated, "it is difficult to try to impose official prices differing radically from prices prevailing in the free market; particularly because in Burma free market prices are heavily influenced by price development in neighbouring countries. Serious consideration should therefore be made to the feasibility of unifying the price system, by raising official prices closer to the free market levels".[28] Responding to the criticisms and because of a variety of other reasons, rice and seven other basic food items were decontrolled in 1977 for a brief period. Contrary to expectation, the result of the decontrol caused free market procurement prices to increase rapidly, compared with a very modest increase in the government procurement prices, and, consequently, official procurement (and hence export) of rice further declined while private free market procurement (and hence illegal export) increased considerably (see Table 1). In the domestic retail trade, however, the government retail price of rice increased at a much higher rate than that of the free market (see Table 2). The reason for such a development was simple. Decontrol of a few basic food items alone without substantial changes in policies, organization, or management system on a scale compatible with the problems was not the correct solution for the underlying problems. Eventually, instead of initiating further reforms, the decontrolled items were again brought under control by the government in 1979. This decontrol was not the first trial. It had been tried several times before when a few items of basic food were decontrolled, and then recontrolled but without any positive results. All these trials also clearly indicated that the potential of Burma's rice industry, and of the rest of the economy, could not be achieved without a wholesale reform of official pricing policies. Recent developments in Burma's domestic prices and market further prove that there is no alternative but genuine and substantial reforms to ensure the survival and growth of the national agricultural economy. The severe destabilization and distortions of prices and markets, and the spiralling of inflation as a consequence, following the "policy changes" towards a "free and open market system" since September 1988 suggest that allowing free market operation and reliance on it alone without substantial overall policy and economic reforms cannot bring about the desired results.

The "policy changes" since September 1988 have included, among other things, officially replacing the "closed and controlled economic system" with the "open market system"; legalizing the previous illegal "black market" trade by formalizing border trade with neighbouring countries, including China and Thailand; and "freeing" private national and international business, trade, and commerce. The policy objectives of all these changes are to boost domestic supplies of food, to hold down prices, and to maintain domestic price and market stability. None of the objectives has yet been achieved as at the end of 1989, and there is little prospect of achieving them in the immediate future under the prevailing socio-economic and political conditions. In a random survey of three markets in Rangoon for 24 items of basic food in July 1989, it was observed that the average increase in retail prices during the three years from 1987 to 1989 was 210 per cent (or more than twice) while the annual increase figures were 67 per cent from 1987 to 1988, and 76 per cent from 1988 to 1989 respectively (see Table 4). An alarming rate of price increase was observed in the basic foods that were most commonly and widely consumed in Burma by a large majority of the population. For commodities, the price increase within a short period of three years was more than three times for all varieties of rice, twice for (cooking) sesame oil, nearly seventeen times for onions, an essential item for all kinds of Burmese dishes, and nearly 1.5 times for meat (excepting goat meat alone), and more than twice for fresh fish, respectively. By the fact that more attention and priority was given to food distribution and supervision of retail prices in Rangoon and fluctuations in retail prices it can be assumed that the problem was more severe in other towns and

TABLE 4

Free Market Retail Prices of Some Essential Food Items in Rangoon between 1987 and 1989

Serial No.	Food Items	Retail Prices (Kyat/Kg) 1987 (July)	1988 (July)	1989 (July)	Percentage Increase between 1987 and 1988	1988 and 1989	1987 and 1989
					(rounded figures)		
I.	**Rice**						
	Superior quality						
	1. *Ngakywe*	3.29	5.17	11.76	57	127	257
	2. *Meedon*	2.82	3.76	10.82	33	188	284
	3. *Emata*	2.82	3.76	10.82	33	188	284
	Inferior quality						
	4. *Ngasein*	1.88	2.35	8.47	25	260	351
II.	**Wheat**						
	5. Wheat-flour	8.96	11.50	14.83	28	29	66
III.	**Cooking oil**						
	6. Groundnut oil	24.54	49.08	42.94	100	–13	75
	7. Seasame oil	12.27	21.47	36.81	75	71	200
IV.	**Other essentials**						
	8. Potato	2.15	3.68	5.52	71	50	157
	9. Chilli	11.04	21.47	21.47	94	0	94
	10. Onion	2.45	9.20	42.94	276	367	1,653
	11. Garlic	7.36	12.27	18.40	67	50	150
	12. Beans (*Kalabe*)	6.75	11.66	15.34	73	32	127

TABLE 4 (*cont'd*)
Free Market Retail Prices of Some Essential Food Items in Rangoon between 1987 and 1989

		Retail Prices (Kyat/Kg)			*Percentage Increase between*		
Serial No.	*Food Items*	*1987 (July)*	*1988 (July)*	*1989 (July)*	*1987 and 1988*	*1988 and 1989*	*1987 and 1989*
						(rounded figures)	
V.	**Meat**						
	13. Beef	15.34	27.61	33.74	80	22	120
	14. Pork	12.27	21.47	30.67	75	43	150
	15. Chicken	18.40	21.47	36.81	17	71	100
	16. Goat meat	24.54	42.94	42.94	75	0	75
	17. Duck	12.27	18.40	27.61	50	50	125
VI.	**Fish** (fresh)						
	18. *Ngagyi*	18.40	30.67	42.94	67	40	133
	19. *Ngakhu*	21.47	30.67	42.94	43	40	100
	20. *Ngayan*	11.04	15.34	24.54	39	60	122
	21. *Ngamyin*	30.67	42.94	73.62	40	71	140
VII.	**Condensed milk & sugar**						
	22. Imported (tinned)	64.27	102.83	128.53	60	25	100
	23. Local made (untinned)	15.34	24.54	30.67	60	25	100
	24. Sugar	15.34	24.54	28.83	60	18	88
			Average increase (%)		67	76	210

SOURCE: Random Survey of Three Markets (Pazundaung, Bogalayzay, and 38th Street Markets) in Rangoon in July of the respective years.

rural areas. Why and how did it happen? Similar to previous problems, the recent problems were also the side-effects of policies, or policy-related ones, which have mostly resulted from ad hoc and deficient and ineffective "reforms".

There are at least four major reasons for the recent increasing distortions of prices and markets in Burma, despite "policy changes". They are: 1) opening of the border trade without proper and sufficient preparation and consideration of all possible consequences, 2) setting in speculative demand and hoarding of food commodities resulting from a lack of confidence in government policies and proper functioning of markets, 3) further deterioration in domestic production and supplies, and 4) insufficient and ineffective policy reforms. These factors are obviously interrelated to one another but for convenience, each one is briefly analysed below to highlight its impact on domestic price and market systems.

In view of the urgent need to boost domestic supply border trade was hurriedly legalized without proper and sufficient preparation and consideration given to restructuring and reforming related organizations, activities and services, as well as the management system to respond effectively to the consequences resulting from this border trade. One of the many short-comings in legalizing the border trade was the lack of prior consideration and arrangement for the transaction system. Foreign exchange control and exchange rates are as rigid as before.[29] As mentioned above, this trade increased so rapidly that the value of the border trade between Burma and China alone was estimated at US$1.5 billion a year, comprising more than 2,000 selected items of merchandise flooding the Burmese market. Taking into account similar trade with other countries, for which estimates are not available, the value and volume of illegal trade alone could not have been less than US$3 billion a year because Thailand has been more important than China as a major source of the illegal border trade with Burma, long before the border trade was formalized. Thus, even assuming that Thailand's relative position in this trade could now decline owing to competition, the combined value of exports from Thailand, Hong Kong, Penang, Malaysia, Bangladesh, and

India could not be less than US$1.5 billion a year. Thus, together with the value of trade with China, the total figure could not be less than US$3 billion a year. To pay for this, private Burmese traders have no alternative but to sell a variety of goods, mainly basic food items and raw materials. Silver bullion, U.S. dollars, and some precious stones, especially jade, are also used as media of transaction but on a limited scale, compared with basic food items such as rice and onions, and raw materials such as teak.[30] This lack of foreign exchange to pay for private import has led to a barter system of trade since the very beginning and is now well established.

The barter system has affected domestic prices in at least three ways. First, a large proportion of basic food items produced domestically, which were supposed to be for domestic consumption, were diverted away for transactions in this border trade. The initial shortage in the domestic supply of these basic food items therefore became acute which dramatically pushed domestic prices upwards, such as the case of rice and onions. The use of rice in the border trade as a means of payment resulted in the halt of the already declining official export, and at the same time, aggravated the situation of domestic rice shortage. Onion, which is mainly produced in central Burma, nearer to China in terms of transportation, and was mainly produced for the domestic market until the opening of the border trade, became an important means of payment for Chinese goods after the opening of the border trade so that a large proportion of onions was diverted away from domestic consumption. This resulted in an acute shortage of onions supply in the domestic market, pushing up the domestic retail price of onions to nearly seventeen times during a short period of three years. Expanding the production of these basic goods to meet the increasing demand in both domestic and foreign markets is practically impossible, at least, in the short-run, owing to a number of major constraints. Because the commodity prices are interrelated, distortion of one or two prices destabilizes other prices and hence the whole economy. Secondly, the external barter terms of trade are naturally unfavourable for the Burmese who mainly sell basic food items to pay for the manufactured items they import. Since the imported items are relatively expensive, the internal terms of trade have become unfavourable especially for the farmers who have to pay high prices for necessary imported manufactured items while they receive less for their farm produce, resulting in stagnation or decline in their real incomes. Thirdly, the border trade has developed an illegal ("black") money market where the local (Burmese) currency, kyat, is highly undervalued while, on the other end, it is highly over-valued in the legal (official) money market. This means that privately exported items from Burma are cheaper in foreign markets and imported items are dearer in the domestic market, contributing to the spiralling upwards of domestic prices.

Since the collapse of the administration and economy in mid-1988 resulting from social unrest and political chaos, stability has not yet been achieved although the administration has been restored. This instability, together with increasing uncertainty and lack of confidence in the government policy and distribution system, has caused increasing instability of prices and the market. This has created a speculative demand for and hoarding of basic food items, this time not only by the consumers and private traders but also by government agencies.

The third reason for the increasing distortions of prices and the market was a further decline in domestic production and deterioration of the already short supply situation. The almost stagnant situation of productive activities, including rice cultivation, since mid-1988 has not recovered yet. A decline or stagnation in overall production in general, and rice cultivation in particular, together with a diversion of a large proportion of basic goods to the border trade while domestic consumption is increasing has aggravated the problems of domestic shortage and price destabilization.

The fourth reason for the rapid distortions of prices and market was the "policy reform" itself. The reform mentioned above has not been followed by substantial changes in price policies — rice prices, for instance. Government procurement prices of rice and the procurement systems remain almost the same as before, and policies on agricultural credit, inputs, and extension services have undergone little or no change. Methods of administration and management of economic activities and organizations have also remained unchanged. All of the formerly ineffective and inefficient state corporations and organizations have been unaffected by the "reforms" although some new "joint-ventures" were established without sufficient means, facilities, expertise, and finance. Under these circumstances it is difficult to expect domestic prices to fall just because the economy has been opened up and free trade allowed.[31]

Some suggestions are given below of how the problems facing the rice industry of Burma can be resolved. As rice is the mainstay of the Burmese economy, rice price policy plays a dominant role in the general economic policy and in agricultural policies, and will most likely continue to dominate in the future. However, given the nature, intensity, and complexity of the problems faced by the Burmese economy, there cannot be a separate solution for the problems of the rice industry alone. Rice price policies and problems have to be tackled in the context of the agricultural price problems as a whole in relation to general economic policies and problems. The problems facing Burmese agriculture and the economy are not unique in the sense that such problems have already been experienced or are still being experienced by many other developing countries in Asia, Africa and Latin America. The suggestions are therefore made on the basis of the past experiences of these countries and Burma, and of overall agricultural price policies rather than the rice price policy alone, in the hope that they may contribute to policy reforms in the future.

One of the major characteristics of price policy in Burma especially after 1962 has been, and still is, an emphasis on equity and stability. As experiences in other developing countries have shown, only resources generated by a high rate of growth can contribute markedly to increase equity and stability. A short-run emphasis on equity and stability alone usually impedes growth and leads to an unmanageable problem of providing equity and stability in the future.[32] This was exactly what Burma experienced in the last quarter century with the result that limited scarce resources were wasted in pursuing the purpose of equity and stability without realizing any of the objectives and impeding growth and creating problems to unmanageable proportions. Thus, long-term considerations must involve short-term balances between policies for growth and those for equity and stability. The maximum use of systematic research and expertise is essential to constantly check these balances, which are obviously lacking in policy formulation, implementation, and evaluation of the progress and consequences in the case of Burma especially since 1962.

The second characteristic of the price policies in Burma was that it neglected the food sector and provided a low rate of growth in demand for labour particularly in the rural areas. As experiences have shown, to meet equity needs in low-income countries like Burma growth must be associated with a rapid increase in the supply of food and demand for labour. Since the poor are substantially deficient in food, their propensity to spend on food is high, but it is only through increased demand for labour that they can earn additional income to purchase food and other basic necessities. However, the relative increase in investment in the food sector especially in Burma was so modest that it failed to create an effective demand for labour in the rural sector. Combined with other factors, the result has been out-migration of rural labour to the already congested urban sector.[33] The consequences have been an increased need for food and other essentials such as housing, transportation, and health care etc., thus contributing to higher food prices, higher government subsidies for food, and decline in real income per person in the urban sector. The farming sector has also been negatively affected in terms of higher wages (and/or more costs) for seasonal labour resulting from the shortage caused by the out-migration of rural labour on the one hand, and sharing the increasing burden of financing the urban sector (in the form of subsidies and other measures) under the government's "equity policy". Since agriculture accounts for a major share of all productive activities and food is an important item in total consumption, fluctuations in agricultural prices are the primary and dominant reasons for fluctuations in income for a substantial proportion of farmers and low-income consumers.

Another notable characteristic of Burmese agricultural price policies has been inherent conflicting policy objectives of production between the government and the farmers. The major policy objective of the government was to maximize yield but that of the farmers was profit maximization. It is important for the government politically to secure sufficient domestic food supply to maintain social equilibrium, and economically, to raise exports to earn badly needed foreign exchange to pay for imports and finance domestic development projects. To achieve this end, the government understandably adopted policies to raise yield such as the introduction of HYVs, and discriminating prices such as low domestic procurement prices compared with export prices. However, high yields with less and less profits owing to higher and higher costs and more work was definitely not attractive to the farmers. In the forty years since Burma's independence in 1948, no concrete evidence has been found to suggest that considerable efforts have been made by the policy-makers to effectively resolve this conflict of interest. It was not a matter of great concern before 1962/63 when costs were still low and cultivation was still profitable. However, after 1962/63, this conflict of interest became a serious problem as costs were rising at an increasing rate compared with that of income. The government raised the official domestic procurement prices of rice first in 1962/63 and several times later to certain levels, but each time the increased procurement prices were far below the level of the increasing costs of cultivation and other general prices. Another conflict lies with the price-stabilization schemes. The price-stabilization schemes only benefited large farmers who sold most of what they produced, but they were income-destabilizing for small farmers who sold only a small proportion of their produce. The extent to which price stabilization schemes destabilize income depends on the price elasticities of demand and the proportion of production marketed.[34] Empirically, the extent of this effect in the case of Burma is not known since there has been no systematic research yet on the demand for agricultural products and no elasticity estimates of demand for food products are available. It has already been mentioned that the government's "guaranteed price" in terms of fixed procurement prices discouraged rather than encouraged farmers to expand their size of cultivation and raise yields after reaching a certain scale and level. More importantly, instead of taking cost-benefit measures to solve the problem, the government imposed by law in 1965, among other things, a maximum limit to the tilling size of rice land to 50 acres (that is, 20 hectares). The consequences of this action were disastrous effects on production and yields resulting from land fragmentation and degradation, and lack of incentives to undertake land improvement activities by the farmers.

Theoretically, at least, since demand for food is relatively more elastic in the developing countries than in the developed countries, and marketable surpluses are much lower, stabilizing prices might have aggravated the instability of income for poor farmers. Since food comprises a high proportion of the expenditures of labourers, price increases slow growth in demand for labour, and a change in food prices has an immediate, inverse, and nearly proportionate effect on the real wage of labour. Empirically, for agriculture using traditional inputs, the aggregate supply response to price is quite inelastic — typically no more than a 0.1 per cent to 0.2 per cent increase in supply for a 1 per cent increase in price.[35] Under the situation of such inelasticity of supply (resulting from diminishing returns or increasing costs that normally arise in agriculture with a fixed land area, a usual case in most agricultural countries in Asia including Burma), if agricultural prices rise, each successive unit of increased production would require successively larger quantities of resources and hence greater cost. Agricultural supply becomes more price responsive with technological change, and the conflict between employment policy and agricultural production policy sharpens.

Governments can maintain depressed food prices in the face of slowly increasing supply if demand is tightly constrained at the same time, as have been tried successfully by the Government of India during the food shortage in the late 1950s and early 1960s,[36] but only for a short period. To prolong this control on food prices for longer periods may be beyond the power of the governments in developing countries. Rising food prices is a clear indication that the supply of food is increasing less rapidly than demand. The correct response to this problem is to put more effective effort to increase the food supply rather than to slow the growth in demand for labour and hence demand for food, with unfavourable growth and equity effects.

Absolute reliance on the free market alone would also not solve all the agricultural problems. There are at least two problems in relying on the market: 1) the market may equate the wrong side of the supply–demand equation; and 2) the lags between action and its effect may be too long to be acceptable.[37] Thus, the task of agricultural policy requires not only to determine appropriate prices in the short run but also to keep diagnosing well ahead of time what development policies are most needed and appropriate in anticipation of the price regimes that would prevail without those actions. Severe disequilibrium between food supply and demand tempts the government to regulate prices rather than deal with the underlying problems, with the consequences of increasing transaction costs and large losses to both producers and consumers resulting from the mechanism of price regulation through public sector trading and the growth of illegal markets. In such circumstances, it is essential to develop the analytic capacity to monitor, evaluate, and recommend policy with respect to agricultural prices. This requires sophisticated analysis and measurement and includes political as well as micro- and macroeconomic analysis because of the involvement of highly technical economic relationships in the problems.

The government often distorts prices by levying commodity taxes, particularly on export commodities which often provide high rates of return to resources relative to their use in production for domestic consumption. Revenues are usually raised by driving a tax wedge between the world price and the domestic price but without sufficient consideration for the fact that 1) it is important that production be kept competitive by effective research, the returns of which could, in any case, be very high, and that 2) too large a tax wedge may shift resources massively out of the export commodity, with a consequent reduction in national output. If export crops are to be taxed for government revenues, it is particularly important that the exchange rates not be overvalued. Taxation under an overvalued exchange rate does not directly provide government revenues but creates an additional price-depressing effect which may drive returns below alternative uses of resources and cause a major supply effect.[38] This was exactly how the cultivation sector in general and the rice sector in particular suffered in Burma for more than a quarter century since 1962. As already pointed out, heavy tax on export crops, particularly rice, in terms of a wide difference between domestic procurement price and export price with a highly overvalued Burmese currency in the official money market has affected both supply and demand, and hence domestic prices and the market. Another use of the overvalued exchange rate in Burma, as in many other developing countries, was as one of the common devices for maintaining a low consumer price. Here again, agriculture was severely penalized without justification by this overvalued exchange rate. Export crops especially rice production suffered the most, as the world price at which sales were made was converted into a relatively low domestic price. The experiences of other countries indicate that a pro-agriculture policy usually requires a devaluation of overvalued currencies. Rapid growth in money supply, perhaps driven by large development expenditures for inefficient projects and unproductive subsidies, and a weak tax system, with a fixed exchange rate have also the same effects. The basic point is that policies made with insufficient consideration for agriculture have a profound effect on farming. Exchange rate misalignment is often the symptom of underlying policies unfavourable to agriculture rather than the cause.

Moreover, the flaws and inconsistencies in the price policies in Burma could have been reduced, if not totally avoided, if the policy-makers could have envisaged beforehand the five major public policy issues that the price policy must face which are associated with technological change initiated since the early 1970s. These issues, briefly, are that 1) increased instability in agricultural production, prices, and incomes tend to accompany accelerated technological change in agriculture and places growing pressures on political systems to respond; 2) technological change may also cause a downward price trend over several years which, no doubt, is beneficial; 3) technological change may lead to increased dependence of farmers on purchased inputs as well as encounter many obstacles in spreading input use since subsidies not only are required for inputs but also for the distributional channels to achieve rapid expansion and public sector investment; 4) government expenditure in agriculture must grow immensely in order to support accelerated technological change and public policy with respect to price stabilization, price support, and input subsidies must all be abandoned or reduced eventually; and 5) the technological change in agriculture may also have a deleterious effect on some of the poor through its effects on non-participating regions and through increased instability (although it is generally desirable that technological change reduces the cost of producing food and hence increases supply). Thus, to the extent that political situations allow, the recommendation here is that further investment is needed in other activities of natural advantage and in education and research as well as policies which are pro-employment and hence strengthen the effective demand for food.

Management problems resulting from the government's intervention in agricultural markets are more or less similar among the developing countries, differing only in scale and intensity. The scale and intensity of management problems in Burma resulting from the government's intervention tend to suggest that the whole system should be overhauled. The successful experiences of some other countries can be used as models, with emphasis especially on the devices to use in intervening the market, the base from which to measure the intervention, and the extent of the intervention.

It has already been noted that financing a food subsidy not only serves as a tax on high-income consumers to benefit the low-income consumers but also reduces the market supply and increases total demand. Low price procurement involves administrative costs and the distinct danger of displacing private trade by an inefficient public-sector marketing agency. If governments are to foster low-priced food to the poor and to avoid spending 15 to 20 per cent of public expenditure on such subsidies, as has happened in Sri Lanka, Egypt, and Bangladesh at various times, a significant effort at targeting to low-income people is essential.[39] An effective approach is to select commodities that comprise a high budget share for the poor and, preferably, a low share for the more well-to-do; particularly appropriate are the poor grades of widely consumed goods. Food-for-work programmes or, more generally, rural employment programmes such as those practised in some countries are a logical means of containing costs of income transfers in the rural areas. Given the need for rural infrastructure and its labour-intensive methods, development objectives are well pursued in this manner. Subsidized employment has favourable effects on human capital and employment, both key factors for growth, and thus should be looked at in the context of a high employment policy rather than as a purely welfare measure.

Public expenditure policies should emphasize the essentials of agricultural technology development and application and broad participation of the people in most regions through massive public investment in infrastructure and education. With those tasks undertaken, other public expenditures will have to be tightly constrained. An approach to monitor the real rate of exchange is to evaluate the domestic inflation rate and the inflation rates of trading partners continually and to operate exchange rate policies consonant with the differential movements of the relative inflation rates. There is evidence to indicate that a departure from international prices has major development costs, and that the use of the international price as a guide for domestic price has a strong logical base. The essentiality of trade to development, the link between each price and all other prices, and the great economic influence of agricultural supply and demand forces reveal that the government (in a developing country) cannot for long maintain prices that differ widely from international prices.[40]

Last but not least is transportation and marketing costs. The commodity consumed in domestic markets may differ in quality from the commodity bought and sold in the world markets; food-grains consumed in the domestic markets of developing countries, for example, are generally inferior to those that are exported. The average national price that is related to the average international price must be translated into various levels of price consistent with a country's spatial and intertemporal diversities in markets. It is here that transportation and marketing costs influence farm and consumer-level prices. A major reason for low producer prices in developing countries is excessively large marketing margins and, in particular, high costs of transportation which, in turn, cause far greater departures in farm-level prices from international prices than the government manipulation of prices. Previous studies in this respect made four recommendations for raising farm prices in a stable manner by: 1) increasing government investment in rural infrastructure; 2) investing in facilities and providing regulation to improve competitiveness in markets; 3) substantially reducing government monopoly in markets and raising the efficiency of government agencies; and 4) operating such programmes with a targeted price band when stabilization in spatial and intertemporal prices becomes essential for economic and political reasons.

So far, price policy in general, and agricultural and rice price policies in particular, in Burma have pulled resources from export commodity production and slowed growth in both farm production (supply) and urban food demand. The decline in major agricultural exports especially rice, and the consequent scarcity of foreign exchange has depressed both food production and consumption as a result of shortages of key imports and transport services, and demand for labour. Eventually, the resultant inefficiencies, corruptions, retarded growth, rapid increase in food prices and distorted market, which require major adjustments in public policy in general and price policy in particular, have also been left unremedied. Under such circumstances, a short-term ad hoc approach and/or piece-meal reforms alone will not solve the problems. The intensity and scale of the problems that Burma is currently encountering demand wholesale and substantial political and economic reforms with short- and long-term perspectives and taking into account both macro- and micro-economic relations and problems. Otherwise the once reputed "Rice-bowl of Asia" would most likely drift along the line of "starvation in a land of plenty".

NOTES

* This paper was first presented to the 33rd Annual Conference of Australian Agricultural Economics Society, Christchurch, New Zealand, 6–9 February 1989. Some revision has been made here especially in the concluding remarks, and data and facts have been updated.

1. The term "rice" is used throughout to refer to husked or milled rice. The available official statistics on production and procurement are all in terms of paddy which are converted into rice by using the conversion ratio of 65 per cent. The term "paddy" is used to refer to unhusked or unmilled rice.
2. Aye Hlaing (1964).
3. Hill and Jayasuriya (1986), p. 8.
4. Steinberg (1981), p. 111.
5. K represents the official Burmese currency, the kyat. The official exchange rate is about K7.5 = US$1.
6. Steinberg (1981), p. 112; and Hill and Jayasuriya (1986), pp. 40–45.
7. Domestic use includes domestic consumption for human and stockfeed use, seeds and wastage. Separate data for human consumption are not available.
8. Steinberg (1981), p. 112.
9. The official procurement function was initially undertaken by the State Agricultural and Marketing Board established in 1946. The Board was reorganized and renamed Trade Corporation No. 1 after 1964. This Corporation became the Agricultural and Farm Produce Trade Corporation up to 1988 and then was changed to Myanmar Agricultural Produce Trading.
10. Although the socialist-minded military government came into power following the *coup d'état* by the army in 1962, the open and free market economic system in Burma practically ended only after 1963–64. The process of nationalization of the means of production on a national scale was "completed" in late 1964 and the reorganization and operation of the economy along socialist lines was started in 1965.
11. "Non-planned" or "non-controlled" crops refer to those crops that were never controlled by the government whereas "de-controlled" crops refer to those crops that were controlled at one time but where control was later released.
12. The information and facts for rice price policies (and agricultural policies too) were drawn from Richter (1973, 1976), IBRD Report (1975), Hill and

Jayasuriya (1986), Kan Zaw (1984), MNPF's two mimeographs (1984), Saito (1981), Tin Soe and Zaw Pe Win (1970), and Tin Soe (1982).

13. IBRD (1975), p. 21.
14. MNPF, *Report to the Pyithu Hluttaw* (1986), p. 4.
15. Mya Than (1983).
16. *Guardian*, 23 June 1965.
17. *Loketha Pyithu*, 14 July 1989.
18. Private land rent was abolished by the Tenancy Amendment Act 1965. Since 1965 farmers need not pay any rent to private landlords. Instead, a fixed land tax is paid to the government in cash. The levels of this tax are low compared with previous levels of rent charged by private landlords.
19. In the two years following the policy changes large amounts of agricultural credit were made available. Supplies of inputs were also boosted. However, after 1964 both credit and input supplies became tight.
20. IBRD (1975), p. 20.
21. Institute of Economics (1980, 1982).
22. IBRD (1975), p. 15.
23. MNPF, *Report to the Pyithu Hluttaw* (1975).
24. MNPF, *Report to the Pyithu Hluttaw* (1988).
25. Institute of Economics (1982).
26. Kan Zaw (1984), p. 57.
27. CSO, *Yearbook 1965*; and MNPF, *Report to the Pyithu Hluttaw* (1988).
28. IBRD (1975), p. 22.
29. Opening a private foreign exchange account at the Myanmar Foreign Trade Bank (MFTB), the only national bank in Burma dealing with foreign exchange matters, is allowed only to those private individuals who earn foreign exchange legally (such as seamen). Such individuals can make transactions through the bank for any payment. However, those who have no legal source of foreign exchange earning but want to start an export-import business, for instance, are not allowed to buy the foreign exchange to open a foreign exchange account. Although the MFTB does not sell foreign exchange to private citizens except in special cases, it buys foreign exchange from private individuals who legally earn them at the official exchange rate which is about 8 to 10 times lower than the prevailing black-market rate.
30. The U.S. dollars are earned from smuggling along the borders with Thailand and Bangladesh. There is also illegal sale of foreign currencies in Rangoon and a few other big cities. The black-market rates for the U.S. dollar are 46–48 kyats in Lashio (in Northern Shan State, Burma) and 50–52 kyats in Rangoon, compared with 36–38 kyats along the Thai-Burma border (Lintner 1989, p. 104).
31. The Minister for National Planning and Finance, and Trade, was optimistic when he claimed in his address at the official opening of (Korea's) Daewoo Corporation's sale of goods at the People's Department Store in Rangoon in July 1989 that Burma would become a developed country within 5 to

10 years' time from 1989. The reasons pointed out by him were that (1) the changed economic policies are on the right track; and (2) Burma is rich with natural resources (*Loketha Pyithu* 27 July 1989, pp. 1–2). However, no elaboration was made.

32. Mellor and Ahmed (1988), pp. 265–66.
33. Maung Suu Zan (1966), pp. 81–104.
34. Mellor and Ahmed (1988), p. 266.
35. Ibid., pp. 271–72.
36. Ibid., p. 267.
37. Ibid., p. 269.
38. Ibid., p. 273.
39. Ibid., pp. 284–85.
40. For further information on the cause and effect, and the possibility of application of each of them to the context of developing countries' agricultural pricing, see, for example, ibid.

REFERENCES

Aye Hlaing, U. "Trends of Economic Growth of Burma: 1870–1940". Mimeographed. Rangoon: Institute of Economics, 1964.

Central Statistical Organisation. *Statistical Year Book 1965*. Rangoon, 1966.

______. *Statistical Year Book* 1975. Rangoon, 1976.

______. *Selected Monthly Economic Indicators*. Rangoon, various issues.

Economic Intelligence Unit. *Country Report. Thailand and Burma*, 1989.

Furnivall, J.S. *An Introduction to the Political Economy of Burma*, 3rd edition. Rangoon: People's Literature House, 1957.

Guardian (Rangoon, Burma), 23 June 1965.

Hill, H. and S.K. Jayasuriya. *An Inward-Looking Economy in Transition: Economic Development in Burma since the 1960s*. Occasional Paper No. 80. Singapore: Institute of Southeast Asian Studies, 1986.

Hla Tun, U, Daw Khin Lay and U Tin Soe. *An Analysis of Rice Distribution and Marketing Activities in Burma*. Research paper prepared in Burmese for the Economic Science Division, Burma Research Congress, Rangoon, 1985.

IBRD. *Current Situations and Prospects of the Socialist Republic of the Union of Burma*. Report No. 565a-BA, 15 January 1975.

Institute of Economics. "Taikgyi Township Rural Survey". Mimeographed, in Burmese. Rangoon, 1980.

Institute of Economics. "Hlegu Township Rural Survey". Mimeographed, in Burmese. Rangoon, Burma, 1981–82.

Jayasuriya, S.K. "Technical Change and the Revival of the Burmese Rice Industry". *The Developing Economies* 22, no. 2 (1984): 137–54.

Kan Zaw. "Agricultural Growth and Regional Development (A Case Study in the Irrawaddy Delta, Burma)". Master of Development Studies degree thesis, Institute of Social Studies, The Hague, Netherlands, 1984.

Khin Win, Nyi Nyi, and E.C. Price. *The Impact of a Special High-Yielding Rice Program*. IRRI Research Paper Series no. 58. The International Rice Research Institute, Los Banos, Philippines, 1981.

Lintner, Bertil. "The Busy Border". *Far Eastern Economic Review*, 8 June 1989.

Loketha Pyithu (Rangoon, Burma), 14, 27 July and various issues in July and August 1989.

Maung Maung Soe. "Rural Institutions and Agricultural Development in Burma: A Case Study of The New High Yielding Varieties Programme". Master of Development Studies degree thesis, Institute of Social Studies, The Hague, Netherlands, 1984.

Maung Suu Zan. *Seebwaye Shudauk* [From Economic Angle]. Rangoon: Kalaung Byan Publishing House, 1966.

Mellor, John W., and Raisuddin Ahmed. "Conclusions — Agricultural Price Policy for Accelerating Growth". In *Agricultural price policy for developing countries*, edited by John W. Mellow and Raisuddin Ahmed. Baltimore: Johns Hopkins University Press, 1988.

Ministry of National Planning and Finance (MNPF). "Planning Procedure in Burma". Mimeographed. Rangoon, 1984.

______. "An Outline of The Directives for the Twenty-Year Plan". Mimeographed. Rangoon, 1973.

______. "Pricing System in Burma". Mimeographed. Rangoon, 1984.

______. *Report to the Revolutionary Council on the Financial, Economic and Social Conditions of the Socialist Republic of the Union of Burma*. Rangoon, various issues.

______. *Report to the Pyithu Hluttaw on the Financial, Economic and Social Conditions of the Socialist Republic of the Union of Burma*. Rangoon, various issues.

Mya Than. "A Review on the Impact of Raising Paddy Prices". Mimeographed, in Burmese. Research Department, Institute of Economics, Rangoon, 1975.

Mya Than. "List of Research Papers read at various Paper Reading Sessions of the Burma Research Congress between 1966 and 1982". Mimeographed, in Burmese. Rangoon, 1983.

Richter, H.V. "The High Yield Program in Burma". In *Technical Change in Asian Agriculture*, edited by R.T. Shand. Canberra: Australian National University Press, 1973.

______. *Burma's Rice Surpluses: Accounting for the Decline*. Occasional Paper, No. 3. Development Studies Centre, Australian National University, Canberra, 1976.

Saito, T. "Farm Household Economy Under Paddy Delivery System in Contemporary Burma". *The Developing Economies* 19, no. 4 (1981): 367–97.

Silverstein, J. *Burma: Military Rule and the Politics of Stagnation*. Ithaca: Cornell University Press, 1977.

Steinberg, D.I. *Burma's Road Towards Development: Growth and Ideology Under Military Rule*. Boulder: Westview Press, 1981.

Tin Soe, U, and U Zaw Pe Win. "Analysis of the Effectiveness of Agricultural Policies in Burma" (in Burmese). Research paper presented at the Fifth Burma Research Congress, Rangoon, 1970.

Tin Soe. "Rice Price Policy: A Comparative Analysis of Burma and Some Asian Countries" (in Burmese). Research paper prepared for the Paper Reading Session at the Social Science Division, Burma Research Congress, Rangoon, 1982.

6

INDUSTRIAL DEVELOPMENT AND INDUSTRIAL POLICY IN MYANMAR
Turning Challenges into Changes

WILFRIED LÜTKENHORST

Overall Structure of the Economy

With a GDP per capita of below US$200 Myanmar is among the poorest developing countries in the world. Despite having relatively rich natural resources and a relatively high literacy rate Myanmar has since 1987 been officially accorded the status of a least developed country.

Data on the sectoral composition of gross domestic product (GDP) for recent years are provided in Table 1. According to the provisional figures for 1988/89[1] slightly more than 40 per cent of GDP originated from agriculture and another 8.3 per cent from livestock and fishery. Processing and manufacturing activities accounted for 8.9 per cent of GDP, services for 16.0 per cent, and trade activities for 22.5 per cent. In the longer-term perspective, looking at the past three decades,[2] the following observations on the changing structure of GDP can be made:

— Compared with most other developing countries the structure of GDP has remained remarkably static. No drastic changes have taken place, the most noticeable ones being

TABLE 1
GDP by Sector
(At 1985/86 constant producers' prices)

Economic sector	Value				Structure				Growth Rate		
	1985/86	*1986/87*	*1987/88*[a]	*1988/89*[a]	*1985/86*	*1986/87*	*1987/88*[a]	*1988/89*[a]	*1986/87*	*1987/88*[a]	*1988/89*[a]
	In million kyat				*Percentage*						
Goods	34,300.6	33,977.0	32,245.2	32,715.9	61.3	61.3	60.8	61.5	(−) 0.9	(−) 5.1	1.5
Agriculture	22,243.5	22,343.3	20.906.8	21,365.7	39.7	40.3	39.4	40.2	0.4	(−) 6.4	2.2
Livestock & Fishery	3,981.9	4,056.8	4,212.5	4,388.0	7.1	7.3	7.9	8.3	1.9	3.8	4.2
Forestry	757.7	719.6	688.2	797.2	1.4	1.3	1.3	1.5	(−) 5.0	(−) 4.4	15.8
Mining	533.5	498.4	428.6	346.3	1.0	0.9	0.8	0.6	(−) 6.6	(−)14.0	(−)19.2
Processing & Manufacturing	5,561.4	5,123.3	4,810.1	4,737.9	9.9	9.3	9.1	8.9	(−) 7.9	(−) 6.1	(−) 1.5
Power	278.0	289.0	300.6	338.6	0.5	0.5	0.6	0.6	4.0	4.0	12.6
Construction	944.6	946.6	898.4	742.2	1.7	1.7	1.7	1.4	0.2	(−) 5.1	(−)17.4
Services	8,300.0	8,600.0	8,869.3	8,494.9	14.8	15.5	16.7	16.0	3.6	3.1	(−) 4.2
Transportation	2,010.4	2,004.1	2,039.0	1,781.0	3.6	3.6	3.8	3.4	(−) 0.3	1.7	(−)12.7
Communications	207.7	254.8	288.5	285.0	0.3	0.4	0.6	0.5	22.7	13.2	(−) 1.2
Financial Institutions	1,332.3	1,421.1	1,498.6	1,602.0	2.4	2.6	2.8	3.0	6.7	5.5	6.9
Social Administrative Services	2,567.8	2,659.3	2,746.9	2,616.2	4.6	4.8	5.2	4.9	3.6	3.3	(−) 4.7
Rentals & other Services	2,181.8	2,260.7	2,296.3	2,210.0	3.9	4.1	4.3	4.2	3.6	1.6	(−) 3.8
Trade	13,388.7	12,819.8	11,932.9	11,944.8	23.9	23.2	22.5	22.5	(−) 4.2	(−) 6.9	0.1
GDP	55,989.3	55,396.8	53,047.4	53,155.6	100.0	100.0	100.0	100.0	(−) 1.1	(−) 4.2	0.2

[a] Provisional.

SOURCE: Ministry of Planning and Finance, *Review of the Financial, Economic and Social Conditions for 1989/90* (Rangoon, 1989).

a 10 per cent decline in the share of trade activities between 1961/62 and 1981/82 and a 3 per cent increase in the share of agriculture in the same period. In the first half of the eighties the structure of GDP has virtually remained unchanged.

— At a very high level of aggregation it can be said that the overall share of commodity producing sectors has slightly increased (from 49 per cent in 1961/62 to 53 per cent in 1985/86) whereas the share of all services and trade activities has declined correspondingly.

With regard to industry it can be noted that — despite the fact that the industrial sector has been assigned a priority role in the country's economic transformation — there was no corresponding increase in its GDP share. Due to the sector's dismal average real growth performance (−7.9 per cent in 1986/87; −6.1 per cent in 1987/88),[3] the share of processing and manufacturing in GDP declined markedly to a record low of only 8.9 per cent in 1988/89. Hence, at least from a macro perspective, that is, ignoring changing patterns of production within the sector, it has not been able to play the expected dynamic role as a driving force of economic development.

Not surprisingly, when looking at the country's export performance, manufactures have as yet not emerged as a significant element. According to UNIDO (United Nations Industrial Development Organization) estimates, manufactures account for less than 5 per cent of total export value and consist mostly of textile products, leather, cement, some pharmaceutical products (such as crude glycerine, alcohol), several petrochemical products and animal feed products. In overall terms, exports account for only a marginal share in GDP (declining from 4.7 per cent in 1985/86 to 2.5 per cent in 1987/88) and have experienced a drastic fall in recent years, partly because of declining prices for major export products.[4] As can be seen from Table 2, total export value (in current prices) went down by 5 per cent in 1986/87 and precipitated by 33 per cent in 1987/88 to reach 1.679 million kyat.[5] In terms of the commodity composition, forest products

TABLE 2
Export Value by Type of Commodity, 1985/86–1987/88
(In million kyat)

	Export value		
Type of commodity	*1985/86*	*1986/87*	*1987/88*[a]
Exports	2,566.1	2,418.5	1,655.2
Agricultural products	1,131.0	800.5	453.5
Animal & marine products	99.8	124.5	76.3
Forest products	1,051.0	1,084.1	754.3
Minerals & gems	205.9	283.9	225.0
Others	78.4	125.5	146.1
Re-exports	87.8	95.4	24.2
TOTAL	2,653.9	2,513.9	1,679.4

[a] Provisional.

SOURCE: Ministry of Planning and Finance, *Review of the Financial, Economic and Social Conditions for 1989/90.*

(mostly teak) have taken over the first ranking position from agricultural products (mostly rice), the former now accounting for 45 per cent, the latter for 27 per cent of total exports.

Throughout the eighties, Myanmar has recorded substantial current account deficits which have mostly ranged around 4 per cent of GDP (3.6 per cent in 1987/88). Debt service payments almost doubled between 1982/83 and 1986/87 to reach some 70 per cent of current receipts. In the same period, the country's gross international reserves went down from SDR 73 million to SDR 36 million, which was equivalent to less than one month of import requirements.[6]

The increasingly precarious foreign exchange situation has led to serious bottlenecks and constraints in the country's economy, especially with regard to essential import requirements of the manufacturing sector. A closer look at the commodity structure of imports shows that they are indeed heavily dominated by industrial input needs. Whereas consumer goods are responsible for only 5 per cent of all recorded imports, the combined share of industrial raw materials and spare parts, construction materials, machinery and equipment, and transport equipment amounts to no less than 92 per cent of total imports (Table 3).

Apart from the foreign exchange gap and the concomitant debt service crisis, the economy has suffered from the inability of the state to mobilize sufficient domestic capital for investment. Investment expenditures went down by 10 per cent in real terms, both in 1987/88 and 1988/89 (provisional figures) which has brought down the investment ratio (share of investment in GDP) to 12.6 per cent. While the key role in promoting economic growth is assigned to the public sector, the GDP share of public revenues has decreased continuously to reach a level slightly below 10 per

TABLE 3
Imports by Type of Commodity, 1985/86–1987/88
(In million kyat)

Type of commodity	*1985/86*	*1986/87*	*1987/88*[a]
Consumer goods	572.2	234.1	222.0
Durable goods	273.0	80.2	106.3
Foodstuffs	63.7	2.5	12.0
Textiles	61.5	16.1	31.0
Medicines & pharmaceuticals	121.9	104.8	50.0
Other consumer goods	52.1	30.5	22.7
Raw materials & spares for inter-industry use	1,484.7	1,158.1	1,207.7
Raw materials	981.8	643.3	499.7
Fuel	0.3	—	—
Tools & spares	502.6	514.8	708.0
Capital goods	2,741.3	2,522.2	2,614.3
Construction materials	505.1	583.5	691.1
Machinery & equipment	1,789.3	1,484.0	1,130.1
Transport equipment	303.3	336.5	695.6
Other capital goods	143.6	118.2	97.5
Commodity unspecified	3.8	21.7	21.7
TOTAL	4,802.0	3,936.1	4,065.7

[a] Provisional.

SOURCE: Ministry of Planning and Finance, *Review of the Financial, Economic and Social Conditions for 1989/90.*

cent in 1988/89. Given that the manufacturing sector has traditionally been the recipient of the largest allocation of state capital expenditures, the negative impact of a decreasing overall capital formation capability on its performance has been significant.

The Manufacturing Sector

Myanmar's manufacturing sector accounts for less than 10 per cent of the country's GDP (8.9 per cent in 1988/89) and employs less than 9 per cent of its labour force. The principal manufacturing activities are related to the processing of natural, mostly agricultural resources and petroleum refining, with food and beverages production generating more than three-quarters of gross manufacturing output and about 40 per cent of manufacturing value added. Private industries — though significantly contributing to industrial production — have in the past been confined to small-scale activities, with a heavy emphasis on agro-processing. The internal structure of the manufacturing sector has remained virtually unchanged during the past two decades. Diversification into entirely new areas has not taken place to a significant extent. Since 1982/83 (with the exception of 1984/85) real manufacturing value added has declined every year; it fell by −7.8 per cent in 1986/87 and again by −6.1 per cent in 1987/88 as production became increasingly constrained by shortages of fuel and essential imported inputs as a result of the increasing foreign exchange scarcity.

A closer look will now be taken at the branch composition, ownership patterns and capacity utilization rates in the manufacturing sector.

Table 4 reviews the long-term trends in the branch composition of gross manufacturing output. It emerges that the dominant position of food and beverages in total output has further increased in the course of time to reach 77 per cent in 1988/89. The only other industrial branches contributing more than 3 per cent of total output are mineral and petroleum products (5.2 per cent, with a declining trend), industrial raw materials (4.6 per cent), and clothing and wearing apparel (3.6 per cent).

TABLE 4

Composition of Gross Manufacturing Output, 1975/76–1988/89

(In percentage and current prices)

	1975/76	*1976/77*	*1977/78*	*1978/79*	*1979/80*	*1980/81*	*1981/82*	*1982/83*	*1983/84*	*1984/85*	*1985/86*	*1986/87*	*1987/88*[a]	*1988/89*[a]
Food and beverages	69.8	66.7	67.4	68.7	67.4	65.8	65.4	64.7	65.6	70.1	72.0	74.0	76.6	76.8
Clothing and wearing apparel	7.8	9.2	9.6	8.3	8.6	8.7	8.2	8.6	7.5	7.1	6.4	5.1	4.3	3.6
Construction materials	3.2	3.3	3.2	3.3	4.4	4.5	4.2	4.1	4.4	3.5	3.5	3.7	3.2	2.6
Personal goods	3.2	3.5	2.8	2.4	2.2	2.7	3.0	2.8	2.2	1.8	1.8	1.5	1.0	0.9
Household goods	0.3	0.4	0.4	0.4	0.4	0.6	0.6	0.7	0.6	0.6	0.5	0.7	0.6	0.6
Printing and publishing	1.1	1.0	1.0	1.0	1.0	1.0	1.0	1.0	1.1	1.0	0.8	1.0	0.8	0.8
Industrial raw materials	3.8	4.4	5.2	5.3	5.4	6.1	6.3	6.5	6.7	6.1	5.5	5.3	4.8	4.6
Mineral and petroleum products	6.5	6.8	6.1	5.5	5.4	5.2	5.1	5.7	5.8	4.4	3.9	3.3	3.3	5.2
Agricultural equipment	0.3	0.5	0.5	0.5	0.5	0.6	0.6	0.5	0.5	0.3	0.3	0.4	0.3	0.3
Machinery and equipment	0.1	0.0	0.0	0.0	0.0	0.1	0.0	0.0	0.2	0.0	0.1	0.1	0.1	0.2
Transport vehicles	1.1	1.4	1.6	1.9	1.9	1.8	2.0	2.1	2.2	1.8	2.0	1.9	1.5	1.8
Electrical goods	0.6	0.7	0.5	0.5	0.5	0.7	0.8	0.7	1.0	0.7	0.9	0.8	0.6	0.6
Miscellaneous	2.2	2.1	1.7	2.2	2.3	2.2	2.8	2.6	2.2	2.6	2.3	2.1	2.9	2.2
TOTAL	100.0	100.0	100.0	100.0	100.0	100.0	100.0	100.0	100.0	100.0	100.0	100.0	100.0	100.0

[a] Provisional.

SOURCE: *Report to the Pyithu Hluttaw*, various issues.

Table 5 and 6 present data on the structure of ownership in the country's industrial sector. As far as the number of establishments is concerned, it can be seen that private factories and establishments account for the overwhelming majority of all industrial units (93.9 per cent), leaving 4.4 per cent for state-owned enterprises and 1.7 per cent for co-operative societies. The share of private establishments is particularly high in light industries producing simple consumer goods whereas state enterprises account for 60 per cent of all units in the case of agricultural equipment and for 70 per cent in the case of machinery and equipment. In general, it must be noted, however, that all industrial activity of any significant size is concentrated in state-owned enterprises. Out of a total of almost 40,000 private establishments there are just

TABLE 5
Ownership Structure of Industrial Establishments by Sector, 1988/89[a]
(Percentage shares)

	Operating factories and establishments		
Sector	*State-owned*	*Co-operative*	*Private*
Food & beverages	1.8	2.6	96.0
Clothing & wearing apparel	0.7	1.8	97.7
Construction materials	7.3	5.8	85.7
Personal goods	0.3	0.2	99.5
Household goods	1.1	1.5	97.2
Printing & publishing	20.0	5.0	75.0
Industrial raw materials	37.6	0.3	62.0
Mineral & petroleum products	0.7	0.3	99.0
Agricultural equipment	60.0	—	40.0
Machinery & equipment	70.0	—	30.0
Transport vehicles	1.9	3.1	95.0
Workshops & dockyards	100	—	—
Miscellaneous	0.2	0.6	99.2
TOTAL	4.4	1.7	93.9

[a] Provisional.

SOURCE: Ministry of Planning and Finance, *Review of the Financial, Economic and Social Conditions for 1989/90.*

TABLE 6
Ownership Structure of Industrial Establishments by Size, 1988/89

Size	*State-owned*	*Co-operatives*	*Private*	*TOTAL*
Below 10 workers	981	409	37,965	39,355
10–50 workers	297	308	1,824	2,429
51–100 workers	150	—	9	159
Over 100 workers	426	—	4	430
TOTAL	1,854	717	39,802	42,373

SOURCE: Ministry of Planning and Finance, *Review of the Financial, Economic and Social Conditions for 1989/90.*

13 employing more than 50 workers and not a single co-operative is to be found in this size segment.

The picture is somewhat different when the corresponding shares of industrial production value are measured.[7] Here, private industries contribute as much as 55 per cent (figure for 1986/87), state-owned industries account for 39 per cent and co-operative societies for another 6 per cent of the total.

The situation with regard to capacity utilization rates has become very bleak. While capacity utilization rates have always tended to be rather low in the past they have now precipitated to levels ranging between 10 and 30 per cent in various branches (Table 7; figures for state-owned industries only). In 5 out of 8 manufacturing branches covered by Ministry of No. 1 Industry, the utilization of installed capacity has fallen below 30 per cent: this applies to textile industries, pharmaceutical industries, metal industries, general industries and jute industries. This may be partly attributable to factors such as inferior technology and weaknesses in organization and management; yet the major determinant has been the acute shortage of foreign exchange to finance essential production-related imports.

The economic realities outlined above — depletion of foreign exchange resources, lack of crucial production inputs not available domestically, inability to generate sufficient domestic investment capital — culminated in 1988 and prompted the new government

TABLE 7
Capacity Utilization Rates of State-owned Industries by Industrial Branches, 1985/86 and 1988/89

Industrial Branch	*1985/86*	*1988/89*
Industries under Ministry of No. 1 Industry		
Myanmar Textile Industries	57.1	29.1
Myanmar Foodstuff Industries	51.4	48.8[a]
Myanmar Pharmaceutical Industries	65.6	28.3
Myanmar Metal Industries	63.0	12.9
Myanmar Ceramic Industries	70.2	51.8
Myanmar General Industries	65.4	20.5
Myanmar Paper & Chemical Industries	57.0	45.6
Myanmar Jute Industries	26.5	24.4
Industries under Ministry of No. 2 Industry	60.7	48.6[a]
Average	57.4	34.4

[a] 1987/88.

SOURCE: Government data provided to UNIDO.

to undertake a wide-ranging revision of the country's economic strategy and policies.

New Economic Strategy and Recent Policy Measures

The economic policy approach adopted in Myanmar in the early sixties was based on comprehensive central planning and state ownership of all important means of production. Public sector investment was to be the main driving force of economic development. The overall economic strategy was geared towards strictly self-reliant development, with priority being assigned to the fulfilment of basic domestic needs within the framework of a virtually closed economy.

Gradual changes occurred during the formulation of the Twenty-Year Long-Term Plan (1971/72–1990/91) which acknowledged the difficulties encountered in generating the resources required for self-sustained growth within the autarkic strategy pursued in the sixties. Consequently, without however allowing significant system changes to take place, it was recognized that it was necessary to rely to a greater degree on foreign trade and to provide incentives for private economic activities. Notwithstanding some marginal changes, the country's economy continued, however, to be largely sealed off from the world market. During the seventies and eighties, when many other Asian developing countries achieved unprecedented economic growth rates and material progress, Myanmar was persistently falling behind in economic terms. The country's industry — effectively shielded off from international competition — remained at extremely low productivity levels and hence was not only unable to tap export markets and generate foreign exchange earnings but also to cater to the needs of the growing population.

While a policy reform had already taken place in September 1987 with the abandoning of price controls for rice and other basic commodities, it was only in September 1988, following a severe economic crisis and widespread political unrest, that dramatic economic policy changes came to be announced. The new State Law and Order Restoration Council (SLORC) officially discarded the centrally planned approach in favour of a more market-oriented and open economic policy framework. While the specific policy changes have yet to be implemented, and the degree of the planned "opening up" of the economy and the precise role to be played by market mechanisms are still unknown, the government is endeavouring, with a view to promote rapid transformation from a low-productivity agricultural to a high-productivity agro-based industrial economy:

- to encourage and enlarge the scope for international industrial co-operation, specifically in the form of foreign direct investment;
- to infuse modern technology into the country's industry in order to increase its productivity and competitiveness and to achieve a diversification towards production and the export of non-traditional manufactured products;
- to partially deregulate the economy by (a) granting more autonomy to private, co-operative and state enterprises in

areas such as trading activities and entering into joint ventures; (b) privatizing and/or commercializing state economic enterprises; and (c) adjusting and increasing the flexibility of the price structure.

More specific economic policy measures taken recently are outlined in the following sections.

General Measures

The present government has officially abolished all existing long-term economic plans in favour of short-term planning on the basis of annual plans. This is done, however, without any clear coherent notion of both the macro policies and the industrial priorities required in the future.

As regards development projects in the industrial sector, preference is accorded to the completion of ongoing projects which are resource-based and foreign-exchange generating or saving. New projects are mainly sought in the form of export-oriented foreign investment utilizing local labour and raw materials.

In March 1989 the SLORC officially revoked the 1965 Law for the Establishment of a Socialist Economic System. At the same time, a new law was enacted which abolishes state monopolies in many industrial branches and allows co-operatives and private entrepreneurs (both domestic and foreign) to engage in the production and trade of most industrial goods. Important areas which continue to be reserved for state economic enterprises are teak, petroleum, natural gas and precious stones. These activities can be conducted either by a wholly government-owned enterprise or as a joint venture with domestic or foreign partners.[8]

While there is a new Foreign Investment Law (see next section), it is to be noted in this context that at present no private enterprise law is in force for *domestic* investment. The old law has been abolished in view of its regulatory and restrictive approach, and a new law is said to be in preparation at present. Measures have been taken, however, under government order to lower income and profit taxes for private industries. While incomes up to 15,000 kyat will not incur any tax during the current fiscal year, private income tax has been reduced from 25 to 20 per cent, foreign company tax from 40 to 30 per cent, and profit taxes for domestic firms from 50 to 30 per cent.

The government further intends to provide access to many public sector support institutions for co-operatives and private industries which have so far been excluded from their services. This would in particular apply to the Central Research Organization (CRO) and to the existing Industrial Training Centres. Such a measure could provide important development stimuli to the country's industrial sector as a whole. In the past, the establishment of private industries had been constrained, *inter alia*, by the lack of access to skilled labour.

Only tentative information is available at present on the government's approach with regard to the future role of state economic enterprises (SEEs) in the industrial sector. In general, privatization of SEEs is being discussed, *inter alia*, by returning some nationalized companies to private hands. Furthermore, SEEs would be required to adopt a commercial business orientation and to generate profits. The implications of this demand for loss-generating SEEs have not been spelled out so far, however. An important change has occurred insofar as SEEs are now allowed to enter into technical co-operation agreements and joint ventures with any other company, be it a private domestic firm or a foreign firm. This may be seen as an important avenue to commercialize some SEEs. Indeed, following the long period of inefficient operations under monopolistic conditions, the gradual commercialization of the SEEs' activities may be more appropriate than their immediate privatization. Management contracts with competent foreign partners may be seen as one possible approach in this respect.

Foreign Investment Policy

The Foreign Investment Law which became effective on 30 November 1988 is certainly among the most important policy measures taken by the present government. The Law allows foreign investors to establish either wholly foreign-owned enterprises or joint ventures in which the foreign partner would be required to take at least a 35 per cent equity stake. All foreign investment applications have to be approved by the new Foreign Investment Commission appointed by the government which is to review the proposed projects in terms of their economic justification and financial viability. The Foreign Investment Commission has been empowered to grant wide-ranging investment incentives, including in particular:

— a tax holiday for three years after start-up of operations, plus a possible extension;
— profit tax exemptions for funds reinvested within one year;
— accelerated depreciation allowances on equipment and buildings;
— tax breaks on export income;
— permission for employers to pay expatriates' personal income taxes and include them as an operating cost;
— equal personal income tax rates for non-residents and locals;
— deductions for research and development;
— the ability to carry forward losses for three years when sustained during the first two years after the tax holiday; and
— customs duty exemptions on machines and materials imported during the construction period.

Furthermore, there are guarantees against nationalization and for the repatriation of profits. The law accords priority to investment projects which promote exports, exploit domestic natural resources, transfer high technology, increase employment, save energy or contribute to economic development in the provinces.

The first industrial joint venture established under the new Law is in the field of woodworking with a partner from Singapore. This may be seen as indicative of an overall high interest from *regional* investors in Myanmar as a new production location.

Further joint ventures under the new Law are being established at present in the framework of activities undertaken by the Union of Myanmar Joint Venture Corporation No. 1 (JVC 1). JVC 1 was recently formed as a limited company with 50 per cent of equity being held by private shareholders and 50 per cent by the State Trading Corporation.[9] Hence, JVC 1 is a mixed company *without* foreign participation. JVC 1 in turn is a partner in three other joint ventures which are being formed under the new Law as private limited companies (the letters of intent have already been signed). The ownership structure of these three joint ventures *with* foreign participation is as follows: 30 per cent JVC 1; 40 per cent foreign investor(s); and 30 per cent concerned state organizations. More specifically, the following three joint ventures are being established:

— Myanmar Agro-Aquatic Resources Development Ltd.
  Equity distribution: 30 per cent JVC 1
  40 per cent foreign partner(s)
  30 per cent Myanmar Fisheries Enterprise
— Myanmar Rubber Wood Industries Ltd.
  Equity distribution: 30 per cent JVC 1
  40 per cent foreign partner(s)
  30 per cent Myanmar Agricultural Service
— Myanmar Bamboo Industries Ltd.
  Equity distribution: 30 per cent JVC 1
  40 per cent foreign partner(s)
  30 per cent General Merchandise Trading

Trade Policy

As mentioned above, trade activities have been substantially liberalized with a view to open the country's economy to the world market. Both co-operatives and private entrepreneurs are now allowed to engage in all domestic and external trading activities, with the exception of trade relating to teak, petroleum, natural gas and precious stones.

A significant departure from previous policies is to be seen particularly in the so-called "border trade". Following negotiations held and arrangements made in November 1988, official border trade has been initiated with China with three trading points opened in Mankham, Muse and Kyohkok. The intention has apparently been to reduce cross-border smuggling which in the past had fuelled a substantial black market. The volume of border trade is estimated at approximately US$300 million annually, comprising mainly exports of agricultural products (such as cotton, dried fish, prawns, fish skins and duck feathers) in exchange for Chinese consumer goods (such as cosmetics, bicycles and household articles). The border trade arrangements immediately triggered off thriving trading activities as the transactions (including customs duties to be paid to the government) are based on a flexible spot market exchange rate rather than on the overvalued official rate.

In general, according to Department of Trade data, there are now approximately 200 registered exporters and approximately 100 registered importers, the majority of them undertaking trade in agricultural products.

Wide-ranging changes have furthermore been undertaken with regard to the allocation of foreign exchange. Exporting state economic enterprises now can claim a portion of their foreign exchange earnings to finance essential imports; the exact amount varies, however, subject to the nature of exports and related import requirements. Private exporters have been allowed to retain 60 per cent of their foreign exchange earnings to finance imports of any kind.

Conclusions and Outlook

At present, the industrial sector — as indeed the whole economy — of the country is at a crossroad. Assuming the proper implementation of the new market-oriented, private sector-encouraging development strategy, it may be possible to mobilize more effectively the country's human resources and efficiently utilize its rich endowment of natural resources for industrial development. It is important to reiterate that Myanmar's economic development had in the past been constrained mainly by the country's isolation from the world economy and the rigid central planning system rather than, for example, by lacking resources or the smallness of its domestic market, as is the case in many other least developed countries. Conversely, there is every reason to believe that the adoption of a conducive development strategy will provide a powerful stimulus to push the country's industry towards higher levels of productivity and competitiveness.

However, to initiate and carry through such a drastic turn in a country's economic strategy is a formidable task requiring wide-ranging changes in policies, institutions, technology acquisition and development, company organization and management, the legal framework and traditional attitudes and modes of behaviour. Every effort should thus be made to gear the international technical assistance programme in the years to come towards providing advice and crucial inputs to this transition process and to minimize the adjustment costs involved.

The success or failure of the initiated transformation process is clearly determined as much by micro-level policy measures (aimed at particular branches, markets, technologies, and so forth) as it is by the overall macro-economic conditions prevailing in the country. In particular, it needs to be emphasized that the issue of a more market-oriented, realistic exchange rate assumes crucial importance in this regard. At present, the country is unable to exploit the comparative advantages existing in a number of resource-based industrial branches due to the negative across-the-board impact of a grossly overvalued currency. There is a danger that — unless corrective action is taken in the initial stage of the new economic strategy — even well-designed export promotion programmes could fail. Moreover, an overvalued exchange rate has the general effect of discouraging foreign capital inflows, notably, foreign direct investment which, however, will need to play a key role in providing the technology and marketing skills required to stimulate export-oriented production.

While the new emphasis on attracting foreign investment is a significant change, it appears important not to neglect the essential role of domestic investment in fulfilling the basic needs and increasing the supply of consumer goods for the population. In this context, the promulgation of a new domestic investment act should be given high priority. At present, with the existence of a liberal Foreign Investment Law, domestic investment has been put at a competitive disadvantage in terms of the eligibility for fiscal and financial incentives. The establishment of an investment climate of confidence and security is a key precondition to boost private domestic investment. In this context, the whole system of taxation for private, co-operative and state enterprises as well as the regulations governing foreign exchange allocations need to be reviewed with a view to eliminating existing distortions. Furthermore, the need to provide investment finance is to be emphasized. Industrial expansion will imply a new and increasing role for the banking system in servicing enterprises. Short-term, and more importantly, medium- and long-term credits must be assigned an active developmental role which implies both responsibility and risk-taking, and thus involvement in investment decisions, for the banking sector.

In terms of sectoral priorities, the government pursues a resource-based industrialization strategy aimed at increasing the domestic value added derived from the processing of natural resources in agriculture, fisheries, forestry and mining. It is in these areas that the greatest export potential can be assumed to exist in the short to medium run. At the same time, a thorough re-assessment is needed of the role of the metalworking and engineering industries in Myanmar's industrial transformation. In-depth analyses will be required to ascertain which metalworking and engineering industries can be economically justified (in terms of economies of scale, technological requirements, import dependence, etc.) in the context of both the country's resource endowments and international market conditions. For these engineering branches to be built up in the country, some degree of temporary infant industry protection may be required. On *prima facie* grounds, a case can be made to produce locally agricultural processing equipment (for example, for rice milling and edible oil processing) and less sophisticated woodworking machinery for which domestic demand is relatively high and can be expected to increase.

Another important area is the need for better structural integration of the industrial sector. It can be noted that hitherto public and private, large-scale and small-scale, urban and rural industries have been operating without substantial linkages. If industrial production is to gain momentum and, above all, if productivity is to be increased, then more specialization and complementarities need to be established. Specifically, sub-contracting potentials will need to be explored and promoted within an overall strategy of building up small- and medium-scale supporting industries which can efficiently produce industrial parts and components for larger enterprises. In this context, the role of industrial co-operative societies deserves special attention.

NOTES

1. The fiscal year extends from 1 April–31 March.
2. Cf. United Nations Industrial Development Organization (UNIDO), *Industrial Development Review Series: Burma*, PPD.65, 16 December 1987 (based on current prices).
3. Compared with a decline in GDP of −1.1 per cent in 1986/87 and −4.2 per cent in 1987/88 (at 1985/86 constant producers' prices).
4. The terms of trade deteriorated by 44 per cent between 1982/83 and 1986/87.
5. At constant 1985/86 producers' prices, exports decreased by 19 per cent in 1987/88.
6. A detailed account of the balance of payments situation is given in International Monetary Fund (IMF), *Burma: Recent Economic Developments*, 16 June 1988.
7. Cf. UNIDO, op. cit.
8. More specifically, the following activities have been listed in the new law as state monopolies: extraction of teak and sale of the same in the country and abroad; cultivation and conservation of forest plantations with the exception of village-owned firewood plantations cultivated by villagers for their personal use; exploration, extraction and sale of petroleum and natural gas and processing of their products; exploration, extraction and export of pearls, jade and precious stones; breeding and production of fish and prawns in fisheries which have been reserved for research by the government; postal and telecommunications services; air and railway transport; banking and insurance; radio and television broadcasting; exploration, extraction and export of metals; electricity generating services other than those permitted by law to private and co-operative electricity generating services; manufacture of products relating to security and defence which the government has, from time to time, prescribed by notification.
9. Total equity shares of JVC 1 amount to 50 million kyat divided into 50,000 shares of 1,000 kyat each.

7

THE UNION OF BURMA FOREIGN INVESTMENT LAW

Prospects of Mobilizing Foreign Capital for Development?

MYA THAN

> *Given the abundant natural resources of the Southeast Asian countries, foreign capital and technical resources are more productive when applied to their primary export industries. It is this higher productivity which gives rise to mutual gains both for the foreign investors and for the countries which receive this type of investment.*
>
> — Hla Myint, 1972

The Union of Burma Investment Law, the first of its kind since the Revolutionary Council took over power in 1962 and formulated ten weeks after the military take-over in September 1988, was promulgated and released to the public on 1 December 1988. This is, historically, a very significant step towards free-market capitalism, after twenty-six years of following an inward-looking and self-isolated socialist path, by allowing foreign capital to flow into the country. More importantly, before this Law was announced, the new military government had abolished the only ruling party, the Burma Socialist Programme Party (BSPP) along with its guiding principle, the "Burmese Way to Socialism"; and the words "Socialist Republic" in the official title of the nation were removed so that Burma has become "The Union of Burma" once again. (This was later changed to "The Union of Myanmar" in June 1989). After introducing this investment law, the government declared, on 31 March 1989, that the socialist economic system had been abolished. In short, the Investment Law is significant in the sense that it has become the symbol of an "open-door policy" and it is remarkable that the authorities could produce such a liberal investment law within a few weeks after they came into power.

Actually, this Law is the second of its kind since Burma gained its independence in 1948. Although all the leaders of the newly independent state were very nationalistic and socialist-oriented, and despite their efforts and strong desire to Burmanize the economy, "By 1949 the desperate fortunes of the insurrection-torn state had led to a plea for private investment from abroad, and the strong passions of Burmanization had somewhat softened the Government's animus toward Burmese business men".[1] It was not until 1955, however, that serious steps were taken to allow foreign investment — that is to say, only after the Investment Policy Statement of the government of June 1955 was issued, were some actual investments made possible in Burma. Then in 1959, the parliament enacted a "Union of Burma Investment Act" which formalized the Investment Policy Statement of 1955 with more incentives for investors, and this became the first investment law of the new Burma.

The objective of this chapter is to review and evaluate the Union of Burma Investment Law of 1988 (the new law); and to compare it with the Union of Burma Investment Act, 1959 (the old law) and those of neighbouring Southeast Asian nations, where necessary. In addition, the chapter will deal with the prospects of foreign direct investment in Burma in the light of the rapidly changing international situation.

Objectives of the Law

There are four objectives mentioned in the Statement on Foreign Investment Law of Burma. They are: 1) to exploit the abundant resources of the country, 2) to export whatever surplus available,

3) to create new employment opportunities and privileges of on-the-job training as well as technical training both inland and abroad for young people; and 4) economic and social development of various regions of the state, together with expansion and improvement of transport and communications.

However, the main aim seems to be to resolve the shortage of foreign earnings much needed in developing the currently deteriorating economy. The government expects, by exploiting the abundant natural resources (especially fishery and forestry) and by expansion of exports, to solve the problem of the shortage of foreign exchange. The second significant factor among the objectives is to resolve the unemployment problem especially for youth and graduates since it poses a critical socio-political problem. The third factor is regional development through the improvement of physical infrastructure which is aimed at relieving the tension between the central government and the minority groups. Technology transfer as an objective is not included in Burma's new Investment Law; however, it is mentioned under the title "Basic Principles" elsewhere (Chapter III, paragraph 4).

On the other hand, the foreign investment laws of other Southeast Asian countries are mostly export-market-oriented, driving for technology transfer and for increasing productivity and standards of living of their own citizens. The Indochinese countries have, in addition to other objectives and those similar to the old investment law of Burma in the 1950s, one more objective: to acquire advanced economic management.

It is not clear, by looking at the objectives, whether the Law of 1988 is export-market-oriented or domestic-market-oriented when it says "exporting whatever surplus is available", although, in general, it appears to be export-oriented.

The Main Features of Investments

According to Chapter III of the new Law, the basic features of foreign investments should be in accordance with the following basic principles:

1. promotion of exports;

2. exploitation of natural resources, which require heavy investment;
3. acquisition of high technology;
4. supporting and assisting production and services involving large capital;
5. opening up of more employment opportunities;
6. development of works which would save energy consumption;
7. regional development.

In fact, the new Law requires that foreign investments should conform with previously described aims and objectives. In Chapter III, two more points are added to those already described as "objectives", namely, the "aquisition of high technology" and the "development of works which would save energy consumption".

It seems obvious that principles for investments mentioned in the new Law are more detailed than in the former. However, compared to Vietnam's Investment Law, Burma's new Law is not development oriented or clearly stated. The Vietnamese law clearly states that it encourages investments in, among others, the implementation of major economic programmes, production of export and import-substituting products, high-technology industries using skilled labour, labour-intensive production using materials and natural resources available in Vietnam, and building of infrastructure and foreign currency-earning services.

Institutional Arrangements

With regard to institutional arrangements, according to the new law, there are two types of foreign investments which can be made in Burma: investment with 100 per cent foreign capital or a joint-venture between a foreigner and a citizen with a minimum requirement for foreign equity of 35 per cent. The investor may form a proprietorship, a partnership or a limited company. This seems to be very liberal compared with some countries in the region where a local majority equity requirement rule is specified. (For example, in Malaysia, if an enterprise exports less than 80 per cent of its production, the share of Malaysian equity should be 70 per cent by 1990.)

Apart from these, it is stated that an economic organization formed under the permit by the investor shall effect insurance with the (State) Myanmar Insurance Corporation in respect of the prescribed types of insurance (Chapter VIII, paragraph 19). As far as matters relating to foreign currency are concerned, the economic organization should open a foreign currency account as well as a kyat account in the bank prescribed by the Commission formed by the government to take care of foreign investment. Moreover, it should carry out all of its financial transactions relating to the business enterprise through the prescribed bank (Chapter XIV, paragraph 17). From this clause, it is obvious that the state intends to remain active in banking and insurance, which means no reduction in red tape. (According to the latest news from the *Working People's Daily*, 22 September 1989, the banking law is being revised to permit foreign banking business.)

In the old investment law of 1959, like in most countries in the region, it was not mentioned what type of investment was allowed, although, in practice, there were two forms of investments, that is, joint-ventures and 100 per cent foreign firms. In the case of the Indochinese states, there are three types of investments: contractual business co-operations, joint-ventures with a minimum requirement of 30 per cent foreign capital, and private enterprises with 100 per cent foreign capital.

With the exception of Burma and Vietnam, foreign firms in any part of the region can carry out their transactions through banks other than the state-designated ones.

Fiscal Incentives

As mentioned earlier, according to the new Law, foreign capital may have a majority equity share (that is, the minimum requirement for foreign equity is 35 per cent) which itself is an attractive incentive for foreign investors. Apart from this, there exist fiscal incentives in the form of tax exemptions and reliefs stated in Chapter X of the new investment law. Income tax exemptions are allowed for a period of three years and more. There is also a provision for income tax exemptions on profits if they are retained in a reserve fund and reinvested within one year. Expatriates are subject to the same income tax as Burmese citizens.

It is not mentioned for how long a contract can be made. However, it is mentioned that "contracts shall be executed as may be necessary" (paragraph 17, Chapter VII) and that "the Commission may, upon application by those concerned allow the extension . . . " (paragraph 18, Chapter VII). In Vietnam's case, the duration of a contract is twenty years and, when necessary, it may be extended for a longer period (Article 15).

According to the new Law, investors will have the following rights: to accelerate depreciation in respect of machinery, equipment, building or other capital assets used in the business; to deduct expatriates' income tax payable to the state from the assessable income; to deduct research and development expenses carried out in Burma from the assessable income; and to carry forward and set-off losses up to three consecutive years from the year the loss is sustained within two years immediately following the enjoyment of exemption of relief from income tax. There is also provision for relief from income tax of up to 50 per cent on the profits from the exports of the firm. Furthermore, exemptions on import duties and other internal taxes are provided on imported machinery, equipment, materials, and so forth during the period of construction, and in the case of raw materials, for the first three years of operation after the construction. It also guarantees that no enterprise under the investment law shall be nationalized during the term of contract or during an extended term, if so extended.

This new Foreign Investment Law is more liberal compared to the one promulgated in 1959 in the sense that the 1959 Act gave a guarantee not to nationalize the firms for a period of up to ten years, or twenty years at the utmost whereas the Law of 1988 guarantees against nationalization as long as the term of the contract exists. Other incentives such as the income-tax exemption period, and customs duty exemption for machinery and raw materials, are similar in both laws except that the Law of 1988 is more detailed and hence more attractive. However, it cannot claim to be "more liberal" than similar laws in other neighbouring

Southeast Asian nations, especially those from ASEAN, even in terms of tax holidays. For example, in Thailand, full exemption is given to foreign investors for three to eight years. *Some studies have questioned the effectiveness of investment incentives and found considerable evidence that fiscal incentives have little effect on investment decisions, except in a few specialized circumstances, especially where similar countries in a region are competing for export-oriented investments.*[2] *And in most of the cases, these fiscal incentives are costly to host country treasuries.*[3] Some specialists, such as Sir William Ryrie,[4] have even suggested that a general move in the direction of eliminating tax incentives and the like, at the same time reducing restrictions on the percentage of ownership permitted to foreign investors, would benefit most developing countries well.[5] It is clear that, apart from financial incentives, there are many other important factors, such as the amount of profit investors can make, the convenience of operation, the extent of government control, and so on.

Economic Activities for Foreign Investors

Concerning the list of economic activities in which foreign investment may be made, there are five remarkable points to note (see Appendix I).

Firstly, the list of economic activities for the new investment law was published on 30 May 1989, exactly six months after the promulgation of the Law. This is probably because the present government wanted to formalize the selling of fishing and logging rights to foreigners before drawing up the proper list of economic activities as Burma needs foreign currency very urgently; and probably partly because the authorities wanted to take time to make sure of the list.

Secondly, the new Law lists 85 activities under eight economic sectors, as defined in the annual reports (the *Report to the Pyithu Hluttaw*) whereas the old law consisted of 69 items under three economic sectors, namely, industrial, mining and services.

Thirdly, the new Investment Law is remarkable in the sense that all economic activities in the agricultural sector, namely, the production, processing and marketing of all crops including plantation crops are available for foreign investment. These were not included in the old law except the rice-milling industry, and the manufacturing of rubber and tobacco products. In the livestock and fishery sector, all economic activities, except the breeding and production of fish and prawns which have been reserved for research by the government, are included. However, in the old law only deep-sea fishing, the sea-food processing industry and the manufacture of dairy products were allowed. With regard to the forestry sector, all economic activities are allowed for all kinds of timber with the exception of the extraction and selling of teak which is monopolized by the state-owned economic organizations. Only the saw mills industry and furniture-making were mentioned in the old law. One more important item in the old law was petroleum and natural gas extraction which has significantly been omitted in the new law.

Fourthly, it is mentioned in the present Investment Law of 1988 that the production and marketing of basic production materials, furniture, parquet, etc., using teak extracted and sold by the state-owned economic organizations may be carried out jointly with the state-owned enterprises (SOEs).

Finally, the new Investment Law mentions neither priority items nor economic activities closed to foreign investors. For example, Thailand has stated that major public utilities and munitions manufacture are the only economic activities closed to foreign investors.

In short, as far as the list of economic activities open to foreign investors is concerned, the new Investment Law seems to be more liberal, in terms of incentives, than the former one although it needs to be clarified much further.

The Foreign Investment Commission

Like its counterparts in the region, such as the Board of Investment in Thailand, the Economic Development Board in Singapore, and the Malaysian Industrial Development Authority in Malaysia, to mention but a few, a Foreign Investment Commission has been formed by the Burmese Government mainly to review investment proposals for the purpose of issuing permits. But unlike its counterparts, it has wide discretionary powers for "the Commission may accept any proposal which in its opinion will promote the interests of the State and which is without prejudice to any existing law" (Chapter VI, paragraph 8). All applications by foreign investors have to be approved by it. It can decide on the suitability of the projects, review extensions and may also evaluate the performance of the enterprise. It will facilitate the investor entitled to invest under the Investment Law. The Commission also has the power to decide on the employment of foreign personnel. It is also stated that the Commission may at any time require an investor to furnish such evidence of facts as the Commission may deem necessary. This fact could deter some investors since it may involve the firm's confidential or secret information which it would not like to disclose. Moreover, the Commission will recommend the bank which shall transact financial matters of the investors and prescribe the insurance organization with which the enterprise shall effect insurance. This seems to indicate that the state, to some extent, will remain active in banking and insurance as in the past under the "Burmese Way to Socialism".

The enormous powers of the Commission can be understood if one looks at the formation of the Commission. According to the Procedures Relating to the Union of Burma Investment Law, the Commission consists of eleven Cabinet members, with the Minister of Planning and Finance as Chairman. The Commission has appointed the Director General of Planning as Secretary, and has provided that meetings should be held at least twice a month.

In 1959, the President had appointed the Union of Burma Investment Committee to review and approve foreign investments. This Committee had had the same function as the Foreign Investment Commission in 1988 except the power to recommend the bank to transact the financial matters of the investors and to prescribe the insurance organization with which the firm shall effect insurance. Thus, compared to the present Commission, the Union of Burma Investment Committee of 1955 did not have as much power.

Assessment

To assess the Foreign Investment Law means, among other things, to assess its "liberalness" and "attractiveness". For this purpose, Table 1 shows the summary of comparative investment incentives in Southeast Asian countries, including the Association of Southeast Asian Nations (ASEAN), the Indochinese states (excluding Kampuchea), and Burma. Investment incentives are divided into nine categories. On the whole, with the exception of protection schemes and priorities given to investors and aliens, and tax credits (direct taxation from corporate income taxes), Burma is not far behind the other neighbouring countries. In short, Burma's new investment law is fairly attractive and liberal, at least according to Burmese standards. However, the following are some shortcomings found in the new law.

1. *It seems that the Investment Law is a short-term measure to solve the shortage of foreign currency problem.* Foreign direct investment can have a longer-term beneficial impact on a country's development as it is generally directly linked to productive investment and also facilitates the transfer of technology and managerial and marketing skills, diffusion of which can have substantial effects on productivity growth.[6] Thus, foreign investment laws usually mention long-term plans, at least in terms of priority industries in which investors are encouraged to invest. But the new Law does not mention a long-term industrialization plan nor state anything about changes in the basic economic policy. Its objective of allowing exploitation of resources appears to mean the selling of rights to extract resources, such as fishery and forestry products, since the government started conducting operations in these areas with Thai, Japanese, Malaysian, Singaporean and Korean merchants soon after the Law was promulgated. Although selling fishing and logging rights is the quickest way of earning foreign currency, there is a danger of draining the country's limited resources if there is no systematic control and management.

The fact that the new Law was promulgated just ten weeks after the military take-over in September 1988, confirms that the

TABLE 1

Summary of Comparative Investment Incentives in Southeast Asian Countries

	Indonesia	*Malaysia*	*Philippines*	*Singapore*	*Thailand*	*Burma*	*Vietnam*
Basic Rights and Guarantees to Investors							
Guarantee against expropriation	×	×	×	×	×	×	×
Guarantee against losses due to:							
a) nationalization	×	×	—	×	×	×	×
b) damage caused by war	×	×	—	—	—	—	—
c) inconvertibility of currency	×	×	—	×	×	—	—
Remittance of foreign exchange earnings and payments	×	×	×	×	×	×	×
Repatriation of capital	×	×	×	×	×	×	×
Protection Schemes and Priorities Given to Investors and Aliens							
Employment of aliens	×	×	×	×	×	×[c]	×[c]
Patent protection	×	×	×	×	×	—	—
Preference in the granting of government loans	—	×	×	×	×	—	—
Protection against unjust competition:							
a) Import competition	×	×	×[a]	—	×	—	—
b) Government competition	—	—	×[a]	—	×	—	—
c) Local competition	×	—	×[a]	—	×	—	—
Real estate ownership by alien investors	—	×	—	×	×	—	—
Exemptions from Taxes and Tariff Duties							
Capital gains tax	—	×	×[a]	—	—	—	—
Corporate income tax	×	×	—	×	×	—	—
Taxes on imported capital goods	×	×	×	—	×	×	×
Taxes on imported raw materials	×	×	×	×	×	×	×
Taxes on royalties	—	×	—	×	×	—	—
Withholding tax on interest on foreign loans	—	×	—	×	×	—	—
Other taxes and fees	×	×	×	×	×	×	×
Deductions from Taxable Corporate Income							
Accelerated depreciation allowance	×	×	—	×	×	×	—
Carry forward of capital allowance during the relief period	—	×	×[a]	×	—	×	×

TABLE 1 (*cont'd*)

Summary of Comparative Investment Incentives in Southeast Asian Countries

	Indonesia	*Malaysia*	*Philippines*	*Singapore*	*Thailand*	*Burma*	*Vietnam*
Carry forward of loss	×	×	×	×	×	×	×
Export allowances/deductions	—	×	×	×	×	×	×
Deduction of organization and pre-operating expenses:							
a) Organization expenses	—	×	×	—	×	×	×
b) Pre-operating expenses	—	—	×	—	×	×	×
Reinvested profits	—	—	×	—	—	×	×
Investment allowance	×	×	—	×	—	—	—
Tax Credits (Direct Reduction from Corporate Income Taxes)							
Investment tax credits	—	×	—	×	—	—	—
Tax credit on domestic capital equipment	—	×	×	—	—	—	—
Other tax credits	—	×	×	—	×	—	—
Extension of Incentive Availment Period	—	×	—	×	—	×	×
Special Incentives							
To multinational companies	—	—	×	—	—	—	—
To exporters	—	×	×	×	×	×	×
To offshore banking units	—	×	×	×	—	—	—
Other laws granting benefits to foreign investors	—	×	×	×	—	—	—
Assistance to Investors							
Joint venture brokerage	×	×	×[a]	×	—	—	×
Technical assistance	—	×	×[b]	×	×	—	×
Processing of application and other requirements	×	×	×	×	×	×	×

[a] Applicable only to BOI-registered enterprises; other incentives are applicable to both EPZA- and other BOI-registered firms.
[b] Applicable only to Filipino investors in firms registered under B.P. 44 and in firms registered as pioneer firms under P.D. 1989.
[c] Only if necessary.

SOURCE: U Tun Wai, *Role of Foreign Capital in Southeast Asian Countries*, RND No. 68 (Institute of Southeast Asian Studies, 1989); The Union of Burma Foreign Investment Law, 1968; and Law on Foreign Investment in Vietnam, 1987.

present regime is desperate for foreign earnings and as a result, economic activities open to foreign investors were not even included at the time of promulgation. The list of economic activities open to foreign investors was released only six months after the new law was promulgated. It seems that the government promulgated the law in a hurry so that it could formalize the negotiations for the selling of the fishing and logging rights which had already been started before the new Investment Law was made public.

Thus, it would appear that the new Investment Law was meant to generate "quick returns" as the foreign currency reserve at the time of the military coup in September 1988 was only about US$57 million (that is, 8.8 per cent of its total imports in 1985), and export earnings had fallen from US$426 million in 1983/84 to US$258 million in 1987/88, according to the official *Union of Burma Review on Financial, Economic and Social Conditions for 1989/90*. The fact that foreign investment has not been integrated as part of the macro-level economic or industrialization plan shows that the Law is not meant for the long-term development of the country. *However, since the present military regime has declared time and again that they are paving the way for a democratically elected government and that they do not intend to stay in power for long, it is natural and appropriate that they promulgate such a foreign investment law meant for the short-term development of the country.*

2. *Although the Investment Law is liberal, other conditions are also important.* It is true that the incentives mentioned in the new investment law are quite attractive, although some ASEAN countries seem to have more to offer (Table 1). A list of economic activities open to foreign investors which accompanied the new law also confirms this (Appendix I). However, as mentioned earlier, fiscal incentives are not the only criteria on which the foreign investor decides to invest or not. Besides the incentives, conditions are also important. These conditions were clearly stated by Myint in the early 1970s, as follows:

> The first thing that should be emphasized is that foreign investors are less influenced by the "hand out" of tax concessions than by

> factors which affect the total business environment. They are more concerned with the reduction of bureaucratic controls and administrative inefficiency which hinders the day-to-day running of their business, and with the longer-term sense of security and freedom from political uncertainties which enable them to make long-term business decisions.[7]

Masao Fujioka, President of the Asian Development Bank, confirms this by saying:

> Developing countries frequently offer special incentives to attract foreign investors, sometimes in counterproductive competition among themselves. But it is the political and economic environment, more than incentives, that draws investors to one country rather than to another. Incentives alone cannot effectively compensate for the lack of polities that allow greater freedom to investors to make their own crucial investment and business decisions. A more open trade regime attracts investment in economically sound projects, away from those that offer artificially high financial profits behind protective walls.[8]

Take some examples. Although there are attractive fiscal incentives, the 1988 Foreign Investment Law indicates the government's intention to place tight control over foreign investment matters. Potential foreign investors will be subjected to strong control, given the fact that the Commission that has been set up to review the investment is powerful and that foreign firms as well as joint-ventures will have to work with the state banks or the state insurance company recommended by the Commission.[9] Such restrictions could lead to the misinterpretation that the government still intends to practise extensive state control and active participation in the economy as in the past twenty-six years under the "Burmese Way to Socialism". As a result, potential investors may be discouraged for there is enough evidence that foreign investments are generally more successful in the countries where the state sector is weak.[10]

The new Law also mentions that foreign currency shall be transferred at the prevailing official rate of exchange. This will definitely have an adverse effect for investors especially when the market rate of the U.S. dollar to the kyat is about seven times higher than the official exchange rate. At the official exchange rate domestic wages would have no comparative advantage against other countries in the region which export the same commodities.

Furthermore, unlike the previous law, the new Investment Law guarantees that the government would not nationalize the foreign firms as long as they are under contract. However, a guarantee not to nationalize is not enough to attract foreign investments. There are some countries which not only give such a guarantee against nationalization but also guarantee against state monopolies on the sale of similar products, and price control (for example, Thailand). Some countries even guarantee to protect foreign investments for a specified period (usually fifteen years) against war and non-commercial risks of expropriation (for example, Singapore).

3. *There seem to be ambiguities in the Investment Law.* In stating the basic principles for foreign investments, the Law uses terms such as "heavy investment", "high technology", and "large capital" which need to be defined in detail. In the case of Vietnam, for example, the term "transferred technology" is defined in Article 41 of the Decrees for the Implementation of the Law on Foreign Investment in Vietnam as follows: 1) The technology transferred to a joint venture shall be one necessary and suitable for the joint venture to produce significant socio-economic effects or to increase the competitive strength of its products in the international market. 2) The transferred technology has to meet one of the following requirements: (a) it must be capable of bringing about a considerable improvement in the appearance and quality of products and an increase in output; (b) it must be capable of creating new products which Vietnam urgently needs or of producing import substitutes; (c) its application will result in a considerable saving in terms of raw materials and energy. There are no such definitions in Burma's new Investment Law.

Then, in paragraph 3 of Chapter II, it is stated that the Commission will prescribe the economic activities allowed to foreign investors from time to time. How can foreign investment flow in if investors do not have prior knowledge of the economic activities allowed? In other words, investors will not be sure of the area of economic activities they would be allowed to invest in. This clause would have been all right had the list of industries in which foreign investments may be allowed been attached to the Law. But, as mentioned previously, only on 1 June 1989, that is, six months after the promulgation of the new Law, did the Commission announce the list of economic activities that foreigners may invest in (see Appendix I). This was probably one of the reasons why foreign investment did not rush in within the six months after the promulgation of the new Law.

The new Law also states that the enterprise is subject to other laws of the state without spelling out which laws are meant. This needs to be spelled out since investors would like to know whether extensive bureaucratic processes would be involved in investing in Burma as the bureaucratic machinery has always been overwhelmingly large and notorious for its inefficiency in the past. (Only five months or more after the new Investment Law was introduced, were booklets such as *Doing Business in Burma*, mentioning the provisions relating to a foreign firm under the Burma Companies Act, the State-Owned Economic Enterprises Law, Types of Economic Activities Allowed for Foreign Investment, Guide to Foreign Investment in Myanmar, and the "Special Company Act of 1950", published.)

The new Law also mentions tax exemption in many cases, but it does not clearly state the taxation system and regulations on taxes such as income tax, corporate tax, sales tax, tax on interest, and so on. Although a new amendment law on income and profit tax was introduced in March 1989, there are still many unanswered questions concerning tax rules.

It is the usual practice that foreign investors acquire land for the construction of factories or the planting of crops and trees or the establishment of fishery production. Unlike in Thailand, the acquisition of real estate is not provided for in the new Law. Even in the Vietnamese investment law, it is mentioned that foreign investors "shall be liable to pay rents for the use of land, water surface or sea surface in Vietnam" (Article 29).

Unlike most of the countries in the region, Burma's Investment Law does not specify priority sectors although one can guess from Chapter III that the extraction of natural resources, export industries, and high technology industries would be given priority. For example, Brunei's priorities are silica-based pharmaceuticals, cement, aluminium, steel, chemicals and equipments. On the other hand, investors can be informed on the types of foreign investments to be discouraged. For example, in Thailand, a list of foreign investments that are not welcomed is provided to investors. This clause is also to be found in Burma's old law of 1955.

4. *There seems to be a conflict between the objectives and realistic possibilities for foreign investments.* One of the objectives of the new Law is to seek high-technology investment. Does a low-income country such as Burma have the technical base to support such investments? The answer is no. Moreover, if one looks at the basic principles of investment mentioned in paragraph 4 of Chapter II of the new Law, it seems that Burma is seeking export-oriented foreign investments along with a transfer of advanced technology. This objective also cannot be achieved since firms with advanced technology very often do not have a comparative advantage that allow them to export from low-income Asian countries. How can a firm with advanced technology in Burma compete with a similar firm from Singapore, not mentioning those from the Western industrialized countries? Another reason why Burma should not seek foreign direct investment with high technology is that if many countries in the region are competing for similar types of investments, this could be counter-productive because of differences in size, per capita income level, and resource base.

What Burma should seek is investments for low-technology, export-oriented labour-intensive industries, which are no longer viable in higher-income countries such as Singapore where labour wage is high. Some multinational firms as well as local firms in Singapore are moving out of the country since Singapore does not have a competitive edge for labour-intensive industries. Although Thailand and Malaysia are enjoying this spill-over effect, they will very soon become unattractive because of rising wages in their respective countries. Naturally, Burma along with the Indochinese countries will then become the target for such industries for they have a comparative advantage in terms of wages, provided that Burma corrects the present artificial foreign exchange rate. Furthermore, the new Law states the creation of new employment opportunities as one of its objectives. How can high-technology investments create more employment opportunities than low-technology labour-intensive investments in a low-income country like Burma?

Nevertheless, although the Investment Law has some shortcomings, it is liberal and surely the first step towards the opening-up of the Burmese economy which had been isolated from the world for more than a quarter of a century. It may turn out to be a means whereby the present military regime obtains urgently needed foreign currency by allowing foreign capital and technology to come in and exploit Burma's natural resources, especially fishery and forestry.

Conclusion: Prospects

According to government press releases, many potential investors from the neighbouring countries have come in to enquire about the possibilities of investing in the country, in the months after the announcement of the Law. Apart from selling fishing and logging rights to businessmen from Thailand, Malaysia, Singapore, Japan and Korea, it is learnt that negotiations are being conducted for oil and agribusiness. It is important to note that, although the oil sector was not included in the new Investment Law, it does not mean that foreign investment would be excluded in that sector. The policy appears to allow case-by-case consideration and is evolving. The Koreans, especially the Daewoo group, are looking at various investments including the opening of a department store, while others are eyeing the area of textiles, shoe manufacturing, hotels, and marine and forest products. According to the *Working People's Daily* (1 April 1989), the Ministry of Trade issued permits to Samsung Co. Ltd. from South Korea and Mitsui & Co. Ltd. from Japan, allowing them to establish and open branch-offices in Burma. Later in June, three more companies from Japan were given similar permits. Furthermore, two departmental stores, one owned by Daewoo and the other by a Singaporean firm, SKS

Marketing Ltd., were opened in Rangoon in July 1989. It is also learnt that the first industrial joint venture has established a woodprocessing industry with a Singaporean partner (Woodwork and Construction Pte. Ltd.) to produce wooden door leaves. Australians are also interested in the building of three new hotels and one agribusiness project involving the sending of maize seeds from Thailand to Burma on credit and taking back part of the maize harvest in exchange. An Austrian company, IAEG, has also signed an agreement to build five-star hotels in Rangoon, Mandalay and Pagan. The main breakthrough came in October and November when the Burmese Government announced production-sharing contracts with a number of foreign oil companies, among them Yukong of South Korea, Idemitsu of Japan, Amoco and Unocal of the United States, Petro-Canada, Britain's Croft Exploration and Dutch Shell.[11] It is estimated that Burma received US$17 million as deposit when fishing licences were issued to eleven foreign firms and it expects to receive US$24.16 million for the whole year.[12] Contracts with nine oil companies for exploration would bring another US$45 million, which is a small amount for these oil giants, but big enough for Burma's almost empty coffer. It is estimated that Burma's foreign reserves has risen from US$64 million at the end of March to about US$150 million in December 1989, which in fact is less than half of the yearly imports. However, big deals from abroad are still lacking, probably because of uncertainties in political stability. In the meantime, the *Strait Times* (20 March 1989) reported that foreigners have invested US$246 million in Vietnam since the introduction of its foreign investment law in January 1988. This shows that Burma's new Investment Law, as a tool to mobilize foreign capital, has not been as effective as expected.

On the other hand, the Burmese Government recently established six joint ventures (Joint Venture Corporation [JVC] No. 1 to No. 6) to mobilize private investment. Under JVC 1, which is a limited company with 50 per cent equity held by private shareholders and 50 per cent by the State Trading Corporation, three joint ventures with foreign participation are being formed. The equity structures are 30 per cent for JVC 1, 40 per cent for the foreign partner and 30 per cent for the state enterprise involved in related economic activities.

It is a well known fact that Japan, the newly industrializing countries (NICs) and some neighbouring ASEAN nations are showing increased interest in investing in this part of the region. Japan, which formulated its "Look Southeast Asia" policy from the beginning of the 1980s, is not only the largest donor country to Burma, but also one of its largest traditional trade partners. Its close ties with Burma were reflected in its prompt recognition of the present regime amidst protests from the United States, the European Community and some human rights groups. It is obvious that its export-oriented, capital-intensive and technology-based investments would flow into the ASEAN nations, but the import-substitution, labour-intensive type of investments are expected to move into countries such as Burma. The NICs, especially Singapore and South Korea, have also started negotiations with Burma (Singapore sent its trade negotiation team in December 1989). Although Burma does not have diplomatic relations with Taiwan, the *Bangkok Post* (1 June 1989) reported that Taiwan is preparing to send a team of "feelers" to Burma. ASEAN manufacturers, especially small-scale enterprises, are also interested in relocating their investments in Burma to preserve their export competitiveness in the world market because of increasing domestic wages. However, others seem to be waiting to see the developments in the political situation of the country.

On the other hand, long-term trends suggest that investments from the OECD (Organization for Economic Co-operation and Development) countries are expected to flow into the region for they are facing rapidly rising domestic wages and appreciating currencies. Quotas on exports are also one of the reasons why firms in these industrialized countries are searching for production locations where labour is cheap and productive. Investments would be mainly in low-wage, labour-intensive export industries such as textiles and garments, which have been subject to quotas on exports from the home country. However, investments from the United States and the EC countries would lag unless democracy is restored to some extent in the country. These countries have suspended economic ties with the Burmese Government because of its handling of the pro-democracy demonstrations in mid-1988. The United States has further suspended Burma's tariff preference under the Generalised System of Preferences (GSP) on the ground that it had failed to protect internationally recognized workers' rights.[13] This is a severe blow to Burma since it would definitely stop potential investors who would have been willing to invest in the country if it had retained its GSP status. Even if the present military government holds elections as promised, it is expected that foreign investments will not flood in; only some small-scale investments will flow in slowly and cautiously.

In conclusion, this new Investment Law would probably fall short of its expectation in attracting much needed foreign investments unless the government creates a suitable atmosphere for foreign investments in which political stability, good infrastructural services, a climate conducive to entry and profitable operation of foreign or joint-venture enterprises are essential. Framing and implementing investment legislation with fairness and impartiality as well as transparency and consistency over time are also necessary. Foreign investors need basic assurances that legislations and their enforcement are unambiguous and predictable in protecting their investments and the profits so generated. In other words, given the present situation, this new Investment Law would not be an effective tool to mobilize foreign capital.[14]

Here, we should learn from the experiences of the 1950s. Despite the fact that the Union of Burma Investment Act of 1959 had been substantially more liberal with attractive incentives than at any time since the independence of the nation, government practices did not seem to be consistent with the provisions of the Act. Taxes continued to be burdensome, labour policies and legislation were unrealistic. Many difficulties were encountered in getting import licences for raw materials, spare parts and operating supplies. There were also many unnecessary production and distribution controls and it was hard to obtain entry and residence permits for foreign employees. The infrastructure was discouraging and investors complained that many government employees and party adherents still needed to be paid off. Other factors significant in investment decisions were as uncertain as before. In general, the climate for investment during that period remained unfavourable.[15] What was the response from foreign investors at that time? "As of January 1961, the Investment Committee had under consideration some fifteen to twenty investment proposals, almost all involving joint ventures with foreign firms, but no definitive action had yet been taken".[16]

Has the situation changed after thirty years? No, at least not in the bureaucratic machinery. There still exist large and often operationally inflexible bureaucratic structures which are generally marked by time lags in decision-making, the processing of unnecessary documentation, having to meet the procedural requirements for foreign exchange and currency control, and so on. All these, at the operational level tend to inhibit the expeditious management of foreign investment. It should also be realized that the Burmese currency, the kyat, is very much overvalued. (The current black-market rate of the U.S. dollar in Rangoon is about 60 kyats, whereas the official exchange rate is about 6.5 kyats.)

Another issue concerns immigration laws since they are very important in attracting foreign investments. Unfortunately, it is hard for potential investors to stay in Burma for more than two weeks and even harder to obtain residence permits. Only recently, tourists (with visa) have been allowed to stay for two weeks, provided they came as a group. How can Burma compete with neighbouring countries, such as Thailand and Malaysia, where exemptions from applying for visa and permission to stay up to 15 days are given to citizens of most countries except the communist countries and others without diplomatic ties? Moreover, the physical as well as institutional infrastructure would create frustrations for potential investors. All of these are serious drawbacks to the realization of a desirable flow of selected foreign investment and therefore need to be revised and even eliminated.

One of the most important issues is political stability. Holding general elections may be one of the factors to create a stable political climate. Unless the government holds free and fair general elections, as it has time and again promised, it would be difficult to persuade foreign investors, particularly those from the United

States and the EC. If these issues are resolved, Burma can expect the much needed foreign direct investment to come in.

On the other hand, the new Investment Law has one advantage over its predecessor in the sense that investors would benefit from exports from Burma to Western industrialized countries because of its least developed country status, the GSP schemes and the export quota imposed on other developing countries.

In terms of socio-cultural factors, Burma can be considered as "investor friendly". Most of its people are Buddhist with traditional respect for elders and seniors. It has a relatively high literacy rate and workers could be easily trained for skilled jobs. People are generally friendly to foreigners but they would resist open commercial exploitation of sex which, in most cases, accompanies an "investment-boom".

What, then, are the attractive areas for investments? Since Burma is very rich in natural resources with a weak manufacturing sector, resource-based industries, such as the manufacture of agricultural-based, forestry-based, and mineral-based products are quite attractive. Areas concerned with the development of infrastructure such as the construction sector, and the telecommunication sector could be attractive too. It is also well-known that Burma is producing only about one quarter of the consumer goods needed for internal consumption by its 40 million inhabitants. Hence, investments in industries producing consumer goods, such as medicines, toiletries, garments and cottage industries could be profitable for foreign investors. Moreover, with its historical and scenic sites, tourism might also be attractive. Among these sectors, the energy sector may have the most attractive potentials. This is because "aside from the unquantifiable gas reserves in the Gulf of Martaban, proven onshore reserves total two billion cubic feet. Large developed gas deposits in the southern Irrawaddy Delta also exist, and extremely large (though unquantified) crude reserves are present onshore throughout Burma. Three fields totalling 1.7 billion barrels already have been tagged, and industry analysts say this is just the tip of the iceberg. . . . The country's hydroelectric potential is equally impressive: A 1983 survey conducted by the Asian Development Bank estimated it at 100,000 MW and identified 25 suitable sites for hydroelectric dams".[17]

However, it should be noted that Burma has to compete with other countries in the region in attracting foreign investments. Therefore, investment promotion is necessary. According to Guisinger (1989), it comprises three main elements: investor-related government services; investment incentives; and investment marketing (advertising, selling, negotiating and all other facets required to convince the investors to sign). Several countries in this region, in a move to attract foreign investment, have liberalized their investment policies, expanded and modernized the existing infrastructure, and simplified procedural requirements and formalities. Some of them are aggressive in investment marketing. What Burma needs is the right mix of these three components. Furthermore, there is one important point to note: there is enough evidence that attracting foreign investment is successful mostly in the countries with a buoyant economy with bright prospects for further growth. *On the other hand, it is of utmost importance for Burma to seek foreign investments that would make economic sense and contribute to its growth and development without draining its limited resources and without disrupting its socio-economic and cultural pattern.*

In any case, as mentioned previously, this Law seems to be aimed for the short-term development of the country, that is, for the period until a new democratically elected government comes in after the general election in May 1990. It is believed that the new government would formulate a new development policy for the country and the present Investment Law would probably be a good start for the new government which can modify it by integrating it with national development policy and long-term industrialization plans and by eliminating its shortcomings.

After all, "There is no easy way to economic development, no alternative to hard work".[18]

APPENDIX I

The Union of Burma Foreign Investment Commission
Notification No 1/89

11th Waning Day of Kason, 1351 B.E.
(30th May 1989)

Subject: Types of economic activities allowed for foreign investment

The Union of Burma Foreign Investment Commission in exercise of the powers conferred under Chapter III, paragraph 5 of the Procedure Relating to the Union of Burma Foreign Investment Law, and with the approval of the Government, announces the following list of economic activities in which foreign investment may be made:

List of Economic Activities

Sr.	*No.*	*Type of Economic Activities*
1		*Agriculture*
	1	Cultivating, producing, processing and marketing of seasonal agricultural crops (including tapioca and tobacco).
	2	Establishing of plantations (including medicinal plants, coffee, tea, palm oil, horticulture, etc.) and producing, processing and marketing of their produce.
2		*Livestock and Fishery*
	1	Livestock, breeding, processing, canning and marketing of livestock and its products (including pig breeding and pork processing, etc.)
	2	Production and marketing of animal feeds, additives, supplements and veterinary medicines.
	3	Breeding, fishing, processing and marketing of fresh water and marine fish, prawns and other aquatic organisms including fish fry, fingerlings, post larvae of shrimp, but not including breeding and production of fish and prawns in fisheries which have been reserved for research by the Government.
	4	Production, processing, marketing of all kinds of fish feeds.
3		*Forestry*
	1	Production and marketing of basic construction materials, furniture, parquet, etc., using teak extracted and sold by the State-owned economic organizations. (To be carried out jointly with the State-owned economic organizations.)

APPENDIX I (*cont'd*)
List of Economic Activities

Sr.	*No.*	*Type of Economic Activities*
	2	Production and marketing of carvings and handicrafts made of teak that has been extracted and sold by State-owned economic organizations engaged in the extraction and marketing of the same.
	3	Production, processing and marketing of hardwoods (other than teak), bamboo, cane/rattan and other forest produce.
	4	Production and marketing of construction material, furniture and other products using hardwoods (other than teak), bamboo, cane/rattan and other forest produce.
4		*Mining*
	1	Exploration, exploitation, production and marketing of non-metallic industrial minerals, such as coal, limestone, gypsum, etc.
	2	Marble quarrying and production and marketing of marble blocks and slabs.
	3	Carrying out other quarrying industries and marketing of products thereof.
5		*Industry*
		(1) Foodstuff
	1	Manufacturing and marketing of bakery products including biscuits, wafers, noodles, macaroni, spaghetti, etc.
	2	Manufacturing and marketing of all kinds of confectionery including those of sweets, cocoa and chocolate.
	3	Preserving, manufacturing, canning and marketing of other food products.
	4	Processing, manufacturing and marketing of oil and fats from vegetables, animals and other substances.
	5	Manufacturing and marketing of soft beverages, aerated and non-aerated products.
	6	Manufacturing and marketing of malt and malt liquors and other brewery products.
	7	Distilling, blending, rectifying, bottling and marketing of all kinds of spirits, beverages and non-beverages.

APPENDIX I (*cont'd*)

List of Economic Activities

Sr. No.	Type of Economic Activities
	(2) Textile
1	Combing, spinning, weaving, finishing and marketing of textile materials of cotton, jute, silk, wool, synthetic fibres, mixed fibres and other fibres of all kinds.
2	Manufacturing and marketing of made-up apparel of all kinds including knitwear.
3	Manufacturing and marketing of made-up apparel materials of all kinds including towels, linens of all kinds, rug and carpets.
4	Manufacturing and marketing of cordage, rope and twine of all kinds.
	(3) Personal Goods
1	Manufacturing and marketing of soap of all kinds, dentifrices, cosmetics, perfume and toilet preparations.
2	Manufacturing and marketing of all kinds of personal goods not elsewhere specified, including umbrella, safety matches, etc.
	(4) Household goods
1	Manufacturing and marketing of household goods such as textiles, glass, plastic, melamine, metal products, ceramic and earthenware.
2	Manufacturing and marketing of non-electrical household goods such as enamel-ware, cutlery, crockery of all kinds.
3	Manufacturing and marketing of electrical household goods and appliances such as refrigerators, air-conditioners, hot plates, irons, cookers, fans and other home use appliances.
4	Manufacturing and marketing of radios, transistors, television receivers, videos, etc.
5	Manufacturing and marketing of electrical fittings and fixtures, electric lamps, bulbs and tubes, etc.
	(5) Leather Products and the Likes
1	Processing of hides, skins and leathers of all kinds, excluding synthetic leather, and manufacturing and marketing thereof, including footwear, handbags, etc.

APPENDIX I (*cont'd*)

List of Economic Activities

Sr. No.		*Type of Economic Activities*
2		Processing of synthetic and artificial leather and manufacturing and marketing thereof, including footwear, handbags, etc.
3		Processing and marketing of furs and skins not elsewhere specified.
	(6)	Transport Equipment
1		Manufacturing and marketing of bicycles, tricycles, and other cycles of all kinds, component parts and accessories.
2		Manufacturing and marketing of scooters, motor cycles, mopeds, etc., component parts and accessories.
3		Manufacturing and marketing of motor cars, buses, trucks, vans, wagons, component parts and accessories.
4		Manufacturing and marketing of tractors of all kinds, ambulances, fire engines, dump trucks, bowsers and other occupational motor vehicles, component parts and accessories.
5		Manufacturing and marketing of tyres, tubes and flaps for all kinds of vehicles and other purposes.
	(7)	Building Materials
1		Manufacturing and marketing of bricks, tiles, floor tiles and wall tiles, refractory bricks, etc.
2		Manufacturing and marketing of asbestos building materials of all kinds.
3		Manufacturing and marketing of cement of all kinds, cement products, lime, plaster and related manufactures.
4		Manufacturing and marketing of pre-stressed concrete pipe, plant and other concrete products.
5		Manufacturing and marketing of all kinds of glass and glass products.
	(8)	Pulp and Paper
1		Manufacturing and marketing of pulp of all kinds, paper and paper board of all kinds including newsprint.
2		Manufacturing and marketing of paper, paper board including carbon paper, waxed paper, toilet paper, etc.

APPENDIX I (*cont'd*)
List of Economic Activities

Sr. No.	*Type of Economic Activities*
	(9) Chemicals, Chemical Products and Pharmaceuticals
1	Manufacturing and marketing of basic chemicals, organic and inorganic, including caustic soda, chlorine, stearic acid, etc.
2	Manufacturing and marketing of all kinds of light chemicals, not elsewhere specified.
3	Manufacturing and marketing of all kinds of plastic wares.
4	Manufacturing and marketing of chemical products, such as paint, varnishes, dyes, thinner and lacquers, etc.
5	Manufacturing and marketing of industrial chemical gases including compressed, liquified and solid forms.
6	Manufacturing and marketing of ice in all forms.
7	Manufacturing and marketing of medicine, pharmaceuticals and drugs, etc.
8	Manufacturing and marketing of insecticides, pesticides, etc.
9	Manufacturing and marketing of rubber products.
10	Recycling of chemicals, plastic wastes and others, and marketing.
	(10) Iron and Steel
1	Manufacturing and marketing of iron and steel products, using iron and steel purchased from State-owned economic organizations or from abroad.
2	Manufacturing and marketing of basic iron and steel products using iron and steel purchased from State-owned economic organizations or from abroad.
3	Manufacturing and marketing of basic non-ferrous metal products of all kinds using metal purchased from State-owned economic organizations or from abroad.
4	Manufacturing and marketing of pre-fabricated and structural products of all kinds including construction and building parts.
	(11) Machinery and Plant
1	Manufacturing and marketing of all kinds of agricultural machinery and agricultural equipment.

APPENDIX I (*cont'd*)

List of Economic Activities

Sr. No.	*Type of Economic Activities*
2	Manufacturing and marketing of all kinds of machinery and equipment used for extraction of timber.
3	Manufacturing and marketing of all kinds of mining machinery and equipment.
4	Manufacturing and marketing of all kinds of machinery and equipment for other industrial purposes including wood-based industries.
5	Manufacturing and marketing of scientific, medical, surgical, optical and all other professional machinery, equipment and accessories.
6	Manufacturing and marketing of all kinds of machinery and equipment and accessories required for the production and distribution of electricity including cable, switches, transformer, generator, battery, etc.
7	Manufacturing and marketing of machinery, equipment and accessories required for all kinds of telecommunication including wireless sets, telephone, etc., and marketing under the permission of the Government.
8	Manufacturing and marketing of pumps of all kinds.
9	Manufacturing and marketing of all kinds of machinery and equipment not elsewhere specified, including piston, piston rings, injection pump and nozzles, casting parts, forging parts, pressure vessels, etc.
10	Manufacture of small plants.
11	Manufacturing and marketing of all kinds of machine tools.
12	Manufacturing and marketing of all kinds of cables, ropes, twine, chain and similar products.
13	Manufacturing and marketing of cinematographic and photographic films, cassette and video tapes and related electronic and electrical products.
14	Manufacturing and marketing of clocks and watches of all kinds.
15	Manufacturing and marketing of fountain pens, ball pens, pencils, and similar writing gears.

APPENDIX I (*cont'd*)
List of Economic Activities

Sr.	No.	*Type of Economic Activities*
	16	Manufacturing and marketing of all kinds of toys, mechanical and non-mechanical.
	17	Manufacturing and marketing of machinery and equipment not elsewhere specified.
6		*Construction*
	1	Construction enterprises undertaking domestic and overseas construction works.
	2	Installation of machinery, plants and equipment and provision of trial and test-run services.
7		*Transport and Communications*
	1	Road transport and vehicles repair services.
	2	Inland water transport services.
	3	Dockyard services.
	4	Shipping agency services.
8		*Trade*
	1	Hotels and Tourist Industries.
9		*Economic activities to which the State-owned Economic Enterprises Law applies*
	1	Economic activities mentioned in section 3 of the State-owned Economic Enterprises Law, provided permission has been obtained under section 4 of the said Law.

NOTE: If proposals for economic activities not specified in the above mentioned list are submitted, they will be considered individually by the Union of Burma Foreign Investment Commission.

By Order,

(Khine Khine)
Secretary
The Union of Burma
Foreign Investment Commission

NOTES

1. Walinsky (1962), p. 502.
2. Asian Development Bank (1987), p. 23.
3. Ibid., p. 24.
4. Executive Vice-President, International Finance Corporation.
5. Asian Development Bank (1987), p. 11.
6. International Monetary Fund (1987), p. 2.
7. Myint (1971), p. 101.
8. Opening address made to a Symposium on Foreign Direct Investment in the Asian and Pacific Region, organized by the ADB and the International Finance Corporation, Manila, 25–27 January 1988.
9. Ten months after the new Foreign Investment Law was made public, Minister of Finance Colonel Abel stated that the bank law was being revised to permit foreign banking business. This could have been the result of the meetings between the Myanmar Foreign Bank and officials from the Thai Bankers' Association (*Business Post*, 25 May 1989) and with the Hong Kong and Shanghai Bank (Economic Intelligence Unit Country Report No. 2, 1989).
10. Singapore is an exceptional case, but it should be noted that the government's intervention is usually through the market.
11. *Far Eastern Economic Review*, 14 December 1989.
12. *Working People's Daily*, 17 June 1989.
13. *Straits Times*, 24 April 1989.
14. The present level of the foreign component of gross capital formation is insignificant, comprising about 4 per cent of GDP whereas that of gross capital formation in 1980/81 was about 20 per cent.
15. Walinsky (1962), p. 503.
16. Ibid., p. 351.
17. *Business Asia*, 30 October 1989, p. 356.
18. Aye Hlaing (1961).

REFERENCES

Asian Development Bank (ADB). *Foreign Direct Investment in the Asian and Pacific Region*. Manila: Asian Development Bank, May 1987.

Asian and Pacific Development Centre (APDC). *Business and Investment Environment in ASEAN-South Pacific: An Overview*. 7 Vols. Kuala Lumpur & Suva: Asian and Pacific Development Centre & South Pacific Bureau for Economic Co-operation, 1987.

Aye Hlaing. "Observations on some Patterns of Economic Development". *Burma Research Society Fiftieth Anniversary Publications No. 1*, pp. 9–25. Rangoon: Burma Research Society, 1961.

Chamber of Commerce and Industry. *Thailand: Guide to Business and Investment,* Paris, 1989.

Guisinger, S. "Promoting Investment: Technical Assistance". Paper presented at the Workshop on ASEAN-U.S. Relations (Phase III), "Private Enterprise as a Means of Development Cooperation", Singapore, 1989.

International Monetary Fund (IMF). *Foreign Private Investment in Developing Countries.* Washington: International Monetary Fund, January 1987.

Myint, H. *Southeast Asia's Economy: Development Policies in the 1970s.* New York: Praeger Publishers, 1971.

Socialist Republic of Vietnam (SRV). *Law on Foreign Investment in Vietnam.* Government of the Socialist Republic of Vietnam, December 1987.

U Tun Wai. *Role of Foreign Capital in Southeast Asian Countries.* Singapore: Institute of Southeast Asian Studies, 1989.

United Nations. *Mobilization of Domestic and External Finance for Development.* New York: United Nations Department of Technical Co-operation for Development, 1987.

Union of Myanmar. *The Union of Burma Foreign Investment Law.* Yangon, November 1988.

______. *Procedures Relating to the Union of Burma Foreign Investment Law.* Yangon, December 1988.

______. *Types of Economic Activities Allowed for Foreign Investment.* Foreign Investment Commission, May 1989.

Walinsky, L.J. *Economic Development in Burma 1951–1960.* New York: Twentieth Century Fund, 1962.

8

BURMA AND ASIA-PACIFIC DYNAMISM
Problems and Prospects of Export-Orientated Growth in the 1990s

RICHARD W.A. VOKES

> *The changes effected in economic policy have now reached the right path and all are expected to work in unity with patriotic spirit. By working thus, the country, which is rich in natural resources, could become an economically developed nation within 5–10 years.*
>
> — D. Abel*

> *the Pacific Rim is where the future lies*
>
> *— Financial Times Survey, The Pacific Rim***

Introduction

The economic crisis that struck Burma in the 1980s has been the most serious since the country achieved independence in 1948. As the decade of the 1980s draws to a close, the economy, like the country as a whole, stands at the crossroads, with a process of radical economic reform already under way and the promise of major political reform, in the shape of multi-party elections scheduled for May 1990. Although overshadowed by subsequent popular unrest and demonstrations in support of democracy, the package of economic reforms agreed at the Emergency Congress of the then governing Burma Socialist Programme Party (BSPP) in July 1988, to which the current military regime remains, at least on paper, committed, represents the complete abandonment of the economic strategy embodied in the "Burmese Way to Socialism". Introduced shortly after General Ne Win's coup in 1962, the key features of the Burmese Way to Socialism were the adoption of an inward-looking economic strategy aimed at eliminating foreign control of the economy, reducing the country's dependence on foreign markets and at restructuring the economy away from its dependence on primary production towards a more balanced industrial state. The state, rather than the private market, was to play the leading role in the process of economic restructuring and development.

That the Burmese Way to Socialism has been an almost complete failure is now widely accepted. In 1987, the year which ironically marked its twenty-fifth "anniversary", the BSPP government was forced to seek least developed country status from the United Nations in the hope of obtaining relief on the country's growing external debt service payments as well as access to increased concessional external aid to help tackle the country's acute economic crisis, caused primarily by a collapse in foreign exchange earnings from its two principal primary commodity exports, timber and rice. Burma's economic decline to near bankruptcy is in marked contrast to the economic performance of the more capitalist and market-orientated open economies of East and Southeast Asia. While the growth of the Asian newly industrializing economies (NIEs) can be attributed, at least in part, to exceptional geopolitical circumstances, Burma's performance is particularly telling when set against the rapid growth and economic transformation achieved since the early 1960s by its neighbours, Thailand and the other members of the Association of Southeast Asian Nations (ASEAN), countries with which Burma shares a similar resource base and pattern of historical economic change prior to independence. Indeed, while the government's growing acceptance of the failure of the Burmese Way to Socialism, coupled with growing pressure from donors such as Japan for major economic reforms to reverse the country's decline, were major factors behind the introduction of the current reform programme, the adoption of a more outward-looking, market-orientated strategy linked to the liberalization of both domestic and foreign private sector participation, can be seen as an attempt to emulate the economic success of the NIEs and ASEAN.

At the same time, the very growth of the NIEs and ASEAN, the changing pattern of trade and industrialization that has accompanied this process, and its links with the rise of Japan as a major economic power, present Burma with a fundamentally different external environment in which to pursue an outward-looking, export-orientated strategy, one that offers both new opportunities and new challenges, given its location on the periphery of the increasingly important Asia-Pacific Rim. The principal objective of this chapter is, therefore, to assess the prospects for Burma's economic development in the 1990s following the adoption of a more outward-looking strategy, with particular reference to the country's links, both existing and potential, with the more dynamic economies of the region. Before doing this it is necessary to examine the background to the rise of the Asia-Pacific Rim and the pattern of industrialization and trade that has emerged.

Asia-Pacific Dynamism and Changing Patterns of Industrialization and Trade

The rapid rate of growth in East and Southeast Asia over the last three decades has not only been in marked contrast to the performance of Burma, but it has also surpassed that of any other region of the world, developed or developing. While the process started with the post-war recovery and subsequent growth of Japan, which remains the region's key economic dynamo, the growth rate of the Asian NIEs — Korea, Taiwan, Hong Kong and Singapore — has surpassed even that of Japan, while other members of ASEAN[1] — Indonesia, Malaysia, the Philippines and Thailand — have, for most of this period, attained growth rates that would place them near the top of any league table of growth among developing countries. Thus, in the period 1968–73, before the downturn caused by the first oil price shock of 1973–74, Japan's gross domestic product (GDP) grew at an average annual rate of 9.8 per cent, while in the same period, growth rates in the NIEs ranged from 8 to 13 per cent and for the four ASEAN countries from 5.5 to 8.0 per cent.[2]

While Japan's growth did slow down substantially following the 1973–74 oil price rise and its adverse impact on the world economy, it still consistently outperformed other industrialized countries, achieving an average growth rate of 4.3 per cent in the period 1974–84. The NIEs and ASEAN have done better than Japan since the early 1970s. In spite of the oil price shock, the NIEs and ASEAN attained average annual growth rates in GDP of between 7 and 9 per cent and 5 and 7 per cent respectively during this period.[3] Thus, the NIEs more than doubled their GDP during the decade of the 1970s, while the four ASEAN countries almost doubled their GDP over the same period, leading to significant increases in per capita incomes.[4]

Although growth rates have been less stable in the 1980s, Japan, the NIEs and the ASEAN countries, with the exception of the Philippines, have still attained growth rates that are well above average. Japan's growth rate in the period 1980–86 was the highest for the industrialized market economies, at almost 4 per cent.[5] For the period 1983–87, the average growth rate of the Asian NIEs ranged from 5.1 per cent in Singapore to 10.2 per cent in Taiwan, while for Indonesia, Malaysia and Thailand, the equivalent rates were 3.4 per cent, 3.9 per cent and 5.9 per cent respectively.[6]

As a result of this rapid growth, the share of East and Southeast Asia in world gross national product (GNP) rose from 10 to 15 per cent between 1962 and 1981[7] and has continued to grow since then. Equally significant has been the increasing shift in the economic focus of the United States towards Asia and the Pacific. In the decade up to 1985, U.S. trade with East and Southeast Asia grew almost fivefold to US$200 billion and, since 1978, the value of its trade across the Pacific has exceeded that across the Atlantic,[8] an indication of the key role played by U.S. transnational corporations (TNCs) and the U.S. market in Asia's recent growth. The highest growth sectors in the U.S. economy, including electronics, are increasingly concentrated on its West Coast, with production and trade links with Asia's fast growing economies. Similar shifts in the pattern of trade and production are visible in Canada, and this, coupled with Australia's rapidly expanding economic and trade links with Asia, has led to the growing focus on the Asia-Pacific region as an economic powerhouse.[9] Between 1962 and 1982 the share of the Asia-Pacific economies in World GNP rose from 41 per cent to 45 per cent despite the relative decline in the importance of North America and Australia in the world economy.[10] Between 1979 and 1985, the Asia-Pacific countries accounted for more than half of the world's economic growth[11] and, with the economies of East and Southeast Asia estimated to have a combined GNP larger than that of Western Europe and as large as that of North America by 1990[12] this region, with more than half the world's population and a substantial resource base, can be expected to continue to increase in importance.

Many factors, both economic and non-economic, have contributed to the successful growth performance of the East and Southeast Asian economies.[13] While there is still much debate over which factors have been most important, it is widely accepted that a key factor contributing to their growth has been the rapid increase in exports, especially of manufactures. In the period 1969–79, for example, Japan, the NIEs and the ASEAN countries all had annual average growth rates in exports close to or above 20 per cent.[14] The choice of an export-orientated industrialization strategy by Japan and the NIEs from the 1960s onwards was largely conditioned by their particular circumstances. Although Japan, and both Korea and Taiwan, did pass through an earlier phase of import-substitution development, helping to provide the foundation for their move into export-orientated industrialization, these three countries are, like Hong Kong and Singapore, relatively resource poor, while only Japan had a substantial domestic market at that time. The export of industrial goods was therefore essential to generate the foreign exchange required to purchase the capital goods and raw materials necessary to sustain the industrialization process. In the case of the Asian NIEs, the success of their export-orientated industrialization strategy can be gauged from the fact that by 1980 these four countries accounted for 50 per cent of all the manufactured exports of developing countries, and as much as 60 per cent of developing country exports to industrialized countries[15] while their overall share of world trade increased from 4 per cent in 1975 to 11 per cent in 1987.[16]

In the case of the four relatively resource rich ASEAN economies, whose economic development through the colonial period had, like that of Burma, been based mainly on the exploitation of natural resources and primary products for export, much of their export growth since the 1960s has been accounted for by an expansion in an increasingly diversified range of such exports. This growth in primary exports has been linked to the rapidly growing demand for such commodities (including oil and gas) in Japan and the NIEs as their industrial development proceeded. This link has been reinforced by extensive investment, especially by Japan, in ASEAN's resource based industries. In ASEAN's case, foreign exchange earnings from natural resource and primary exports were used to build up and sustain their industrial sectors. While high growth rates were achieved, especially within manufacturing, industry remained biased towards import-substitution in spite of small domestic markets, because of the high protection offered. Even so, the growth of manufactured exports has been increasingly important to ASEAN. Between 1969 and 1979 the share of industrial exports in total exports grew significantly in all but Indonesia,[17] where the growth in industrial exports was dwarfed by the more rapid growth in first timber and then oil exports. In the 1980s, however, the export of manufactures has become increasingly important to all of the ASEAN countries, reflecting the much greater priority now being given to export-orientated industrialization.

Sound macro-economic policies, including, in particular, appropriate fiscal, monetary and exchange rate policies have been vital to the success of the export-orientated development strategy.[18]

However, rapid growth in the manufactured exports of the NIEs and ASEAN has coincided with, and been closely linked to, the growing importance of TNCs as production, particularly within the manufacturing sector, has become increasingly global in nature. In the face of rising labour costs which undermined their international competitiveness, and technological developments which allowed production processes to be broken down into sub-units of varying factor intensities, whole industries or parts of industries were gradually moved offshore from the 1960s onwards by companies in the United States and subsequently Europe and Japan. This industrial restructuring was facilitated either by direct investment in subsidiaries overseas by TNCs, often in the form of joint ventures, or through licensing agreements covering technology transfer and access to export markets.[19] The subsequent rapid industrialization in at least some parts of the developing world has led to what is termed a "New International Division of Labour" (NIDL). The Asian NIEs and the ASEAN countries have been among the major "beneficiaries" of this process of restructuring,[20] and what is significant in the context of this chapter, is the way the NIDL has been mirrored within East and Southeast Asia.

In the case of Japan, the development of new industries is said to have followed a typical "Catching-Up Product Cycle" pattern whereby imports of a product give way in time to import-substitution production, aimed at replacing imports and meeting growing domestic demand, and finally to production for export. Final goods industries are the first to develop, followed by the growth of intermediate and capital goods industries in response to rising domestic demand as industrialization proceeds.[21] As this process occurs, so a country's comparative advantage shifts from more simple labour-intensive products to more high value, sophisticated, capital- and technology-intensive products. Thus, as Japan's industrialization progressed, so the production of more-labour intensive products was shifted offshore, particularly to the NIEs, to which Japan then supplied intermediate and capital goods.

Although the pattern of development for the NIEs has been somewhat different because of their greater reliance on TNCs and export-led growth, they too have sought to move up the technological ladder into capital and technology-intensive products, both in response to increased competition from other low-cost production bases, such as the ASEAN countries, and the desire of their governments to broaden and deepen their industrial base so as to maintain long-term growth potential.[22] As a result, investment in these countries has been increasingly directed into the capital goods and high-technology sectors, with investment, including investment by the Japanese and the NIEs themselves, in more labour- intensive assembly type industries increasingly being concentrated in the ASEAN countries. Assuming this so-called multi-tier catching-up process continues, the ASEAN countries should start to lose their comparative advantage in labour-intensive products and will have to intensify their, as yet limited, efforts to shift into higher value capital and technology-based industries,[23] providing opportunities for lower-income developing countries, such as Burma and Vietnam, to move into or expand the production of labour-intensive goods for export.

However, the ability of other countries to emulate this pattern of development, and even for the ASEAN countries to maintain their current high rates of growth, depends crucially upon the continued viability of the export-orientated industrialization strategy, and this is increasingly being questioned in the light of both growing protectionism in the industrialized countries (prompted to a considerable extent by the very success of Japan and the NIEs) and the growing pressure on the United States to reduce its trade deficit. The latter may be viewed as particularly serious in this respect, since the United States has been the principal export market for Japan and the NIEs, and its willingness to run up large trade deficits with these countries, while having its access to their domestic markets restricted, has been vital to their export success.[24] Given slower growth in world trade, some economists have already argued that there is a need to move away from export-orientated industrialization towards a more balanced strategy based on growth in domestic markets.[25]

Since the slower growth in world trade is likely to continue into the 1990s, there clearly are dangers for countries such as

Burma seeking to rely heavily on an export-led strategy. However, in contrast to the bleaker global trade environment, the prospects for trade and export growth within the Asia-Pacific region are more positive. This is mainly due to the fact that, as a result of the rapid growth and changing patterns of industrialization and trade over the last three decades, the region has begun to develop its own internal growth potential, resulting in a reduction in dependence on the performance of other industrialized countries.[26] Japan is very much at the centre of this process. It is already the most important source of imports for all of the Asian NIEs and for the ASEAN countries, with the exception of the Philippines.[27] More importantly, it is becoming an increasingly important market for their exports as domestic demand begins to take over from exports as the prime engine of growth.[28] Japan is currently the second most important export market for Taiwan, Korea and Singapore and the third most important for Hong Kong,[29] and exports of the NIEs to Japan are growing rapidly, with exports to Japan for all four countries up by 40 per cent or more in 1987.[30]

In the case of the ASEAN countries, Japan is already the most important export market, with the single exception of the Philippines, where it comes second to the United States.[31] There has also been a rapid growth of trade between the NIEs and ASEAN as well as growing trade among the two groupings themselves. At least in the case of ASEAN, the pattern of trade with Japan and the NIEs is still of a largely vertical nature, consisting of exports of primary commodities and raw materials in exchange for manufactures and capital goods. The volume of such exports is likely to continue to grow in line with continued economic growth in Japan and the NIEs, and there has been much new investment in ASEAN's resource and energy sectors by these countries. However, as the process of industrialization within ASEAN continues, so the scope for an expansion in more horizontal trade in manufactures is increased. This is especially so in view of the new wave of offshore investment by TNCs from Japan and the NIEs, much of it in ASEAN.

The current upsurge in such investment is partly a response

to rising protectionism levelled against Japanese and NIE exports, but also reflects the impact of currency appreciation and rising wages and labour shortages within the manufacturing sectors of these countries. Significantly too, much of the production from new offshore units is aimed not only at the world market but also at the countries' own domestic markets. Pressure from the United States and Europe, as well as other developing countries, including those in ASEAN, for further liberalization of access to domestic markets, plus growing pressure for further currency appreciation, especially of the Korean and Taiwanese currencies, can be expected to further increase the level of offshore investment over the next few years. Finally, the opening up of the region's socialist economies, notably China, Vietnam, Laos and Burma, can itself be expected to contribute to the growth in regional trade, even if the pace of economic liberalization in China will be slower in the aftermath of its recent political upheavals. Fear of Japanese economic domination and conflicts over technology transfer are among a number of issues that could undermine the present pattern of growth and development in the region, but given the existing efforts to improve economic co-operation within the Asia-Pacific region and Japan's sensitivity to its dominant position, these are unlikely to affect seriously the region's development.[32]

Burma's Path to Development and its Links with Asia's Dynamic Economies

Since the economic policies adopted by the Burmese Government in 1962 were essentially designed to sever the country's links with the world economy in preference for an inward-looking strategy emphasizing self-sufficiency and self-reliance, the country has been largely by-passed by the rapid growth and industrial and trade restructuring within the Asia-Pacific region. Burma has not, however, been entirely isolated from these events. Ironically, this has reflected the fact that Burma's development since 1962 has been consistently undermined by the weakness of the country's trade sector and the resultant acute shortage in foreign exchange. As a result, even before the present crisis, the government had been forced to make compromises in its original quest for autarchy.

In the years immediately following the 1962 coup, priority was given to the development of an import-substitution industrial base and to the provision of social services. At the same time, the country's three major production sectors, agriculture, forestry and mining (all important as the traditional source of exports) were neglected. Exports of rice, the country's major export at the time of the 1962 coup, fell from 1.68 million tons in 1961/62 to only 0.85 million tons in 1970/71.[33] Coupled with the decline in the production and export of other primary products, which together with rice accounted for more than 80 per cent of export earnings in 1970, the country soon faced an acute shortage of foreign exchange. This situation was aggravated still further by the poor performance (in spite of the priority it received in terms of investment) of the industrial sector. With the production of consumer goods in particular falling far short of demand, a black market linked to illegal imports from Thailand and China developed.

The country's economic problems in this period forced a major reassessment of economic policy. In September 1972, the central committee of the BSPP approved a new policy document entitled "Long-Term and Short-Term Economic Policies of the Burma Socialist Programme Party", which marked a significant retreat from the original ideals of the Burmese Way to Socialism. In addition to a relaxation of restrictions on private sector activities, the new policy, significantly, gave priority to the production and export of primary products. Equally significant was the government's recognition that the country's economic isolation had contributed to the poor performance of the economy by limiting access to both capital and technology.[34] However, with the government still unwilling to allow direct foreign investment (in its efforts to minimize foreign control) emphasis was given to raising the level of foreign aid.[35]

The BSPP government was initially very successful in boosting the level of such aid. During the first decade of military rule, foreign aid to Burma was limited to very small amounts provided largely by China and Japan, the latter remaining important because of war-time reparations. The level of foreign assistance, which totalled only US$21.7 million in 1970/71, reached US$460 million by 1977/78 and US$505 million in 1980/81. Although an increase in aid from multilateral donors has been important, the majority of the increased aid has come from bilateral donors, particularly Japan and West Germany.[36] The level of Japanese aid has, however, dwarfed that of all other donors. Apart from being able to build on its existing links with the Burmese Government, the rapid growth in Japanese aid was intended not only as part of its long-term strategy to secure export markets for its industry, but also to secure more assured access to the raw materials needed to sustain that industry.

The increased supply of foreign aid after 1972 enabled the Burmese Government to boost the level of development expenditure and imports of capital goods and industrial raw materials. This did lead to a marked improvement in the economy's performance. Since most of the bilateral aid was in the form of tied project aid or programme loans to fund imports, it also affected the country's trade patterns. Thus, Japan, already the principal source of the country's imports prior to the 1972 reforms, has become increasingly dominant in the country's import trade. In the period 1980–86, 34 per cent of Burma's imports came from Japan, an increase from around 25 per cent prior to the reforms.[37] There was also a sharp increase in Burma's exports to Japan after 1972. Between 1973 and 1979 Japan became the country's principal export market, although since 1980 it has been pushed into second place by Singapore. Nonetheless, the close trade and aid links between Burma and Japan can be expected to provide the foundation for an expansion in economic ties, including increased Japanese investment, as the country opens up. There has also been a marked increase in Burma's imports from West Germany, the second most import source of bilateral aid, especially since 1977. In the period 1980–86, West Germany accounted for 11 per cent of Burma's imports, an increase from around 7.8 per cent in 1972–73, making West Germany the second most important source of imports in this period.[38] While Burma's exports to West Germany have also risen, they have increased less rapidly than exports to Japan and other Asian countries.

Within Asia, traditionally the most important destination for Burma's exports, apart from the increase in exports to Japan, there has also been a marked increase in exports to the NIEs and ASEAN. As noted earlier, since 1980, Singapore has been the country's major export market, while exports to Hong Kong, the country's third most important market, also increased significantly in the early 1980s. In the case of the ASEAN countries other than Singapore, exports to both Malaysia and Thailand have shown a strong upward trend, these two being the country's next most important export markets in the 1980s after China. Trade with Indonesia, a major export market between 1974 and 1984, fell dramatically after that date in response to the cut-back in Indonesia's rice imports as it achieved self-sufficiency.[39] Burma's exports to ASEAN grew by an average of 11 per cent per annum between 1974 and 1985, above the overall rate of export growth, with ASEAN absorbing an average of some 25 per cent of Burma's exports during the 1980s.[40] Overall, Asia, including Japan, absorbed almost 50 per cent of Burma's exports in the period 1984–86.[41]

In the case of Burma's imports, the dominance of Japan means that, in spite of the pre-eminence of the industrialized countries as a source of imports, those imports from Asia account for at least 60 per cent of the country's total imports. Even excluding Japan, the share of imports coming from Asia has increased in the period since the reforms, from 18 per cent in 1970–72 to 25 per cent in 1984–86.[42] Again, much of this has been accounted for by increased imports from the NIEs and ASEAN, although there has also been a marked increase in the level of imports from China. On the import side, Singapore is once again the major trading partner among the NIEs, and the second most important partner overall after Japan. However, the level of imports from Korea has risen significantly since 1975, so much so that Korea is now the country's fourth most important source of imports after West Germany.[43] It is worth noting that the increase in Burma's imports from Korea in the 1980s has also been related to increased aid to Burma from Korea.

Among the other ASEAN countries, Thailand and Malaysia

are again the most important, although imports from Indonesia also increased in the 1980s. Burma's imports from ASEAN (including Singapore) grew by an average 8 per cent per annum between 1974 and 1985. Even so, ASEAN's share of Burma's imports for the period 1981–85 was only about 12 per cent, although it is worth noting that, while these imports still consist mainly of primary commodities, there has been a marked increase in imports of industrial goods from the ASEAN countries as their own industrialization progressed.[44] In practice, imports from ASEAN are much more important than the above data suggest in view of Burma's very substantial and largely unrecorded non-legal trade. While China has become the main source of non-legal imports supplying the country's black market, Thailand remains the second most important source of smuggled goods, while traders from Singapore and Malaysia are also active in the trade. Although consumer goods form the major part of non-legal imports, intermediate and capital goods, such as machinery, spare parts and chemicals, are also imported in exchange for timber, jade, gems, precious metals, rice, rubber, livestock, opium and heroin.[45]

With the exception of illegal drugs, there is very little difference between the items making up Burma's legal and illegal trade, and while the relative importance of different items does vary, the basic structure of legal and non-legal trade is the same. This reveals that Burma continues to depend upon a vertical trade structure in which it exports low value primary commodities in exchange for imports of high value capital goods, industrial raw materials and manufactures from the industrialized countries, leaving it in a relatively weak position given the long-term downward trend in the terms of trade between primary commodities and industrial goods. While there has been some change and diversification in Burma's import and export markets since 1972, there has been no significant diversification in the country's export base. This partly reflects the renewed emphasis the government was forced to give to traditional exports after 1972, but it also reflects the fact that much of the new investment made possible through external assistance was still directed to the country's inefficient state-owned, import-dependent, import-substitution industrial sector, rather than into sectors such as agriculture and resource-based industries in which the country had or could develop a comparative advantage.[46] As a result, there has been little growth in manufactured exports. In 1987, such exports, which included simple processing of primary commodities, accounted for only 6 per cent of the country's exports.[47] Even more seriously, there has been no significant diversification in the primary export sector itself. This has left Burma with an extremely narrow export base, dominated by rice and timber, which together continue to account for more than 70 per cent of the country's export earnings,[48] leaving the country dangerously vulnerable to fluctuations in world demand and prices.[49]

This danger was realized after 1982. Burmese Government figures show that prices for rice, teak, hardwoods and minerals (which account for a further 8 per cent of Burma's exports) fell by more than 30 per cent between 1981/82 and 1986/87[50] while the country's overall terms of trade fell by 41 per cent in the period[51] adding to the country's already serious trade and current account deficits. Coupled with the rapid growth in the country's external debt, resulting from increased foreign assistance (and, in particular, the country's reliance on aid rather than foreign investment as a source of external capital), Burma was plunged into a debt and balance of payments crisis from which it has yet to recover.[52] With official imports consisting mainly of essential production and capital goods, attempts to tackle the crisis by cutbacks in imports only further aggravated the economy's decline, finally forcing the government ignominously to seek least developed country status and then to introduce the new economic reform programme in the hope that a more outward-looking strategy supported by foreign investment could provide the basis for Burma's economic recovery and future development.

Problems and Prospects of Export-Orientated Growth in Burma in the 1990s

Burma's current economic reform programme goes much further than that of 1972 and follows on the heels of earlier decisions to end the government's long-standing monopoly on first the internal rice trade (in September 1987) and then rice exports (in February 1988). Under the new package of reforms, private sector participation is now allowed in all but a few key sectors, notably communications, energy, teak forestry, precious stones, pearls, and banking. Even more striking, in view of the Burmese Government's earlier hostility towards foreign investment, is the new open-door policy on such investments. A new Foreign Investment Law was passed in November 1988 and, significantly, joint-venture foreign investment will be allowed even in those sectors from which the domestic private sector is excluded.[53] In seeking to encourage foreign investment, it is clear that priority is to be given to the promotion of exports.

Although the new package of reforms is indeed radical by Burmese standards, it does not, as yet, provide all of the ingredients necessary for economic recovery and export-oriented growth. It is clear from the experience of the NIEs and ASEAN that an outward looking strategy is a necessary, but not sufficient, condition for the success of an export-oriented strategy. Other factors, including appropriate fiscal, monetary and exchange rate policies, are also necessary. As yet, there have been no major shifts in these key aspects of macro-economic policy. Burma's hopelessly overvalued exchange rate is a key problem in this respect, since, in the absence of a major devaluation, the potential for free market exports will remain extremely limited.[54] The overvalued exchange rate has already caused the failure of the policy designed to liberalize rice exports, since rice exports were unprofitable at the official exchange rate.[55] Although in January 1989 the managing director of the Foreign Trade Bank indicated that the government was considering an exchange rate adjustment, it now appears that the question has been shelved until after the proposed elections in May 1990, a move that no doubt reflects the likely short-term inflationary impact of a major devaluation and the effect this might have on political stability.

A major problem affecting Burma in this respect is that it currently lacks the necessary external aid to fund the complete structural adjustment that is necessary. All of the country's major

Western donors suspended aid payments following the September 1988 coup and the violent suppression of the popular protests for political reform. Although the Japanese recognized the new regime in early 1989, aid payments are being limited to existing projects. The Japanese, like most other Western donors, are awaiting the outcome of the proposed elections before considering a full resumption of aid ties. The success of the reform programme is, therefore, effectively a hostage to political reform, since a massive new inflow of donor assistance will be vital to ease the country's debt problem and support the balance of payments, rebuild economic infrastructure, up-grade managerial and technical skills and promote administrative reform, all of which is necessary to raise the country's absorptive capacity and provide the necessary economic foundation for increased foreign investment.[56]

The reform programme is hostage to the political reforms in other respects too. Since the present regime is effectively a continuation of the old BSPP military-dominated government in another guise, there is still widespread distrust of the government and a questioning of its commitment to the reforms. This is especially so in relation to the liberalization of private sector activity, since the confidence of private traders and businessmen (as well as the population at large) was all but destroyed by the currency demonetizations of November 1985 and September 1987. Furthermore, apart from retaining its monopoly in a number of key sectors, recent statements suggest that the state also intends to maintain a dominant role in other sectors, such as tourism, which were to be opened to the private sector.[57] Moreover, as a result of the failure of the earlier trade liberalization reforms and the problem of rapidly rising rice prices, the government has reimposed restrictions on both the domestic and external trade in rice. There are also signs that the present regime remains ambivalent towards foreign investment and the "corrupting" effect of foreign influence. Finally, major political reforms will be necessary to bring an end to Burma's civil war between the government and the minorities. Not only does this constitute a severe drain on government resources, with defence expenditure reported to be currently absorbing some 40 per cent of the nation's budget, the continuing civil war and insecurity along wide tracts of the country's border also deprive the government of access to much of the country's forestry and mineral reserves and disrupt moves to expand official cross-border trade.

In view of the above, forecasting Burma's likely prospects, even over the next five years, is a hazardous undertaking. The economic reform programme, however desirable, itself increases the risk of potential instability in the short-term because of increased prices and the hardship it will impose on sections of the population, a problem that would equally face a popular democratically elected government. Even with a co-ordinated programme of donor support to rebuild the country's broken down infrastructure and ease the debt burden, it would take most of the next five years to lay the foundations for economic recovery, given the extent of the economy's decline. All this precludes an optimistic prognosis. What is offered below is rather an outline not only of the possible direction of change in the short-term, but also of the problems and prospects of export-oriented growth in Burma following the adoption of a more outward-looking strategy, especially in the light of the changing division of labour in the Asia-Pacific region and Burma's existing links with that region.

A priority facing Burma as it goes into the 1990s is the need to rebuild and diversify its export sector and at the same time build up and restructure its very small and inefficient industrial sector. However, at least in the short to medium-term, it is the country's primary commodity and natural resource base which offers the best hope for boosting vital export earnings and which holds most attraction for foreign investors. This is particularly true in relation to the Japan and NIE markets, but also for the ASEAN markets, since although primary exports remain important for the ASEAN countries, they are now experiencing raw material supply shortages in many of their resource-based industries, for example, timber and fisheries, while as noted earlier, their trade sectors are becoming less competitive with that of Burma as their industrialization progresses. Even before the passing of the Foreign Investment Law in November 1988, General Saw Maung's government had signed agreements with Thai and Korean firms covering the exploitation of both timber and fisheries resources. Since the Law was passed various agreements in the mineral and gem sector have been reported. Then, in October 1989, in another reversal of long-standing policy, the government signed the first onshore production sharing agreement for oil exploration with a Korean company. This is expected to be the first of a number of such deals with foreign companies, including some from Japan, although the impact of this development, even assuming oil is found, will only be felt in the long-term.[58]

Boosting the country's agricultural export earnings, which is also vital, given that agricultural exports account for more than 40 per cent of total exports, is a more difficult task. In the case of rice, the chief agricultural export, Burma obviously faces strong competition in both regional and international markets from Thailand and now also from Vietnam (which has recently re-emerged as a major exporter) as well as from the United States. Raising the earnings from rice exports will depend mainly on efforts to expand sales to markets in Africa and the Middle East and on efforts to raise the quality of rice exports. For the latter, additional aid for the rehabilitation and upgrading of the country's rice milling industry could well be obtained, especially from Japan, although the setting up of a new joint venture between one of Burma's state-owned companies and a Thai company to produce rice-milling equipment for both the domestic and export markets was announced in October 1989.[59] In the case of rubber, the level of Burma's production and exports is such that it does not really present serious competition to the key producers in ASEAN; thus, the possibility of technical assistance and even investment from the ASEAN countries in this sector exists. The same is true of other agricultural exports, such as pulses, beans, animal feeds and livestock, where the potential for both expansion into regional markets and the setting up of joint ventures is good.

While the stress on primary and natural resource exports is inevitable in the short-term, such a strategy clearly leaves Burma vulnerable to commodity price falls and in the position of the supplier of generally low value-added products. It also exposes

Burma to the danger of environmental degradation from over-exploitation which it has largely avoided to date.[60] The rapid depletion of forestry, marine and other resources in the ASEAN countries, especially Thailand, is a major reason for the current interest of regional investors in Burma's resource base. While this is working to Burma's advantage now, there is a real danger of over-exploitation in the short-term rush to maximize foreign exchange earnings. Burma should, in fact, be in a position to capitalize on the growing concern over environmental matters among both bilateral and multilateral donors to draw up a more sustainable resource development programme. However, the above problems also emphasize the need to set up resource-based industries as a means of both raising value-added and strengthening the country's industrial base. The main potential here lies in the forestry and fisheries sectors, although there are possibilities for export or import-substituting industries with the agricultural sector, particularly with such commodities as rubber and oil seeds. Given the extensive experience and continued involvement of investors from the ASEAN countries in resource-based industries, investors from ASEAN could be responsive while investment and aid to help set up such industries could also come from Japan and the NIEs.

Even the development of resource-based industries would leave the economy dependent on a fairly narrow resource-aid production base, so that the development of a more broad-based industrial sector ought to receive some priority. What further prospects exist either for economically efficient export-oriented or import substitution industries, given that an export-orientated strategy does not rule out economically efficient import-substitution production? On the import substitution side the country's major imports, including non-legal imports, consist of capital goods, some 60 per cent of official imports, and consumer goods. Even with an economic recovery, the demand for most capital goods would not be sufficient to justify economic production. In addition, such industries would be import-dependent and require a technological-skills base that would take time to build up. Some potential does exist for the production of simpler capital goods for agriculture and resource-based industries, such as farm machinery and rice processing equipment, and these should not be ignored, since they could provide the basis for the subsequent development of the capital goods sectors. In the case of consumer goods, the existence of a massive black market is indicative of the existing demand for such goods, which can also be expected to grow as the economy recovers. Yet here it will be difficult for Burmese production to compete with the cheap, high quality goods available from China and Thailand that are now well established in the country, although an exchange rate adjustment would, by raising import prices, choke off at least some of the demand for imported goods. This again emphasizes the importance of exchange rate policy to the success of any recovery programme. Clearly, there will be some sub-sectors of industry, such as textiles and processed foods, where Burma either has or could develop a comparative advantage for both import substitution and export with the help of foreign aid and investment.[61] However, Burma's move into export-orientated industrialization is more likely to come through the gradual relocation of labour-intensive assembly type industries from the ASEAN countries as wage levels rise there and these countries move further up the ladder of industrial technology.

With the emergence of large conglomerates within the ASEAN countries and even TNCs, this process of relocation could involve ASEAN investors as well as foreign-owned firms in ASEAN. Some investment in new offshore production facilities by investors from Japan and the NIEs is also possible. However, all such investment would be limited until Burma's economic and communications infrastructure has been radically improved.

Burma's oil and gas resources could also be important to the country's development in the longer term, particularly if new onshore oil reserves are found.[62] Both are potentially important export commodities but, more importantly, offer significant opportunities for downstream developments in energy-based industries. However, the economics of such industries, as Thailand's experience with its Eastern Seaboard Development Programme reveals, are extremely sensitive to world prices, while development costs are so high as to be prohibitive for Burma until the economy has recovered and it has overcome its debt crisis.

The service sector, in contrast, does offer the potential for more rapid growth in the short term. This could partly come from the growth of the industrial sector itself. However, the main potential lies in tourism. Tourism has been an important industry in ASEAN, both as a source of foreign exchange earnings and employment. In Thailand, earnings from tourism currently constitute the principal source of foreign exchange, with the country attracting more than 3 million visitors in 1987 compared to only around 40,000 for Burma in 1986/87. Burma has much to offer tourists, but again the infrastructure necessary to support tourism, including hotels, airports and aircraft, would all need to be improved and expanded before any dramatic increase in tourist arrivals will be possible. The ongoing insurgencies and the insecurity associated with them also act as a constraint on the development of tourism, as does the continued concern over the country's political stability. However, negotiations are already under way between the government and a number of big Thai hotel chains and other foreign companies for hotel and other tourism projects in Burma. While expansion in tourism offers the potential for increased foreign exchange earnings and employment growth, since it is a labour-intensive industry, to offset this, it has limited linkage effects and a high import content.

Some of the potential scope for growth and development in Burma under an export-orientated strategy, has been outlined above. Before concluding, it is necessary to emphasize that, however necessary such a strategy is, given Burma's current economic crisis, such a path brings its own problems. Whatever the growth potential of the export-oriented industrialization strategy, it still exposes the country to fluctuations in the level of global economic activity, even though the effect of these will be less intense than when the country is relying solely on primary commodity exports. Furthermore, though capable of significant employment generation, export-orientated industrialization, especially in its early stages, has few other linkages with the domestic economy and can, as a result of high import dependence, have only a limited net effect on foreign exchange. These problems can be equally true of import-substitution industrialization, which is why export-orientated, resource-based industries have been given such priority in ASEAN, and why they will be equally important to Burma.

Other problems, such as the heavy reliance on foreign technology, the difficulty of ensuring effective technology transfer and avoiding a capital-intensive bias in the choice of technique, though again not confined to export-orientated industrialization, are made more difficult by the crucial role played by foreign investment and TNCs in the process. Even in the ASEAN countries there is concern over foreign control and dominance of the economy. In Burma, there is a real risk that a major influx of foreign investment could result in a resurgence of fear of foreign control, given both the weakness of the Burmese private sector, and the way the military regimes have played on such fear in the past. Effective government direction will, therefore, be needed, not only to foster the domestic private sector and an increased flow of foreign investment, but also to ensure that a fair share of the benefits of Burma's new road accrue to the country and its people, and that the foundation for sustainable long-term growth and development is laid.

NOTES

* Minister of Planning, Finance and Trade, Burma. See *Working People's Daily*, 27 July 1989, p. 1.

** 20 October 1986, p. 1.

1. Brunei, the sixth member of ASEAN, is ignored in the following discussion owing to its small size and the fact that its economy is dependent almost entirely on oil and gas exports. Although Singapore is a member of ASEAN, it is regarded as one of the four Asian NIEs and is grouped with them in most of the following discussion. The term "ASEAN" in this chapter therefore generally applies to Indonesia, Malaysia, the Philippines and Thailand.
2. Ichimura (1988), p. 10.
3. Ibid.
4. In the case of the NIEs, per capita income doubled in the period in all but Hong Kong. The ASEAN countries experienced a slower rate of growth in per capita incomes due to population growth, but it still ranged from 3.7 per cent in the Philippines to 5.1 per cent in Indonesia over this period.
5. World Bank (1988), p. 224.

6. *Asia Yearbook 1989*, p. 6; and Asian Development Bank (1988), p. 7. This period includes the recession years of 1985 and 1986. Both Singapore and Malaysia experienced negative growth in 1985 and very low growth in 1986. The growth rates in all of the ASEAN countries have improved significantly since 1986.
7. Anderson et al. (1985), p. 7.
8. Financial Times (1986), p. 1.
9. The term "Asia-Pacific region" seems preferable to "Pacific Rim" since it is not so clear where the Pacific boundary should end. We take "Asia-Pacific" to include all countries in or bordering the Pacific Ocean plus all of the ASEAN countries.
10. Anderson et al. (1985), p. 8.
11. Financial Times (1986), p. 1, 7.
12. Financial Times (1988), p. 1.
13. Ichimura, for example, lists ten economic and political factors, both internal and external, as causal factors in their fast growth (Ichimura 1988, p. 17). There is much debate on the importance of different factors. Some stress the favourable external environment, others sound macro-policies. The role of the state, though mentioned only implicitly by Ichimura, is widely regarded as having been of crucial importance, especially in the NIEs. See notes 20 and 22 below.
14. Kojima and Nakauchi (1988), p. 114.
15. Wong (1985), p. 7.
16. Financial Times (1988), p. 10.
17. Kojima and Nakauchi (1988), p. 114.
18. This is sometimes referred to simply as "getting prices right". However, since undervalued exchange rates have been an important factor in the success of the NIEs, especially Korea and Taiwan, it may be more appropriate to talk about "getting the right prices wrong in the right way"!
19. This process of restructuring has also been linked to the rise of "original equipment manufacturing" (OEM) whereby companies produce goods to the design and specification of a foreign buyer which then sells under its own brand name.
20. A number of countries in South America and a few African countries, such as Kenya, have also experiencd industrial growth in this manner. For a radical perspective of the NIDL and the role of the state in export-orientated industrialization especially in so far as it affects Southeast Asia, see Higgott and Robison, eds. (1985).
21. Yamazawa and Watanabe (1988), pp. 217–19.
22. It is particularly in the field of technological development that the state has played a key role in the NIEs, with the possible exception of Hong Kong. Even in Hong Kong, the government has recently become more interventionist in an effort to promote increased research and development within

the electronics sector, seen as a key to moving into higher technology products. See OECD (1988).

23. As examples of attempts by the ASEAN countries to move up the technological ladder and of some of the difficulties involved, see Fong (1984), and Shiowattana (1989). For a less positive view of the prospects for technological development and future industrialization in the ASEAN countries, see Yoshihara (1988).
24. In 1986, in spite of efforts to reduce their dependence, exports to the United States still accounted for 48 per cent, 39 per cent, 31 per cent and 23 per cent respectively of Taiwan's, Korea's, Hong Kong's and Singapore's exports.
25. See Kojima and Nakauchi (1988), p. 130. They also give other reasons for moving away from a reliance on export-orientated industrialization. These include the problem of the divergence between the growth rate of exports and the growth rate of domestic value added because of dependence on imported raw materials and capital goods (p. 109) and the need to give greater priority to the growth of the service sector (p. 115).
26. Writing in 1985, Anderson et al. noted that more than half of the trade of East Asia and other Pacific economies was with other countries in the region and that "This bias towards inter-regional trade ensures that a disproportionately large share of the benefits of strong trade growth in East Asia accrue within the Pacific region" (p. 16). A more recent source indicated that Pacific countries now transact 65 per cent of their trade with each other. See *Far Eastern Economic Review*, 16 November 1989, p. 14.
27. Asian Development Bank (1988).
28. World Bank (1988), p. 22.
29. Asian Development Bank (1988).
30. Financial Times (1988), p. 10.
31. Asian Development Bank (1988).
32. The Pacific Basin Economic Council and the Pacific Economic Co-operation Conference were both established in the late 1960s to try and improve economic co-operation. In November 1989, Australia hosted a ministerial conference designed to lay the foundations for a new Asia-Pacific Economic Co-operation Forum. Trade liberalization was a key issue at the meeting.
33. See Table 1a in the chapter by Tin Soe and Fisher in this volume.
34. Steinberg (1981), p. 48.
35. Small amounts of foreign investment were tolerated in the early 1970s as the government sought to encourage offshore oil exploration. Since foreign participation in this sector was suspended in late the 1970s, the only foreign investment, prior to the current reforms, was a joint venture between the Burmese Government and a West German engineering firm entered into in 1984.
36. For a more detailed discussion of Burma's aid relations, see Vokes (1989).
37. Khin Maung Nyunt (1988), pp. 68, 127.

38. Ibid.
39. Ibid., p. 126. Burma's exports to Singapore increased from US$11 million in 1972 to US$58 million in 1986, the latter figure equivalent to 11.4 per cent of total exports in that year. The equivalent figures for Hong Kong were US$3.5 million and US$31 million (6.1 per cent). In the case of Malaysia, Burma's exports rose from US$3 million in 1972 to a peak of US$25 million in 1984, since when they have tailed off. In Thailand, they increased from less than one million in 1972 to US$30 million (5.9 per cent of total imports) and slightly less than the peak figure of 1985. Exports to Indonesia amounted to less than one million tons in both 1985 and 1986. Burma has very little trade either on the export or the import side with the Philippines. See Khin Maung Nyunt (1988), pp. 57, 126.
40. Mya Than (forthcoming), pp. 51, 55.
41. Khin Maung Nyunt (1988), p. 57.
42. Ibid., p. 67.
43. Ibid., p. 127.
44. Mya Than (forthcoming), p. 50, 55.
45. Mya Than (1989), p. 66. A mid-1980's estimate of non-legal trade put the value at more than US$200 million or more than one-quarter of official imports. See Hill and Jayasuriya (1986).
46. Considerable investment was made in agriculture in the 1970s but this was mainly channelled into the rice sector to promote the use of high-yielding varieties to boost supplies for both domestic consumption and export. The success of this programme was a major factor in the economy's improved performance between 1976 and 1982. However, little effort was made to diversify agricultural production or exports or to develop other resource-based industries.
47. UNIDO (1987), p. 20.
48. Mya Than (1989), p. 47.
49. The only significant change in the export structure since the 1970s has been the gradual increase in the importance of timber product exports. In 1985, earnings from teak and other forest products exceeded those of rice for the first time.
50. *Report to the Pyithu Hluttaw, 1987/88.*
51. IMF (1987), p. 40.
52. Though less important, other factors, notably the stagnation of agricultural production and a fall in oil production and growing fuel shortages, also contributed to the crisis; set-backs in both sectors were also aggravated by the growing foreign exchange shortage after 1982.
53. See chapter 7 of this volume by Mya Than.
54. The official exchange rate is 6.7 kyat = US$1.00. The black market rate is more than 50 kyat to the dollar (see also note 18).
55. It has been estimated that in mid-1988, rice sold domestically in Burma

would have fetched some 80 per cent more than if it was exported at the official exchange rate (see Asian Development Bank 1989).

56. Most of this new aid would need to be in grant form or on highly concessional terms, at least during the early stages of recovery, for Burma to avoid the risk of another debt crisis. Given the country's low per capita income, at around US$190, it would be eligible for grant aid.
57. *Bangkok Post*, 15 October 1989, p. 2.
58. *Far Eastern Economic Review*, 26 October 1989, pp. 120–21.
59. Ibid., p. 109.
60. Burma has a long history of conservation measures in the forestry sector including plantations for teak. In recent years, however, production has been reported to be running ahead of conservation, particularly as the country's foreign exchange shortage deepened.
61. Burma's industrial sector is currently dominated by the food and beverages sub-sector which accounted for almost 72 per cent of gross manufacturing output in 1986/87 compared to 60 per cent in 1961/62. The textile sub-sector is the next most important but accounts for just 6 per cent of gross manufacturing output compared with 15 per cent in 1961/62. Industrial raw materials and mining and petroleum products are the only other sub-sectors of significance, together accounting for 9.4 per cent of gross manufacturing output in 1986/87. See UNIDO (1987).
62. Burma already has extensive reserves of natural gas. According to government figures there was a significant increase in gas production from the country's onshore fields in the decade up to 1986/87. Although extensive offshore gas fields were discovered in the Gulf of Martaban in 1982 and 1983, their development has been postponed because of weak world prices and the very high development costs which would have added significantly to the country's external debt.

REFERENCES

Anderson, K., et al. *Pacific Economic Growth and the Prospects for Australian Trade*. Pacific Economic Papers No. 122. Canberra: Australian National University, 1985.

Asia Yearbook 1989. Hong Kong: Far Eastern Economic Review, 1989.

Asian Development Bank (ADB). *Asian Development Outlook*. Manila, 1989.

———. *Key Indicators of Developing Member Countries of ADB*, Vol. 19. Manila, 1988.

Bangkok Post (Bangkok), 15 October 1989.

Butwell, R. "Ne Win's Burma: At the End of the First Decade". *Asian Survey* 12, no. 10 (1972).

Far Eastern Economic Review (Hong Kong), 26 October 1989.

Financial Times. *Survey of the Pacific Rim*. London, 20 October 1986.

______. *Report on Asia's Pacific Rim*. London, 30 June 1989.

Fong Chan Onn. *Technological Leap: Malaysian Industry in Transition*. Kuala Lumpur: University of Malaya, 1984.

Higgott, R.A. and R. Robison, eds. *South East Asia: Essays in the Political Economy of Structural Change*. London: Allen and Unwin, 1985.

Hill, H. and S. Jayasuriya. *An Inward Looking Economy in Transition: Economic Development in Burma since the 1960s*. Occasional Paper No. 80. Singapore: Institute of Southeast Asian Studies, 1986.

Ichimura, S. "The Pattern and Prospects of Asian Economic Development". In *Challenge of Asian Developing Countries: Issues and Analysis*, edited by S. Ichimura. Tokyo: Asian Productivity Organization, 1988.

International Monetary Fund (IMF). *Burma. Recent Economic Developments*. Washington, 1987.

Khin Maung Nyunt. *Market Research of Principal Exports of Burma with Special Reference to Thailand (1970/71 to 1985/86)*. Asian Studies Monograph No. 40. Bangkok: Chulalongkorn University, 1988.

Kojima, K. and T. Nakauchi. "Economic Conditions in East and Southeast Asia and Development Perspective". In *Challenge of Asian Development Countries: Issues and Analysis*, edited by S. Ichimura. Tokyo: Asian Productivity Organization, 1988.

Ministry of Planning and Finance. *Report of the Pyithu Hluttaw on the Financial, Economic and Social Conditions of the Socialist Republic of the Union of Burma, 1987/88*. Rangoon, 1988.

Mya Than. *Burma's External Trade. An Optimistic Trend for ASEAN?* Singapore: Institute of Southeast Asian Studies, forthcoming.

Organization for Economic Co-operation and Development (OECD). *The Newly Industrializing Countries. Challenge and Opportunity for OECD Industries*. Paris, 1988.

Shiowattana, Prayoon. "Japanese Technology Transfer in Thailand" . Paper presented at the Joint Seminar of Thammasat and Kyoto Universities on Japanese-Thai Relations, Kyoto, 20–21 October 1989.

Steinberg, D. *Burma's Road Toward Development: Growth and Ideology Under Military Rule*. Boulder: Westview Press, 1981.

United Nations Industrial Development Organization (UNIDO). *Burma Industrial Development Review.* Vienna, 1987.

Vokes, R.W.A. "The Economy of Burma". In *Far East and Australasia 1990.* London, 1989.

Wong, J. "Trade Opportunities and Problems with Other Regions". Background report to the Sixth ICC Annual Conference, Korea, 25–28 March 1985.

World Bank. *World Development Report 1988.* Oxford University Press, 1988.

Yamazawa, I. and T. Watanabe. "Industrial Restructuring and Technology Transfer". In *Challenge of Asian Developing Countries: Issues and Analysis*, edited by S. Ichimura. Tokyo: Asian Productivity Organization, 1988.

Yoshihara, K. *The Rise of Ersatz Capitalism in Southeast Asia.* Oxford University Press, 1988.

9

UNITED NATIONS TECHNICAL AID AND ECONOMIC DEVELOPMENT IN BURMA*

SOE SAING

An Overview of Burma and the United Nations System

Background

Burma and the United Nations have held a long and fruitful relationship for forty years. When Burma joined the United Nations in 1948 there were 58 members. That number has grown to 159 in 1986. In the early 1950s, the United Nations Children's Fund (UNICEF), the World Health Organization (WHO) and the United Nations Technical Assistance Board (UNTAB) set up offices in Rangoon. When the UNTAB and the United Nations Special Fund for Economic Development (SUNFED) were merged, the resulting United Nations Development Programme (UNDP) opened its office in Rangoon in January 1966.

Co-operation between the U.N. agencies and Burma increased dramatically; from an annual average of US$30,000 for technical aid in the 1950s, it rose nearly a hundredfold in the 1980s, with prospects of more to come.

The UNDP is the most important United Nations agency in Burma, and the UNDP Resident Representative is, by virtue of the

United Nations General Assembly mandate of 1977, also the resident co-ordinator of all the U.N. system's operational activities in the country. He has the role of *primus inter pares* among the heads of the various U.N. agencies in the country. He also serves as the representative of the United Nations Fund for Drug Abuse Control (UNFDAC), and several other U.N. agencies.

United Nations' technical assistance consists of a four-element mixed package of advisory services and consultants, feasibility studies, equipment, and fellowships. In 1986 about three hundred government officials received fellowships to attend U.N.-sponsored training courses, study tours, seminars, and workshops abroad, and in the same year there were about one hundred and twenty international personnel and consultants based in the country, while another one hundred came on missions. More than ninety Burmese nationals are serving in about a dozen countries as United Nations Volunteers (UNV), a sort of reverse technical aid, mainly in the fields of medicine, engineering and education.

The UNDP

The UNDP's role is unique: to be catalytic and pivotal because of the special nature of its partnership with the government. In contrast to the bilateral aid donors, the UNDP has no sectoral bias; it can direct its resources towards any area of national priority, at the government's request.

Since 1974 the UNDP has played a new vital role for public investment. Together with the World Bank and the Asian Development Bank as executing agencies, it has financed wide-ranging multi-purpose pre-investment technical feasibility projects aimed at mobilizing financial resources to meet Burma's development needs. This project, called Burma "Umbrella Project", was in its third phase (Umbrella III) for the period from 1982–87. To date, such UNDP-financed projects have generated substantial follow-up investments in a number of economic sub-sectors.

For the period 1961–66 Burma received US$15 million of assistance from the United Nations Technical Assistance Board, as well as US$7 million from the United Nations Special Fund. From the time the UNDP became the sole integrated agency in 1966, Burma has received technical assistance amounting to US$102 million (up to 1986). The total amount received, therefore, was US$124 million.

UNICEF

UNICEF's assistance to Burma initially concentrated in the child health field. By the 1960s its mandate was extended to child education and social welfare. Two decades later into the 1980s the theme was on integrated basic health services. The UNICEF programme for Burma now has a new orientation towards activities which reach directly to the communities, in support of education and social welfare, with emphasis on intermediate technology, especially in water supply and sanitation.

FAO

All aspects of agriculture (which include livestock, fisheries and forestry) are in the realm of the Food and Agriculture Organization (FAO), a specialized agency of the United Nations formed to raise the nutritional and living standards of all people by more efficient means of production and distribution of food.

In Burma, the FAO is involved in a variegated range of activities from the improvement of paddy and other cereal grains, to better livestock breeding, inland and offshore fisheries, and forestry. It provides direct funding under its own Technical Co-operation Programme and Special Action Programme. The UNDP also "employs" the FAO to act as its executive agency in some projects.

WHO

Established in 1948 as a United Nations Specialized Agency to protect and promote the health of people globally, the World Health Organization in Burma encompasses programmes in the joint spheres of health and medicine. It has assisted in the formulation of the successive National Health Plans. Its assistance ranges from disease control to the training of medical and paramedical personnel, and promotion of rural health care. The WHO works with the government to achieve primary health care throughout the country as part of the world-wide theme "Health for All by the Year 2000" (HFA 2000).

Other United Nations Agencies

Among the other U.N. agencies involved in Burma for major project execution are the International Civil Aviation Organization (ICAO), the International Telecommunications Union (ITU), the International Labour Organization (ILO), the United Nations Educational, Scientific and Cultural Organization (UNESCO), the United Nations Industrial Development Organization (UNIDO), the World Meteorological Organization (WMO), the United Nations Conference for Trade and Development (UNCTAD), and several others.

To indicate the diverse activities of the United Nations in Burma, an extract of the sectoral allocation of UNDP Country Programme IV (1982–86) is shown in Table 1.

Overview

Though Burma is one of the ten largest recipients of the U.N. technical aid, the amount received has not been large in relation to its needs. The U.N. system's contribution can be significant only if it has a multiplier, catalytic effect on the country's development efforts.

Various intergovernmental forums have repeatedly stressed the enhancement of self-reliance as a key to development. They have also reasserted the need to make the U.N. system's technical co-operation more effective; and to strive for more rigorous and timely evaluations to find out if the implementation efforts did accomplish what they were meant to do.

In a way, the UNDP's own *ex-post facto* functional evaluations

TABLE 1
United Nations Programme Classification, 1982–86
(In million US$)

General development issues, policy and planning	10
Natural resources	7
Agriculture, forestry and fisheries	17
Industry	7
Transport and communications	10
International trade and development finance	1
Human settlements	1
Health	7
Education	7
Employment	1
Social conditions and equity	1
Culture	2
Science and technology	2
Total (Figures do not tally because of rounding)	76

SOURCE: *UNDP Country Programmes*

of the projects did shed some light on the project patterns and problems. Nevertheless, an evaluation of the United Nations technical aid activities in Burma is needed to provide a clearer picture. After all, it is at the country level that the U.N. system's contributions combine with national resources to make things work. On this basis, and relying upon the successive UNDP Country Programmes for Burma spanning more than twenty years, a brief sketch is outlined below.

In doing so, it has to be borne in mind that the quantum of U.N. technical co-operation is comparatively small; that there is perennial difficulty in determining what the so-called "impact" of technical assistance comprises; what "catalytic" effects there may be; and not lastly, the paucity of even basic national socio-economic data sources. There is also one other difficulty inherent in the structural diversity of the projects which differ in form, scope, complexity, purpose, and duration. In Burma, there are no "replicate" projects, and no "average" or "standard-sized" projects, for comparative purposes. Curiously enough, each U.N. agency has its own technical concepts, documentation, procedures and policies.

Faced with these difficulties and qualifications, the overview sketch is directed towards the recurrent topic of self-reliance, and the strength and weakness of the United Nations system. Self-reliance is always of topical interest because it never fails to touch the core of nationalistic and chauvinistic feelings, especially of the post-World-War II independent countries like Burma, which furthermore, is also historically bent towards insularity.

Impediments in the path of self-reliance in Burma have been many: nationalizations of economic sectors and centralized social welfare, which, *inter alia*, resulted in the loss of public initiative and drive; almost mind-numbing red tape; and low quality over-crowded nationalized education system, are but some that exist at the national level. The aid process itself encourages nationals not to be self-reliant but to turn to "foreign experts" rather than to tackle the problems themselves. The circumstances are such that the risks of failure are many and the rewards few. It is thus more prudent and self-protective to rely on "foreign experts".

Fellowships from all sources have been less than adequate, and scattered thin over many sectors. And fellowships have been found to be not helpful towards self-reliance. Fellowship foul-ups; fellowships awarded not necessarily to the most deserving; fellowships superficially prepared; absence of fellowship monitoring and follow-up, have not been uncommon. Overcoming all that, and after much hard work abroad, to have to return to the same work environment, the same old rules, and the same old jobs, could not but be discouraging to the returnees, and hardly conducive to fostering initiative that could lead to self-reliance.

The statements made here are not new. They have been repeatedly discussed throughout the United Nations system. It is of no consolation to know that other countries are also afflicted with similar malaise. But the issues are so crucial, and because the remedial measures have been less than effective, that it is deemed useful to reiterate them.

Assessment

The role of U.N. technical aid reflects both the strength and weakness of the system itself. The positive factors are the competence of the system to proffer relatively unbiased aid and consultation on development problems (in contrast to the national interest-dominant aid of bilateral donors), and the world-wide means at its disposal to provide comprehensive technical services on almost any economic and social sector.

The negative factors are the relatively small size of U.N. inputs, as well as its complex process, and lack of cost-effectiveness (not all its fault). The United Nations agencies have less manoeuvrability, and less leverage than the big bilateral and multilateral donors.

The role of the United Nations system differs in both degree and kind from that of the other donors. Major projects are usually linked to the specific interests of the bilateral country donors, while the remainder — the small, the difficult, the specialized, or the sensitive (and usually the less desirable) ones — are left more by default than deference to the United Nations system. Though the United Nations is not a residual donor, it has come to be associated as a filler of gaps, and a handler of needed but unwanted tasks — a role which is unnoticed, but special for the United Nations system and also one that is beneficial to Burma.

Taken as a whole, it is hard to specify the economic impact of the United Nations system (except perhaps in the UNICEF, WHO and FAO projects where specific subjects handled are amenable to quantification). Nonetheless, but for the United Nations' assistance (with all its inadequacies), it is arguable if Burma could have achieved whatever economic and (especially) social progress it has had. Put differently, Burma might have had to seek least developed country status earlier than it did, but for such assistance received in various forms.

Of the U.N. agencies, the UNICEF is the best known, followed by the FAO and the WHO. The above-average quality of these agencies' field staffs, their advisory assistance to institutions, their "grassroots" exposure and community approaches, have made their mark, and are well known throughout the small towns and villages.

Financial resources and technology transferred, experts provided, equipment delivered, and expenditures spent, are all very well. However, they are but *indicators* of technical co-operation *activity*, and no more than that. Concentration on "*inputs*" and "*programme delivery*" should not override the fact that effective *results* are the true measure of the success of technical co-operation in the final analysis.

Structural Maladjustments in the Burmese Economy

Burma is at present standing on sticky ground with no discernable destination in sight. At this point there is as yet nothing promising to look forward to except for a "promised" election in the offing for mid-1990. But the forthcoming elections will be different because for the first time in thirty years, it will be a multi-party one.

However, after the election is held, and whatever the outcome thereof, or whoever may "win", the country will still be in the same moribund state, unless the economy can be resurrected. For that to happen, Burma cannot go it alone. The conclusion is therefore clear: substantial and prompt infusion of appropriate foreign aid is a *sine qua non.*

Previous experience of Burma's capability in handling the economy hardly inspires confidence. Despite the fact that Burma was the twenty-fourth largest recipient of overseas development aid (ODA), amounting to US$2.2 billion for the period 1973–83, the economy is what it is. That fact alone says enough. Laudable objectives and industriousness (at least at the beginning) were sufficiently present. What was not conspicuously present was the sound institutional set-up for economic policy formulation and management. The road to economic fiasco was paved with good intentions.

Before any future large-scale foreign aid can be fruitfully and effectively utilized, it is imperative that the country's absorptive capacity, no matter how defined, must first be expanded. To enable this to come about, the economic management machinery (in all aspects) will have to be drastically overhauled, and improved. This restructured machinery must be independent, be shielded from, and made impervious to, interventions in the name of some sacrosanct ideological "ism", be it "leftism", "rightism" or whatever. Non-ideological pragmatism must be the name of the new game.

In the presence of not unreasonably favourable economic conditions then prevailing thirty years ago, the puzzle was how the structural maladjustments could have occurred. To find out, one will have to go back to the aftermath of World War II, and the successive governments thereafter. The last twenty-six years spent in the vain pursuit of an elusive "ism" were the "years of futility", and form the penultimate chapter of the contemporary "Burmese Economic History", still unfolding.

Table 2 illustrates the deterioration of the economy during the last decade. While the newly industrializing economies (NIEs) and middle income countries (MICs) in Asia were vying for double-digit growth rates in their economies (except, of course, in inflation), the presence of numerous minus signs in the table indicates the situation in Burma.

Distortions

It will be useful to identify some of the more glaring distortions that have become embedded in the economy:

- Primacy of politics over the economy;
- Weakened administration;
- Consequences of the nationalization of trade, industry, and banking and education sectors;
- Unviable and inefficient state economic enterprises;
- Over-valued currency;
- Inflation and the black market;
- Restrictive trade, and unrealistic pricing policy.

Of the above, which were the causes and which the effects are the ultimate questions, to which cogent answers must be

TABLE 2
Trends in Economic Performance
(at 1969/70 constant producers' prices)
(In per cent)

	1982/83	*1983/84*	*1984/85*	*1985/86*	*1986/87*	*1987/88*
Real GDP	5.6	4.4	5.6	3.2	1.0	2.2
Productive sectors	6.2	4.6	5.9	2.3	0.4	1.8
Services	6.1	4.2	5.5	4.9	4.1	4.4
Trade	3.5	4.1	4.9	3.4	− 1.6	0.3
Total consumption	7.3	5.4	8.2	2.5	1.0	2.1
Total investment	13.6	−10.2	−6.5	1.2	− 0.5	1.5
Export (FOB)	0.6	12.7	−10.6	−1.7	13.5	−8.4
Import (CIF)	10.4	−18.7	− 3.0	−5.2	−18.5	3.5

NOTE: Figures relating to the performance of the Burmese economy must be cautiously interpreted, given the not inconsiderable shares of both the black market and the subsistence sectors in the economy, undefined and unreflected in official data.

SOURCE: *Report to the Pyithu Hluttaw*, various issues.

found, or else there can be little hope for solutions to "cure" the country's ills.

Misdirections

Recapitulation of the "wrong" economic direction taken initially and subsequently might prove both enlightening and instructive.

In the 1960s the perceived view was that developing countries should pursue import-substitution with the ultimate aim of industrialization. The United Nations Conference on Trade and Development (UNCTAD 1964, newly formed at that time) also gave impetus to this trend, owing to the Latin American influence under Raul Prebisch, then dominating. All this readily found favour with the historically-inclined inward-looking economic thought processes then resurgent in Burma.

Following the adopted trend, 30 per cent or more of foreign aid and borrowings were allocated to the various consumer goods industries. More by default than design, this resulted in the relative neglect of the core sectors of agriculture, energy and transport. The hardest hit was agriculture, which happened to be not only the largest sector, but also the leading foreign exchange earner.

A mini-version of a green revolution combined with some agricultural diversification crash programmes, higher allocation of capital to some consumer industries, resulted for a while in the higher production of paddy, other grains, and some consumer goods. The increases, however, were sporadic and not sustained. Lack of energy in more ways than one, in later years, was one reason. This misallocation of foreign resources changed the character and the composition of imports, which led to uncalculated detrimental consequences.

At the same time, as the demand rose for the import of intermediate "essential" items such as raw materials, and spare parts for the consumer goods industries, foreign exchange earnings dropped because of the decline in almost all exports both in relative and absolute terms. The terms of trade were also highly negative. Thus, when importation of the essential goods had to be reduced (as they frequently were), for whatever reason, snags and bottlenecks cropped up. At first, these occurrences were sporadic, isolated and limited to particular sectors. Eventually, the shortages became cumulative and the snowball effect took place across the board, and chain-reaction set in. The agricultural sector declined further, manufacturing industries were more and more under-utilized, and the transportation system became erratic. The whole situation became desperate to the extent that foreign exchange expenditure had to be rationed. The result was that various macro- and micro-economic plans went awry.

The over-centralized government planning machinery was too cumbersome to be capable of fine-tuning the controls. To obtain some relief, short-term palliative measures were resorted to, including more drastic selective cuts in imports. By this time the rot had set in, resulting in even worse shortages.

Slogans and exhortations, decrees, price controls, restrictive measures — all were brought out and employed, but almost all ineffectual. Market forces (being anathema to "socialistic" thinking), were politically ignored. They, however, prevailed, notwithstanding the quixotic tilts at the windmill. Prices spiralled. The one market that truly flourished was the black market.

This picture gives a lesson in paradox. It was the very fear of undue dependence upon external sources by way of imports that impelled the original direction towards the import-substitution line of action. The results turned out to be the opposite of expectations.

Nodal Points

Now that the "misdirections" have been described, the question is what next to do? If it is accepted that the absorptive capacity of the country must be expanded, and that the economic management machinery should also be reconstructed as the precursor, then the following inter-linked nodal points can be identified as those that must be dealt with in concert:

- Macro-economic policy co-ordination;
- Re-orientation and streamlining of the planning role, concurrently with an improvement in statistical data base;
- Government budget structure and resource mobilization;
- Trade and pricing policy;
- Banking and external finance management;
- Inflation and the black market;
- Upgrading of the educational system.

The economic situation is in such disarray that it is difficult to make out which of the above choke-points should be tackled first. What is clear, however, is that all must be dealt with, not just some. The nodal points are so cross-linked to one another that either/or is no more a viable option. The cross-linkages are so inter-twined that any change in one nodal point entails changes in all the others — a case of one and all.

Economic reform, under any definition, cannot be a single-handed effort. In any such attempt, development of the national institutional capacity to act flexibly and react speedily to the ever-changing circumstances of internal and external stimuli will have to be the very first cornerstone set down. Since Burma cannot do this by itself, the next logical step is to consider from where, when and how succour can be obtained.

In doing this, time, cost (including the hidden ones), and ease of availability are the relevant factors to keep in view. Using these criteria in looking through the relative merits of multilateral and bilateral possibilities, the choice almost inevitably falls on the United Nations system for a number of reasons: firstly, the country's needs are urgent, and prolonged delays must be avoided. It is less likely to be so with the United Nations, than with the bilateral donors, because the former has little or no bias, whereas the latter will inevitably have their respective national interests to advance, and *quid pro quo* to extract. A poor but proud country like Burma is more prone to sensitivity regarding moral (apart from any financial) debt and obligation to pay back. In the case of the United Nations this will not be so.

Prospects of Technical Aid from the United Nations System

Taken that technical aid is best sought from the United Nations system, at least for Burma, the sources, and the resources obtainable from them are briefly described below.

Among the U.N. agencies, the automatic choice would have to be the UNDP, for two reasons: the first for what it can offer, and another for what it can perform as a co-ordination centre. By virtue of it being *in situ* within the country, its familiarity with the past as well as the prevailing country situations, its contacts with the counterpart national departments, its world-wide capacity to provide any expert or service required, and with the General Assembly mandate to be the resident co-ordinator for all the United Nations activities in the country, no agency other than the UNDP can be the initiator and implementor for many facets of the technical aid packages to be brought in.

By itself too, the UNDP can offer a number of important aid packages. In 1988, through no fault of its own, the UNDP had to suspend its ongoing projects. These can be re-activated at very short notice. It can then accelerate, taking up fresh projects in the pipeline. This is one of the special attractions of the UNDP. It always has under its wings a backlog of ready-made projects in advanced stages of preparedness. It can, therefore, save considerable time-lag.

Recently, the UNDP has been allotted new funds, mainly for the benefit of least developed countries, which therefore suits Burma. These funds are for emergency post-crisis rehabilitation; for management development facility; for special programme reserve resources. All these will add up to a set of useful starting tools for Burma in its immediate need for rehabilitation.

At the same time, the UNDP can mount by itself any kind of mission, staffed not only by its own personnel but also by outside experts, or in *tandem* with other agencies, such as the World Bank and the Asian Development Bank — as had been successfully implemented previously under the Burma "Umbrella" projects.

Perhaps what the UNDP can do best to assist Burma is to organize a Special Round Table, to which it can invite prospective donors, not limiting it to the ODA countries, as in the Consultative Group meetings chaired and organized by the World Bank. The UNDP can include at the Special Round Table the neighbouring and the regional countries also as they can possibly offer capital aid (though not on the ODA scale), or at least technical aid, in whichever fields they are expert in. The catalytic effect of such a meeting can be enormous, and far-reaching.

Besides this, there are the Bretton Woods twin superpowers of the financial and economic development spheres of the United Nations system: the International Monetary Fund (IMF) and the World Bank. They are the acknowledged authorities in their respective fields, which embrace practically all that pertain to economic and financial development. Being twin organizations they co-operate well. The most important joint mission they have performed for a country is the Structural Adjustment Facility (SAF), which was set up by the IMF in 1986 to cater to the financial needs of the poorest economies, especially those beset by deep-seated foreign exchange difficulties, just as Burma's is.

The SAF has several innovative features of which the most appropriate and useful one is the preparation of the Policy Framework Paper (PFP), a document of joint effort by the IMF, with the World Bank, and the country concerned. The PFP spells out the conditions and steps the applicant country must undertake to be eligible for the facility. When agreed to by the three parties (the Fund, the Bank and the country concerned) the PFP becomes a "certified document" of economic changes which will be more readily accepted by the rest of the ODA financial community and other donors. Being a party to the PFP, the World Bank will have impelling cause to make it a success. It will, therefore, more extensively offer its own "Structural Adjustment Loan" (SAL), in addition to the usual sector or programme loans. The SAF of the Fund will, therefore, be followed by the SALs of the World Bank. These are then usually followed by ODA and other loans. Thus, the World Bank makes itself the lead donor. This PFP "certificate" will therefore be very valuable for a least developed country in search of foreign capital aid. Without it the task will be that much harder, if not impossible.

By way of a curious nomenclature, it is interesting to note that it is the International Monetary Fund that handles the *banking* aspect, and it is the World Bank which does the *funding* of the development projects. That is why the saying is that the Fund is not a fund but a bank; and that the Bank is not a bank but a development fund.

On the training side of technical aid, the IMF Institute is there to train higher echelon personnel of the ministries of finance and the central banks of the developing countries in the intricacies of banking and finance, especially in the external finance and foreign exchange fields.

The World Bank, on its part, can mount high-powered missions covering all aspects of the economic development of a country, ranging from the overall economic survey to that of any economic and social sector. These studies are in-depth efforts, comprehensive and authoritative. These reports are always used as reference documents by all the other donors because the World Bank possesses a reservoir of top class staff with unrivalled experience in all branches of development, continuously honed for more than four decades in the difficult situations in the various developing countries all over the globe.

On the training side, the World Bank has the Economic Development Institute (EDI), a premier institution for the training of development practitioners. Like the IMF Institute, which it predates, it not only trains and holds workshops in its headquarters in Washington, but also in the different regions and sometimes in the countries themselves. Holding a workshop in a country is doubly valuable to it, because of the larger number of staff that can participate, it is more convenient, and on-site training is always to be preferred.

These two pre-eminent institutes offer the kind of technical aid that Burma needs to keep its technocrats abreast of the external world and its latest developments. Without possession of this specialized knowledge, Burma would be playing Blindman's Buff in sophisticated surroundings which have gone beyond such antiquated games.

Another United Nations specialized agency of importance to Burma is UNCTAD with which it maintains liaison for matters concerning business related to least developed country status, as well as international trade. In 1989 UNCTAD organized a preparatory meeting in anticipation of the United Nations Conference for the Least Developed Countries, to be held in Paris in 1991. The previous (and the first) United Nations Conference on Least Developed Countries was also held in Paris, in 1981. From this first Conference emanated the blueprint for the Special New Programme of Action (SNPA) which spelled out significant concessions to least developed countries by way of debt relief measures, softer ODA loans with higher grant elements, and many others.

UNCTAD singly and jointly with the International Trade Centre (ITC) and General Agreement on Tariffs and Trade (GATT) offer various kinds of technical aid, in the form of consultants, training on international trade, Generalized System of Preference (GSP) Rounds, and allied subjects, both at their respective headquarters and in the country concerned. As a matter of fact, all other specialized agencies of the United Nations do offer a variety of packages of technical aid along similar lines, in their respective special fields.

The regional arm of the United Nations itself, the Economic and Social Commission for Asia and the Pacific (ESCAP), of which Burma is a full member, holds throughout the year either at its headquarters in Bangkok or in the regional countries, many seminars and training workshops, on a whole range of subjects on development. The pilot project is also a valuable tool of technical aid offered by ESCAP. It is implemented within the country, usually in conjunction with another United Nations agency. There are also several institutions affiliated to, and under the wing of ESCAP, such as the Asian and Pacific Development Centre (APDC) in Kuala Lumpur, the Statistical Institute (SIAP) in Tokyo, which offer general and specialized courses to ESCAP member countries. The United Nations University in Tokyo also offers fellowships, but of a different nature, and only to mature and top-level echelon.

Ideology should not be allowed to occupy undue importance as it impedes progress in the path to economic and social development. Moreover, technology does not recognize any "ism". For a variety of reasons (some obvious, some not), Burma failed in the past to take up all that were offered as technical aid to the detriment of its technocrats and overall human resource development. Be that as it may, this time round, Burma cannot afford not to make good use of all within its reach. Officially, as a full member of the United Nations and being also a least developed country, Burma is, *ipso facto*, entitled to take up as many technical aid measures as are made available. Burma need have no compunction or sense of obligation whatsoever in accepting them.

At this juncture, the plight Burma is in and the predicament Burma faces, may perhaps be summed up in a Shakespearian quote:

> What to come is still unsure
> In delay there lies no plenty. . . .

NOTE

* The name of the country of Burma has been changed in June 1989 from "The Union of *Burma*" to "The Union of *Myanmar*". As the events described in this paper pre-dates the name change, the original name "Burma" is retained throughout, in order to avoid confusion, and to preserve chronological sequence.

REFERENCES

Arnold, Steve. *Implementing Development Needs*. Westview Replica Editions. Boulder: Praeger, 1982.

Asian Development Bank (ADB). *Annual Report of the ADB*, various issues.

Bryant and White. *Managing Development in the Third World*. Boulder, Colorado: Westview Press, 1982.

Cassen and Associates. *Does Aid Work*? Clarendon Oxford: Oxford University Press, 1986.

de Silva, V. *Information for Development Planning*. Bangkok: UNADPI, 1979.

Development Co-operation 1986. OECD Press, 1986.

Girling, Robert H. *Multilateral Institutions and the Third World*. New York: Praeger, 1986.

Gosovic, Branislav. *UNCTAD — Conflict and Compromise*. Seiden: Sijitoff, 1972.

______. *Guide to Practical Projects Appraisal*. New York, 1978.

Government of the Union of Burma. *Report to the People's Congress* (annual), various issues.

______. *Report of the Central Statistical Organization*, various issues.

Hassan M. Selim. *Development Assistance Policies & the Performance of Aid Agencies*. London: McMillan Press, 1983.

International Monetary Fund (IMF). *Annual Report of the IMF*, various issues.

______. *The Finance & Development Journal*, various issues.

Lamb, Geoffrey. *Managing Economic Policy Change*. World Bank Discussion Paper 14. Washington D.C.: World Bank, 1987.

Lethem and Cooper. *Managing Project-Related Technical Assistance*. World Bank Staff Working Paper 586. Washington D.C.: World Bank, 1983.

Menon, B.R. *Bridges Across the South: Technical Co-operation*. London: Pergamon Press, 1972.

Mikesell, R.M. *The Economics of Foreign Aid: Self-Sustaining Development.* Boulder, Colorado: Westview Press, 1983.

Pine, B., ed. *A World without a UN.* New York: The Heritage Foundation, 1984.

Riddel, R. *Foreign Aid Reconsidered.* Baltimore: John Hopkins University Press, 1986.

Shand, R.G., and H.V. Richter. *International Aid: Some Political, Administration, and Technical Realities.* Canberra: Australian National University, 1979.

Silvermann, Jerry M. *Technical Assistance & Aid Agency Staff.* World Bank Technical Paper 28. Washington D.C.: World Bank, 1984.

Sottas, Eric. *The Least Developed Countries.* Geneva: United Nations, 1985.

Technical Aid: Proceedings of Truman Seminar. Harry S. Truman Institute, Hebrew University of Jerusalem, 1971.

United Nations. *United Nations Handbook 1988.* New York, 1988.

______. *Guide to Practical Projects Appraisal.* New York, 1978.

______. *Report of UNDP Office, Rangoon*, various issues.

______. *Report of FAO Office, Rangoon*, various issues.

______. *Report of UNICEF Office, Rangoon*, various issues.

______. *Report of WHO Office, Rangoon*, various issues.

White, J. *The Politics of Aid.* London: Bodley Head, 1979.

Williams, D. *Specialized Agencies and the United Nations.* London: C. Hurst & Co., 1985.

World Bank. *Annual Report of the World Bank*, various issues.

______. *The World Bank Economic Review*, various issues.

______. *The World Bank Research Observer*, various issues.

10

REMODELLING MYANMAR

JOHN BADGLEY

I

Can a people remodel their state? By changing their government, can they hope to change their pattern of economic behaviour? And most particularly, can the Myanmar people hope to accomplish both these changes in this century? It is the premise of this chapter that these two actions are essential if Myanmar is to escape from the tortured path the country has followed since independence. The poverty, the collapse of public morale, the demise of a respectable civil service, judiciary, and professional military, the corruption of party democracy, and the continuing erosion of the people's confidence in the government in the eyes of the world: these conditions work against constructive change. Yet, it is possible, just barely possible, within the 1990s that fundamental economic and constitutional changes will so transform the country that this heartbreaking period will be seen as an essential phase in the political maturation of a people struggling to find their own path to modernity.

Matching a new government successfully with any traditional society is a creative task. Rarely is the fit acceptable the first time; indeed, in this regard most political history in the past two centuries is a record of failure. Rebellions, revolutions, constitutional revisions, even elections are modes of political change whereby leaders often wiggle out of past encumbrances and design new ways of achieving private gain in the name of the public good. Recognizing this human foible, the democracies have devised constitutions under which the citizens can change politicians, as well as laws non-violently by representing their factions and interests within legislative bodies; but they retain for themselves the power to elect, or reject by their choice, leaders better able to meet the challenges of changing times.

Of the twenty-three European states, only Switzerland has retained the same constitution since the seventeenth century. The British claim a political system of comparable duration, but the transformation of their laws and society in the nineteenth century significantly altered the roles of parliament, the crown, and the courts. Indeed, all other European countries have changed their constitutions during the current century; therefore, it should be no surprise that Asian states have experienced fundamental changes in this same period.

Myanmar is no exception to this generality, with two failed constitutions since independence, and a current regime in power only through martial law. The *coup d'etat* of 18 September 1988 was imposed by the Defence Minister, General Saw Maung. His junta restrained and finally imprisoned its major opponents through regulations enforced by the State Law and Order Council (SLORC) in which the Director of Intelligence, Brigadier Khin Nyunt, is also Secretary. These measures are only the latest wrinkle overwhelming the positive impulses that once drove U Ne Win to seek power as comrade-in-arms with General Aung San. A half-century ago these two youthful patriots were peers among the Thirty Comrades who led the independence movement against the British. After General Aung San's assassination in 1947, and following defection of several key army units in 1948–50, he clung to power and held the state by uniting remnants of the *Tatmadaw* (military) together against the ethnic and communist insurgents — he subsequently believed the domestic political reality was shifting.[1]

U Ne Win once saw Burmese citizens as naturally born to freedom, but gradually came to perceive his people as a threatening mass, incapable of self-government, a "tiger which I hold by the tail". Thereafter, he governed harshly to save his people from themselves. Foreign capitalist-imperialists (British, Americans,

Japanese), as well as adventurous communist giants (China and the Soviet Union), and expansionist socialist powers (India) have been his foils at various times to justify increased control designed to protect the people from internationl "exploiters". Seemingly a plot to retain, then pass on, power to those of kindred spirit grew within the Burmese Socialist Programme Party (BSPP), and currently as the *Tatmadaw* spirit practised by the SLORC leadership. In fact, the world responded to the appeal for democracy by hundreds of thousands of citizens during the 1988 demonstrations. Most of Myanmar's middle class was persuaded to support General Aung San's eloquent daughter, Aung San Suu Kyi, the prodigal who returned to nurse, then bury her mother.

In the post-Ne Win era, *Tatmadaw* officers must choose: will they join with elements of a civilian leadership to form a new coalition of military and civilian heroes; or will they continue the self-defeating practices that have brought Myanmar to its knees, and thereby bring opprobrium on themselves? Contrary to their recurrent assertion that the *Tatmadaw* is above politics, General Ne Win established it as the dominant faction in the landscape of politics by seizing the reins of civil power back in 1958 and again in 1962. This blatant truth is no less obvious than it was in Bismark's Germany, Cromwell's England, or dozens of other praetorian regimes in Africa, the Middle East, and Asia. Indeed, Myanmar was merely part of a global trend when its army became political; now a global revulsion against military rule raises the hopes of civilian leaders that democracy need not be guided by uniformed guardians of the national spirit.

The process of succession, under way for most of the past decade, is messy because U Ne Win ignored his own constitutional prescriptions by clinging to power through various cliques of senior officers. They govern by holding the centre as U Ne Win's heirs, and compete with other retired military leaders who accept Aung San Suu Kyi as their spokesperson and claim democracy as their goal. These men, led by retired General Tin Oo, seek Bogyoke Aung San's mantle through political coalitions with elements in the government as well as among key insurgent leaders. Still on the periphery, but now with world media attention, are the key ethnic insurgent armies — Karen, Shan, Kachin — and smaller armed bands from other communal groups — Mon, Arakanese, Pa-O, Wa, Kayah,Lisu — all demanding a restructured constitution that will guarantee political representation and economic equity through laws their leaders want to help create.

The once formidable Burma Communist Party (BCP), which self-destructed in 1968 through savage infighting, then rebuilt with China's aid, again destroyed itself in April 1989 following an intense struggle between Wa-dominated units and the Sino-Burman top command. Reduced to dependence on the opium trade for its funds, the BCP lost its control of territory along the China border, its authority as a revolutionary party, and its potential as an alternative government. General Saw Maung's junta denies this collapse of the *Tatmadaw*'s old enemy, for it undermines their rationale for holding power; he contends that the internecine struggle was all a diabolic plot designed to exploit (yet again) gullible citizens. To commemorate the massive demonstrations of 8 August 1988, Brigadier Khin Nyunt published a long document on 8 August 1989 which argued that the "riots and violence" were hatched in the minds of the BCP leadership in collaboration with "a major foreign power". The foreign power, through the BCP, paid agitators to represent the lie that the people of Myanmar were dissatisfied with the *Tatmadaw*'s benevolent care during the transition to elections.[2] Meanwhile, the key opposition party leaders and members have been imprisoned.

> Only when the rule of law and order and peace and tranquillity (*sic*) prevail, would the lives, homes and property of the people be safe and secure; only then would they be able to earn their livelihood in peace and freedom. The Tatmadaw is carrying out this duty and all nationalities of the Union are urged to give all co-operation and assistance in this great task (Masthead of *Working People's Daily*).

II

The rich mosaic of cultures and communal traditions that make up Myanmar requires a new political architecture, a design not previously established. Under the Burman (and Shan) kings, the vast majority were villagers, both minorities and the Burmans, who lived at arms length from government. They were subjects of monarchies within an imperial system where power was justified by inheritance, military skill, and karma, not by votes. The non-Burman peoples were tied to the empire through various alliances, and occasionally by Burman armies of occupation that established no enduring legacy of civil harmony. This system of rule was similar to other Theravada polities in the medieval era and prevailed until the nineteenth century, when Burma was colonized by the British; then two distinct administrations were created to rule (and divide) Burmans and "frontier peoples". Consequently, despite the nationalist movement which pressed the British to make political reforms before the war, the independence gained in 1948 rested on a very shaky foundation. The fledgling pre-war parliament and party system was patterned after that in India; the leadership had no indigenous model, no Burmese political invention that accommodated the diverse nationalities in an enduringly peaceful state.

Political innovation is an essential step if the post-independence conflicts are to be settled, but without concomitant economic growth no government can last. Therefore, this essay addresses the kind of role the state (meaning the public bodies of government, the constitutionally derived institutions) should play. What political economy is best suited to Myanmar's constituent peoples? The answer to this query rests on a critique of what Burmese political behaviour requires. Political architecture should be designed to fit the people, not the reverse as has been assumed by determinist theorists whose faith in state socialism was unshakeable.

These prescriptions are written to stimulate thinking about the political economy best suited to Myanmar's experience. Although the cultures are unique within this richly diverse land, other nations in recent years have faced comparably desperate conditions. Some remain mired in despair, others have successfully pressed forward with both expanded freedoms and economic growth. Yet others have experienced high productivity with governments granted only limited political freedom, and that under duress from an impatient citizenry.

In the first flush of development theory after World War II, many social scientists prescribed the"stages of growth" principle, which they believed would lead agrarian nations to rapid industrialization. They hoped to bypass the pitfalls which led to global wars in the first half of the century. Hundreds of rebellions, regional wars, and state terrorism have since humbled most intellectuals who expected to guide politicians and bureaucrats with sustained growth models. Still, South Korea, Taiwan, Hong Kong, and Singapore have transformed themselves into the new industrializing countries (NICs), and now enjoy the same economic miracle that transformed Japan after World War II. Few scholars still contend that a single ideology, economic theory, or management model accounts for their rapid economic growth and expanding political freedoms. As one examines the details of their industrialization, each society functions differently. And two other Southeast Asian countries, Malaysia and Thailand, which are approaching NIC status, have significantly different social and political systems. While all of the NICs are overcoming the planet's two most devastating global trends, the population explosion and natural resource depletion, it is depressing that Myanmar continues to ignore them.

Free markets, efficient productivity, revolutionary information and transportation technologies, participant societies — writers now use these catchwords as if by application, they alone are sufficient answers to the negative forces that have defeated Myanmar's development plans in the past. But the coming decade will be as bleak as the past four without a legitimate constitution, a viable political system, an even-handed judiciary, and a professional civil service. No vision of progress makes sense without the practical application of public policies through laws that fit the complex ethnic and environmental reality of Myanmar. And no laws will be acceptable unless they are administered by sincere leaders working to earn the trust of their own people. Has Myanmar been administered in this manner? Will it be so in the future?

III

This chapter is built on the assumption that Myanmar's current junta is loosing its legitimacy and the confidence of the people, that it has no political base apart from its allies within the military. It may be displaced in the elections of 1990, but if not, then eventually by some broader coalition with greater legitimacy. If the state does not split asunder in the interim, a goal no faction now seeks, the people will support any leadership that can stabilize the economy, improve the socio-economic infrastructure, and demonstrate equity in their allocation of resources. It is reasonable to expect the citizens to be drawn towards a vision of communal co-operation, which can be engendered by new leaders who have faith in the nation's capacity to escape its painful past. With luck they will also have the capacity to conjure a productive economic system linked to a global market, with a commitment to the human rights articles of the United Nations Charter.

This scenario, which would have seemed excessively rosy even a half-decade ago, reflects the movement elsewhere, as well as within Myanmar, towards democracy and an open market system. Thanks to *perestroika*, *glastnost*, and "people power" moving onto centre stage from Brazil to the USSR, and from Eastern Europe to the Philippines, it is realistic to expect the people of Myanmar to respond in kind. World-wide communication informs them of this historic shift, and allows leaders little time to evade the issue.

The dramatic 1988 demonstrations for democracy in Burma revealed the strength of the freedom movement among Myanmar's citizens. Their massive scope was in part stimulated by U Ne Win himself, who, in his resignation speech from the BSPP, blamed socialism for many of Burma's failures, and recommended consideration of a multi-party political system with a new constitution.[3] His immediate successor, General Sein Lwin, was a disastrous choice who survived just 18 days, but was followed by a former chief justice, Dr Maung Maung (U Ne Win's biographer and confidant for thirty years), who released key commodities from government controls, opened the country to foreign investment, expanded the freedom of citizens to travel and form private businesses, and encouraged the formation of independent political parties and a free press: all during a brief five-week tenure as head of state. General Saw Maung's "coup" curtailed features of that liberal trend, but in time the junta affirmed several of Dr Maung Maung's progressive steps. Perhaps most important was their promise of elections in the spring of 1990.

Political campaigning reached a feverish pitch in the winter and spring of 1989, with large crowds turning out despite a SLORC regulation forbidding assemblages of five or more. Pamphleteering, videotapes, audio cassettes — the accoutrements of a party-building effort in any modern democratic society — seized the imagination of townspeople. The international media reported these events, as their reporters witnessed them personally during visits to some of the more than 200 party headquarters that opened in Yangon during this period. One coalition, the League for Democracy, became dominant through the charisma of Aung San Suu Kyi and the enthusiasm, loyalty, and intelligence of their organizers, mostly volunteers. Their experience paralleled that of Poland's Solidarity in 1980–81, a movement also repressed by older, conservative, uniformed men steeped in their own habits of rule. Those reformist organizers, too, risked their careers, and lives in the same passionate quest for freedom, public trust, and votes.

This is not to ignore the violent military measures in 1988, which anticipated very similar acts by China's military in 1989. But those costs can be seen as the stakes many students and citizens are willing to pay. They have accepted the axiom that the value of liberty is invariably correlated to the amount of effort citizens exert to gain it. In Myanmar, as in China, students led the movement which cost many their own lives. In both countries, unified military commands have contained the reformers; however, the seeds of transformation have been planted.

In earlier days the lack of alternative sources of information prevented the oppositions in both countries from prevailing; however, as is evident from the governments' strident efforts to spurn the reporting of foreign correspondents on BBC, Voice of America, and All India Radio, neither regime can tolerate much truth at the grass-roots level. Their Achilles' heel, as is the case for all totalitarian rulers in our time, is mass communications. As radios and VCRs reach into the villages, once the world press begins to cover domestic issues governments can no longer dupe their public for a lengthy period.

However, inflation is the issue most undermining the power of the lingering U Ne Win junta. Shortages in the cities of key items — rice, fish, cooking oil, gasoline — deepens the hostility towards and frustration with the military junta's economic policies. While doubts about the 1988 events can be created among some of the public by a disinformation programme, and the popularity of particular opposition leaders can be affected thereby, the daily grind of earning a living has the most profound impact on people. While shortly after the coup wages for the lower civil service ranks were doubled, and salaries for more senior officials increased by half, inflation has since reduced the value of everyone's income. As at November 1989 a *pyi* of rice on the open market in Rangoon costs a labourer three days wages (60 kyats), a litre of petrol costs one and a half days wage, one egg equals three hours labour, and a *viss* of pork costs five days labour. U Ne Win had used demonetization schemes three times in the past decade to slow the inflation rate; but it had only temporary effect and contributed greatly to the distrust of the government by merchants, ordinary housewives, and the international financial community as well. They readily recognized the monetary ruse for what it was, a deception played on the public to reduce the power of those with wealth who might oppose the controlling junta.

IV

Because this exploitative system has become entrenched in Myanmar, it is fruitless to try to disconnect political and economic issues. The country's difficulties are inextricably linked; consequently, the key assumption underlying the following propositions is that a radical departure is needed to regain public trust in government.

The Political System

1. That the manner in which a new government assumes power will determine how far the leadership can proceed in remodelling

the state. Anybody designing a new constitution, whether by election or appointment, should be drawn together in a fashion suitable to Myanmar's complex political landscape.

2. That democracy has proved to be a flexible political system adaptable to cultures throughout the world, for it is based on representation of both individual and community views. It is important that human rights and the legislative, executive, and judicial functions be institutionalized separately in the new constitution; that the body of representatives chosen to write it understand the entire range of sentiments within the polity; and that the actual structure fit the multi-ethnic nature of the peoples in Myanmar.

3. While many societies encourage multi-party modes of election, it is critical to remember that parties primarily exist to produce candidates for election, and that many forms of single, dual, and multiple party systems function badly, or well, depending on the congruence of the constitution and the society.

4. That access to information is crucial to a democracy's success. Freedom to investigate and report facts, opinions, and research findings has been profoundly restricted for three decades; opening the society to mass communication is irreversible, and therefore the issue facing the next government is not whether, but how that opening should take place to engender the greatest stability. The world press and mass media is as much a part of Myanmar's future as is village gossip, and is uncontrollable.

The Economic System

1. That the projects planned by the international consulting teams during the first fifteen years of Myanmar's independence be reviewed, evaluated, and applied where appropriate. A commission of objective, professional, world-class economists and financiers should conduct this task and recommend immediate steps to recapture Myanmar's comparative economic advantages. These include rich agricultural and renewable forest resources, ample fresh water for irrigation and hydropower, underdeveloped petroleum and mineral resources, and perhaps most importantly, an

inexpensive labour force moving into urban settlements (due to population pressures forcing youth out of the villages).

2. That employment of restive youth is critical if the country is to enjoy political stability, and as Myanmar's neighbours — Thailand, Malaysia, India — are demonstrating, rapid economic growth is feasible in urban areas where domestic and foreign businesses can link up, creating new enterprises to supply expanding domestic and international markets. Their products can serve as import substitutes and save foreign exchange. However, their chief benefit is to broaden the economic base and increase the rate of growth. Responding to the needs of a society where 40 million people have long been deprived of consumer goods will be profitable for many new businesses in the coming decade. Imports from China, Thailand, Japan, India, Singapore, and Malaysia partially fill these needs — however, domestic entrepreneurs can respond even more efficiently to pent-up consumer demands, once capital is available through liberalized investment laws. The value added to primary products through indigenous manufacturing is critical to building the economy, the tax base, and employee training in modern production.

3. Since rice farming is the predominant economic activity in the country, and because both the quality and quantity of rice produced has greatly declined due to price manipulations and deteriorated mills and storage facilities, rehabilitation loans and expert technicians should be available at reasonable cost to individual, co-operative, and corporate producers. Alternative grains and crop substitutions for rice have been introduced in central Myanmar; these programmes should be expanded as the world rice market is saturated at present.

4. Because environmental destruction now ranks among the most critical issues globally, and Myanmar faces enormous devastation of its forests, soils, river systems, and unique flora and fauna within the coming decade unless biologically sustainable policies are enforced, an advisory commission of experts should be established to propose legislative and administrative steps needed to accomplish this goal.

5. That private banking be re-established so that foreign investors can be attracted. The single public bank available for corporate and joint-venture firms not only inhibits the flow of funds because of archaic banking practices, but it reveals a suspicion of business that intimidates most international firms who have plentiful opportunities to invest elsewhere.

6. That the black/grey market system be dropped and replaced with regulated free trade in a currency of negotiable international value. The impact of these two steps will challenge the viability of the subsidized government trade corporations, but will substantially increase the flow of goods in the private sector, reduce inflation due to greater market efficiencies, and secure tax receipts that have been lost for nearly three decades. Perhaps most importantly, these measures will link legitimate entrepreneurs from abroad with experienced traders and producers throughout Myanmar, who have been considered illegal smugglers under U Ne Win's socialist regimes.

Transportation System

1. That a commission be established to analyse Myanmar's infrastructure of highways and waterways, and recommend priorities for major capital improvements, based on a commitment to equitable economic growth throughout the country. An example of the immediate benefits to such strategic thinking is found in the explosive expansion of trade across the Yunnan border over the past two years. It started with a political understanding between Yangon and Beijing to eliminate the Burma Communist Party (BCP), for the insurgent force had controlled the major cross border traffic and used their tax on smuggling to pay for arms; that situation blocked any consideration of legal commerce in the past. With the collapse of the BCP, the Kunming–Rangoon highway was freed for market-responsive truck traffic, a profound transformation as the road had been perceived primarily as an invasion route in the past. Now its value as a commercial link between the two countries has become apparent. This trade is a significant stimulant to the economies of Lashio, Mandalay, and

towns along the way, as well as to new investors in Singapore, Malaysia, and Thailand who are shipping goods in both directions.

2. Comparable agreements to legalize trade between Myanmar and Thailand raise the possibility of bridging the rivers and opening the Three Pagodas Pass road for large-scale commerce; while in the isthmus, new Thai-Myanmar roads to Tavoy and Mergui will have a profound impact on peoples throughout the Tennasserim.

3. Alternatives to the deadly Golden Triangle opium trade become feasible if better roads, with concomitant socio-economic investments, are introduced in the Shan, Karen, and Mon areas. Such a massive effort requires collaboration with international lending agencies as well as larger corporations and officials in Thailand, Laos, and China; but funding becomes realistic once political accommodations are established between Yangon and the insurgent leadership struggling for greater control over their future. While the opium "lords" have formidable armies, it is in the interest of all governments in the region to overcome this challenge to their rule; and it is of particular interest to the United States, with its dreadful drug problem, to offer financial assistance. The commercial "back door to China" was a dream fostered by British and French empire builders in the nineteenth century. Now it is being affirmed as an integrated mainland Southeast Asian market. Recent meetings between Myanmar's regional military commanders and their counterparts in these countries suggest that this prospect has become politically feasible.

4. While no comparable exchange has happened with India and Bangladesh, the amount of smuggling over their borders has nonetheless expanded. With legalized trade and a revalued currency, the western portion of Myanmar could enjoy the same strategic economic benefits as the eastern. The economies of Arakan, the Chin and Naga hills, and especially the Kachin region will improve dramatically with the construction of an integrated road and Chindwin-Irrawaddy rivers transportation system. Again, this critical issue is as much political as economic in content.

5. The creation of a new set of ports and rail links will streamline Myanmar's transportation system, and offer great opportunity for economic growth in the delta, the Tennasserim, lower Arakan,

and the arid lands to the west of the Irrawaddy towns of Prome, Myingyan, and up to Monywa. The existing ports of Yangon, Moulmein, and Bassein lack deep water facilities and long-range planning for north-south as well as east-west linkages holds promise of more equitable economic growth between regions. Large projects of this nature must have heavy foreign investment, which can come if Myanmar's isolationist policies are retired and both indigenous and foreign contractors are required to meet generally established international performance standards.

The Administrative System

1. That a stable relationship between government and the citizenry is essential if sufficient foreign investment is to be secured. The crisis management that has characterized Myanmar's administrative practices over the past two years must be replaced. A professional civil service was established prior to Burma's independence, and while nationalists wanted those officials to be more responsive to indigenous values, it is a tragedy that the tradition of relative incorruptibility within the Indian Civil Service (ICS) has been severely compromised. By casting military officers in civil service roles to enforce law and order, the civilians were further diminished in stature. The functional efficiency of capable officials can only be regained by recruiting administrators qualified to perform their jobs, and sufficiently educated to grasp the complexities of the society they are expected to serve. To that end it is essential that a rigorous examination system, ongoing performance evaluations, and above all, a pay scale appropriate to their responsibilities be established. An ad hoc commission should conduct a comparative study of Myanmar's civil service system with other Asian states that have enjoyed successful economic development, and recommend appropriate changes.

2. That a new administrative code be drawn up, suitable to the *laissez faire* policies characteristic of free market systems. The deep corruption that developed during the quarter century when the Burmese Way to Socialism prevailed can only be removed by

freeing civil servants and investors alike from the red tape of autarchic socialism. A bureaucrat should be paid to protect the public interest, not trap the entrepreneur into paying a second salary. A commission of professionally qualified citizens should be established to review and recommend such a code.

3. That a tax commission be established to reformulate the tax code in accordance with the needs of an economy being rebuilt on free enterprise principles. While these fiscal and monetary issues have been considered in much more detail in other chapters, it is critical that the new government recognize the close linkage between the laws, regulations, legal profit-margins, and investment incentives. In large measure, Myanmar's dismal economic performance in the past was due to contradictory public policies in this area.

The Education System

1. That the education system be revised to suit Myanmar's predominantly agrarian society with reasonable goals for the coming decade. It is tragic that primary and secondary curricula direct all students towards college, yet only a tenth are permitted entry. This is an enormous waste of the talents and time of teachers and students alike, and squanders public funds. Mandatory instruction in English at the senior high and university levels creates even deeper frustrations since the vast majority of the populace will develop insufficient skill to use English. In the past four decades every government had expanded the number of teachers, students, and educational administrators; however, their training had not been suited to the employment awaiting most students, except for the children of the new élite class. By taking costly private tuition, they alone could pass the stiff entrance examinations for the professional schools. The ranks of anarchists and rebels are swollen with frustrated high school dropouts, as well as arts and science graduates who never had meaningful work, and who must take on two or three jobs to survive. Again, a review commission should be established immediately to lay before the new government recommendations for a reformed educational programme.

2. That private educational institutions should be encouraged as part of the free market system. Myanmar had strong traditions of Buddhist monastic as well as Christian mission schools, and some locally financed "national" high schools rivalled the quality of British public schools in pre-independence years. These private and local traditions offer potent alternative models that will permit parents and local communities to regain control over their children's future.

3. That every language community should have the opportunity to instruct their children in their language, culture, and religion, recognizing that accountability for future generation's skills is a shared responsibility of parents, teachers, and administrators. This issue has been one of the most explosive undergirding the ethnic conflicts that have eroded Myanmar's economy since independence. The central government should prepare indigenous language texts and encourage multi-cultural education throughout Myanmar. This will sensitize future generations to the realities of their complex heritage of nationalities. The School for Ethnic Minorities in Sagaing is only a symbol of the kind of institutional response needed for this problem. An Institute of Myanmar Cultures should be established to research and recommend ongoing changes needed in all educational fields to stay abreast of this feature of education.

4. That the university system should be reviewed by a commission equipped to consider pedagogical as well as economic, security, and political issues. One of Myanmar's tragedies is the fissure that evolved between civilian and military education. The élite within the military is drawn from the Maymyo academy which has recruited highly qualified cadets, but trained them to see the military as the last bastion of nationalism. The civilian arts and science graduates are viewed with particular suspicion, which contributes to the rift currently dividing the country. More generally, the education system is designed to help students pass examinations; it serves them ill in preparing them for jobs or citizenship. Again, comparative evaluation of other national systems is essential. Many features of Myanmar's educational tradition are worthy and must be conserved; however, the basic

philosophy of pedagogy should be reconsidered in view of the change from a closed socialist system to an open, information-oriented society.

The Legal System

1. Cultural considerations should undergird laws and regulations whenever possible: this is to recognize that the state can survive only if a sense of commonwealth prevails; however, Myanmar has suffered insurgencies from the outset of independence because central governments were unable to acknowledge the legitimate concern among ethnic communities for the integrity of their traditions and desire for self-government. Determining which common laws should be applicable to all citizens is clearly a political task; however, to view demands for distinctive civil codes suitable to each community as threatening Myanmar's sovereignty is to invite continued insurrection. While a common criminal code must be applied if civility is to prevail, it is equally critical that each religious and ethnic group should feel that its traditions are recognized by the legal system. A commission to evaluate this sensitive and complex issue is essential to the future integration of local common law with a national code. Only through acknowledging the cultural diversity can future governments hope to achieve unity. An appropriate legal system is the crux of successful integration.

2. Buddhism is the predominant religious expression in Myanmar, and the Buddhist *dhammathat* tradition is central to customary law. The relationship of the Buddhist *sangha*, the *dhamma*, and the *vinaya* to the legal system should be reviewed to resolve contradictions that have arisen due to the heavily ideological nature of government since independence. The creation of a more liberal legal system may reduce tensions between state and religious authorities, thereby contributing to greater social harmony. That Myanmar might have a more inviting investment climate as a result should not be lost on political and *sangha* leaders alike.

Law Enforcement

1. That police functions should be returned to police organizations, and their members should be drawn, as much as possible, from the communities where they serve. The creation, within the past decade, of parapolice units by using junior military officers as commanders, and manning them with ill-trained village youths for "crowd suppression" activities, undermines the morale of professional law enforcement officers as well as residents in the communities where they serve. These special forces, armed with automatic weapons and untrained in crowd control have kept their senior commanders in power, but badly served the country. The traditional separation between police and military functions was deeply ingrained in Burma during the colonial and immediate post-colonial period. A return to that institutional division is essential.

2. That pay scales and training of police officers should reflect the requirements of their duties. Again, corruption that has permeated every feature of Myanmar life has caused law enforcement to become a farce. A reassessment and reorganization of the police forces can recapture the professional ethic and loyalty required to sustain the law.

The Welfare System

Welfare measures — health care and nutritional aid for poor children and mothers, the aged, and the handicapped; rehabilitation and retraining of veterans; continuing education for the thousands of under- and unemployed civil servants during Myanmar's transition to a market-driven economy — these activities require government intervention. If programmes are carefully evaluated and introduced in a fiscally responsible fashion, the entire workforce will benefit, markedly improving Myanmar's competitive position in gaining new industries. Again, a mixed commission or public and private experts should be formed to recommend policies that address these issues. The cost of major welfare reforms is well beyond the tax capability of any government in the near future, no matter how well intentioned; however, inequities can be removed and efficiencies gained as the fractures within the society are healed.

The Military

1. The military, as the major political actor in Myanmar during the past three decades, as well as the largest sector in the budget, must itself be restructured if the state is to be remodelled. By returning troops to the barracks, and releasing the officers of their many non-military functions, substantial budget reductions will be possible.

2. In effect, the country can declare peace within itself by negotiating an end to the communal conflicts that have persisted. The original structure of Burma's army was sound. The threefold division of tasks between the navy, air force, and army is problematic due to the dominance of the army; however, the professional competence of the Burma army in its first decade of life was substantial. Continued warfare with ideological, communal, and opium armies gave them battlefield experience that was denied to most Asian armies at the time.

3. The sociology of Myanmar's military is similar to that of most agrarian societies in that troops are recruited from the ranks of underemployed villagers, non-commissioned officers are drawn from those troops who adapt to the discipline of army life (most enlisted men resign after three to five years of service), while most officers are university graduates, either from the military academy or the University Training Corps. Because of the high risks involved in Myanmar's ongoing struggles, and the low pay received in the lower ranks, the senior military is given perquisites that exceed that of their civilian counterparts (chauffeured cars, housing, food rations, medical care, and retirement benefits sufficient to establish a business). To gain these entitlements the mid-level officers must show battlefield skills, loyal units, and unquestioned loyalty. Abuses of rank privileges, corruption in managing civilian corporations, and flagrant violation of human rights can only be stopped by a fresh leadership, loyal to the constitution and willing to serve it, and not rise above the law.

4. Myanmar's military training programmes are professional, and the quality of most servicemen is adequate to their job, if that job is limited to maintaining a monopoly of violence and not trying to accomplish a hundred other tasks. By reducing the overall strength to suit the security needs once the new political leadership settles the major insurgencies, the budget needs of the military can fall to the equivilant of most Asian states, which is 10–15 per cent rather than the current 40 per cent of government revenues.[4]

V

This is a necessarily brief assessment of Myanmar's current situation and the changes needed to achieve a brighter future. While suggesting radical departures, it builds on the assumption that rapid economic growth is possible. The inclusion of unreported and illegal commercial activities will at least double the worth of the gross national product. The systematic collection of taxes because of more professional behaviour, increased productivity by farmers responding to price incentives based on real market conditions, the rationalization of the commercial sector of the economy — these activities will substantially improve the welfare of all. Myanmar's reported per capita income in *Asian Development Outlook, 1989* is less than US$200. The government reduced its estimated literacy rate in 1987 from 60 per cent to 20 per cent to qualify for least developed country status and thereby gain reductions in loan costs; however, most analysts peg the first rate as more accurate, given the cultural emphasis among Buddhists on literacy.

The significance of these qualities within the populace, and the potential of the economy if most of the problems outlined above are dealt with, suggests a change is pending. It is possible that by the end of the century, just a decade from now, per capita income will exceed US$700, that the gross national product will be reported, accurately, as three times its current value, and that it could even amount to a fourfold increase. Such a goal by any government that takes power after the elections is realistic, if the political will is there to make it happen. There is no structural reason, nor any behavioural quality among the people, nor any lack of investment capital, nor lack of management experience among Burmese who could be recruited from around the world to serve an administration with such a goal.

Even more impressive are the consequences in the following decade if this "first decade" goal is achieved. The NICs and both Thailand and Malaysia have established models of economic growth that Myanmar can emulate during the first quarter of the twenty-first century, which suggest improvements well beyond anything discussed in this chapter. In short, the future is bright if the correct measures are taken now.

However, it seems at present the clouds hang low over Myanmar.

NOTES

1. See General Ne Win, *Annual Report to the Burma Socialist Programme Party, 1974.*
2. Brigadier General Khin Nyunt, *Burma Communist Party's Conspiracy to take over State Power* (Yangon: State Law and Order Council, 8 August 1989); later published by the Ministry of Information of the Union of Myanmar, 8 September 1989.
3. See *Working People's Daily*, 23 July 1989.
4. Editors' note: According to the International Institute of Strategic Studies', *The Military Balance 1989/90*, Myanmar's defence expenditure constitutes about 30 per cent of GDP.

REFERENCES

Amnesty International. *Burma: Extrajudicial Execution and Torture of Members of Ethnic Minorities*, 1988.

Asian Development Bank. *Asian Development Outlook 1989. Burma 1987 Report.* 1988.

Aye Saung. *A Burman: In the Back Row.* Bangkok: White Lotus, 1989.

Brig. Gen. Khin Nyunt, State Law and Order Restoration Council Secretary. *Burma Communist Party's Conspiracy to Take Over State Power.* 8 August 1989.

Burma Review, No. 1–8, 1989.

Economist Intelligence Unit. *Country Profile: Thailand, Burma, 1988/89.*

MacDougall, Hugh C., ed. *Burma Press Summary* (extracts from *Working People's Daily*), Vols. I–III, 1987–89.

Ministry of Planning and Finance, Union of Burma. *Report to the Pyithu Hluttaw 1988/89*. Rangoon, 1988.

Project Maije. *Burma — Reports on Human Rights, Abuses, Insurgency and Karen State*, edited by Edith Mirante, 1987–89.

United Nations Development Program. *Development Co-operation: 1987 Report*. July 1988.

Working People's Daily, 1988–89.